C0-CCB-604

Computers in English and the Language Arts

NCTE Committee on Instructional Technology

Cynthia L. Selfe, Chair
Janet M. Eldred
Elizabeth Foster
Mary Louise Gomez
Deane M. Hargrave
Gail E. Hawisher
Kenneth C. Holvig
Nancy Kaplan
Patricia A. Malinowski
John G. McDaid
Rick Monroe
William R. Oates
Dawn Rodrigues
Michael Spitzer
James Strickland
Marcia Juskiewicz Ulloa
William Wresch
Patricia A. Slagle, Executive Committee Liaison
Robert L. Hamm, NCTE Staff Liaison

Computers in English and the Language Arts

The Challenge of Teacher Education

Edited by

Cynthia L. Selfe
Michigan Technological University

Dawn Rodrigues
Colorado State University

William R. Oates
American Welding Society

National Council of Teachers of English
1111 Kenyon Road, Urbana, Illinois 61801

Staff Editors: Jane M. Curran, Robert A. Heister

Book Design: Tom Kovacs for TGK Design

NCTE Stock Number 08172–3020

It is the policy of NCTE in its journals and other publications to provide a forum for the open discussion of ideas concerning the content and the teaching of English and the language arts. Publicity accorded to any particular point of view does not imply endorsement by the Executive Committee, the Board of Directors, or the membership at large, except in announcements of policy, where such endorsement is clearly specified.

Library of Congress Cataloging in Publication Data

Computers in English and language arts : the challenge of teacher education / edited by Cynthia L. Selfe, Dawn Rodrigues, William R. Oates.

p. cm.

ISBN 0–8141–0817–2

1. Language arts—Computer-assisted instruction. 2. English language—Computer-assisted instruction. 3. English teachers—Training of. 4. English language—Study and teaching. I. Selfe, Cynthia L., 1951– . II. Rodrigues, Dawn. III. Oates, William R. (William Robert), 1943– .

LB1576.7.C68 1989

428.4′078—dc20

89–12716

CIP

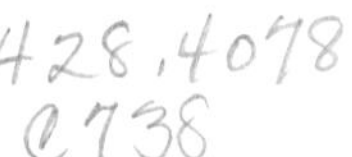

Contents

Appendixes

Acknowledgments

The editors would like to thank the authors of the chapters in this book for contributing their time and energy to this endeavor. We also are grateful to the leaders of the National Council of Teachers of English for supporting and sustaining the work of the Committee on Instructional Technology. Finally, our thanks go to those teachers, staff members, friends, and family members who encouraged us to produce this book.

C.L.S.
D.R.
W.R.O.

Foreword

During 1969–73 while I served as the first editor of *English Education*, the editorial board and I were already aware of the beginnings of the electronic revolution. Try as we might, we were unsuccessful in our efforts to secure articles which would help English educators prepare themselves, as well as future teachers of English, to use electronic instruments to improve their teaching. The closest we came was an article in 1972 which discussed some pioneering work in computer-assisted instruction.

Knowing how long it takes a new idea to be implemented in education, no one should be surprised to note that it has taken almost two decades for a volume to emerge which will provide an answer to the question, How can we use computers to improve the teaching of English?

The present volume is distinctive in a number of ways. One of its editors, William R. Oates, presented the first paper at the 1979 Annual Convention of the National Council of Teachers of English on the importance of using computers to teach the language arts more effectively. Within two years, the NCTE Committee on Instructional Technology was formed. The other two editors, Dawn Rodrigues and Cynthia L. Selfe, have published books about ongoing research and lessons learned by teachers who were early adopters of computers in the classroom. Committee members set to work to discover where computers were being used successfully in teaching English and, more importantly, who was preparing English teachers to do this. Now we have a source to which we can turn to obtain ideas of how to improve our educational programs in English through the use of computers.

The twofold approach used in this volume is to be commended. In the first section, twelve existing programs for teacher preparation and inservice are described, covering activity in eight different states. Here teachers will find programs geared to teachers at all levels: elementary, secondary, and college. In the second section, the collection attempts to define components of model teacher education programs. In this section, chapters are included that fill in details concerning such items as word processing and networked classrooms. At the end of this section, there is a chapter devoted to evaluation, that ever-knotty problem in education.

One of the virtues of this volume is that it stresses the importance of active participation by the learner. In the past, when we were excited about the possibilities of using radio, motion pictures, and TV as aids to learning, we soon became disenchanted when we learned that many students responded by becoming passive sponges of assimilation. The computer places stress on student-response pedagogy, for the student is forced to respond to the computer, thus actively engaging in the learning process.

Our work as a profession, however, continues. It is unfortunate to discover in William Wresch's survey of teacher education institutions reported in Appendix A that little is being done to prepare future teachers to use computers. George Bernard Shaw was right when he once remarked that educators are putting "tacks" where the "carpet" had been some time before. If the contents of this volume are taken seriously by teachers of English, there is hope that we will soon bring the "carpet" and the "tacks" closer together. The National Council of Teachers of English and those who have contributed to this volume are to be commended for the seminal work that they have done.

Oscar M. Haugh
Professor Emeritus
University of Kansas

Introduction: A History and Overview of This Collection

William R. Oates, American Welding Society

A Brief History of This Book

Most English teachers who have used computers in their classes have until recently been self-taught. They have been pioneers, some adventurous and some reluctant, charged with finding effective ways to use technology in their classrooms. Few of these pioneers believe that they have yet reached the promised land; most are still trying to chart their way through the wilderness. Many share a vision, however, that computers can have a strong positive impact on the quality and scope of their work in teaching English and language arts. Some have begun to map the territory and to post warning and directional signs toward this goal.

This pioneer community has grown throughout the 1980s to include a meaningful part of the teacher community in English and English education. Special and few among the pioneers have been English educators who have developed teacher-preparation programs for integrating computers into English curricula. The settlement of this new land requires new college-level English education programs, modernized inservice training programs, and other ways to share knowledge with the larger teacher community. The tendency to teach as we ourselves were taught, while always questionable, is clearly inadequate in today's computerized classrooms.

This book shares knowledge learned by numerous of these pioneers in using computers to help teach English and language arts. Many of the contributors have designed new teacher education programs and conducted computer workshops for small groups of teachers. The aim here is to multiply these efforts at improving teacher preparation for using computers with English classes. Most resources to date have been directed toward the individual English teacher. The authors believe a greater benefit may be achieved now by directing this book toward those who will prepare teachers for integrating computers into the English and language arts curricula. Nevertheless, the book still is largely by teachers and for teachers. Many of the pioneers are teachers themselves who had to pull themselves up by their own technological and pedagogical bootstraps. English education and training programs should now operate so that others do not have to learn the hard way. Such a productive sharing by both experienced teachers and teacher trainers is the goal of the contributors and of the editors.

Such sharing and dissemination is also part of the mission of the National Council of Teachers of English, whose Committee on Instructional Technology is responsible for this book. In 1981, NCTE created the Committee on Instructional Technology, and this group began to work actively to explore how technology was currently being used in the nation's English and language arts classrooms.

This committee was not alone, however, in its work. In 1984, NCTE's Task Force on Excellence in Education expressed concern that uses of computers in teaching English and language arts might undercut rather than advance excellence. It passed a formal action stating, "The Task Force is alarmed that schools seem more enchanted with using computers for random drill and practice, testing, instructional management, and practice of low-level skills, rather than for composing, thought processes, text analysis, and creative uses of language" (quoted in Oates et al. 1985). Nevertheless, the task force members also said they believed that "if properly employed, the microcomputer might have a greater impact on English teaching than on mathematics."

The Committee on Instructional Technology agreed with the task force on both counts. The success that English teachers would have in improving education through using computers hinged mightily on the phrase "if properly employed." Experience suggested that the positive goals envisioned for computers in the English classroom would not be widely reached by individual English teachers trying to cope on their own with a dizzying complex of educational technology and instructional change. The typical pioneering teacher had to compete with math and science teachers for computer access and had to wade through a labyrinth of software of widely varying quality. In short, teachers had, and still have, little time to rethink curricula or pedagogy as a part of using computers in classes.

Experience also suggested to the Committee on Instructional Technology that the solution for the late 1980s and 1990s would be to encourage institutional and programmatic approaches to using computers in teaching English. The committee, believing that individual

English and language arts teachers should not have to reinvent the wheel every time they integrated computers into their classrooms, set out to collect and publish a series of essays that would describe existing teacher education programs and that would help our profession move toward model programs of this kind. The committee published a call for manuscripts in the major journals of our field, did a blind review of fifty-nine abstracts, and began the lengthy process of writing, rewriting, and editing the collection. Our effort began in 1985 and comes to fruition with this volume.

An Overview of the Book

This collection has two major parts. Part I is devoted to describing a dozen teacher-training and education programs around the country that are already helping teachers integrate computers meaningfully into their curricula. Part II lays out a "game plan" that others may follow in designing new teacher-training programs, and discusses the process of evaluating computer-writing curriculum projects. The appendixes contain the results of a survey of computer uses in English education programs, conducted by William Wresch of the University of Wisconsin–Stevens Point, and a list of tips for improving computer access for English classes, prepared by three members of NCTE's Committee on Instructional Technology.

Part I: Existing Teacher-Preparation Programs and Inservice Programs

The first three programs described in Part I are conducted at teacher education institutions. These teacher-preparation programs represent a range of approaches that have been successful, and share some strikingly similar ideas with respect to the proper role of computers in the English curriculum.

The first chapter, authored by David Humphreys, past chair of the NCTE Assembly on Computers in English, describes a "computer loan" program conducted at Cuyahoga Community College in Warrensville Township, Ohio. This program, which is cosponsored by the Urban Initiatives Action Program, is attached to a teacher education course which endeavors to show English instructors at the elementary and secondary levels how "technology, particularly computer-based instruction, can be used to supplement or expand the learning of language skills." In Chapter 2, Joan Dunfey of Lesley College in Cambridge, Massachusetts, describes a graduate English education course for elementary teachers interested in integrating computers into the language arts curriculum. Dunfey says that school administrators are just beginning to see that buying hardware is not enough, that funds and time are needed for teacher training.

Elizabeth A. Sommers and James L. Collins, in Chapter 3, describe the English education graduate course they have developed at the State University of New York at Buffalo. The course prepares teachers of writing, reading, and literature to integrate computers into their language arts programs. Sommers and Collins emphasize that computers are instructional resources and must not determine what teachers and students do. A computer program should be used only when it enhances a goal that the teacher or the class is pursuing.

The next two chapters in this section describe programs that combine the resources of teacher education institutions with the energy of writing centers patterned after the National Writing Project. In Chapter 4, Amy L. Heebner tells readers about a joint teacher education project between the Teachers College Writing Project and the Center for Intelligent Tools in Education. The project has developed a graduate course, "Computers in Writing," for practicing teachers in elementary, secondary, or collegiate settings. It also supports English teachers in selected New York public schools in integrating computers into their classes as a part of its case-study research. Notable about this project is the extent to which it attempts to combine research about computers in education with teacher practices in English classrooms. Chapter 5, authored by Jane Zeni Flinn of the University of Missouri–St. Louis and Chris Madigan, describes the Gateway Writing Project, which has taught some three hundred teachers of grades K–12 ways to integrate computers with composition instruction. Collaboration and recursion, themes important in the writing process, are the same themes that have emerged as important to teacher training in the Gateway Writing Project.

This theme of articulation between public schools and teacher education institutions is carried further in Chapter 6. Barbara L. Cambridge and Ulla Connor describe a collaborative staff-development program in which junior high and high school English teachers joined with composition teachers from Indiana University–Purdue University at Indianapolis to develop innovative computer-assisted instruction designed to meet the needs of composition teachers and their students.

This concept of consistent and ongoing teacher education leads nicely into the last five chapters in this section. These chapters remind us that teacher education is certainly not limited to teacher-training institutions, that much of our education takes place within our own schools and classrooms—in elementary, junior high, high school, and college English classrooms.

Staff development at the high school level, for example, is described in Chapters 7 and 8. In Chapter 7, Sandra Hooven of Glendora High School in California provides a look at a unique program of staff development involving a low budget and minimal planning and featuring a student as a teacher trainer. Chapter 8, authored by W. Edward Bureau, language arts supervisor at Springfield High School in Pennsylvania, describes an inservice project designed to teach instructors new computer methods while at the same time revamping the writing curriculum. Bureau stresses that the simple availability of computers does not lead to their effective integration into English instruction. He attributes Springfield High School's success to the foresight involved in creating a highly structured, three-year inservice program. Unfortunately, many schools lack the resources needed to undertake such a large project.

The last four chapters in this section describe inservice education in university settings, where such programs are far less common than in public school settings. Chapter 9, written by Paul LeBlanc of Springfield College and Charles Moran of the University of Massachusetts at Amherst, describes a series of inservice workshops to train teachers in providing quick feedback to students' on-screen, in-process writing. These workshops challenge earlier assumptions about the kinds of reading and critiques necessary to help student writers in computer-supported writing environments, and the sessions focus on helping teachers make rapid diagnoses of text and oral response to writers. In Chapter 10, Deborah H. Holdstein of Governors State University in Illinois talks generally about the variables involved in setting up and implementing inservice computer education programs for English composition faculty. She stresses the importance of tailoring such programs to meet the needs of the university, department, and faculty. In agreement with this advice, in Chapter 11, Stephen A. Bernhardt and Bruce C. Appleby describe an inservice educational program at Southern Illinois University–Carbondale. The program is particularly notable because of its richness and its support by administrators.

In the final chapter of this section, Eleanor Berry, William Van Pelt, and Neil A. Trilling describe an unusual program that addresses the educational needs of tenure-track and non–tenure-track faculty, as well as graduate students. This multifaceted program at the University of Wisconsin–Milwaukee was planned carefully to avoid wasteful expenditures of administrative support, budgetary resources, and faculty expertise.

Part II: Toward Model Programs

The chapters in Part I of this collection all focus on meaningful ways that working teachers have integrated computers into their English curricula. Part II of the collection is designed to help teachers and teacher educators take a closer look at those specific components that characterize successful programs. The chapters in this section suggest specific ways readers might implement some of the key components of these teacher education programs as they create programs suited to the needs of their own individual schools and curricula.

In Chapter 13, which leads off this section, Dawn Rodrigues of Colorado State University suggests characteristics of model training programs in her opening "game plan." While she notes there is no single "right" way to implement a computer-based writing project, she does identify some criteria that seem essential for most programs. In particular, all should be rooted in writing-process theory; all should stress language, not computers; and all need administrative support.

The next three chapters in this section focus on how teachers can use word-processing programs, prewriting software, and style-analysis programs to enhance their writing instruction. In Chapter 14, Helen J. Schwartz of Indiana University–Purdue University at Indianapolis explains how teachers can create their own writing activities and classroom exercises around the word processor. She reviews some of the reasons for stressing the word processor as the central piece of software in the English classroom. In Chapter 15, Michael Spitzer of the New York Institute of Technology gives readers a comprehensive overview of the uses of prewriting software in the English class. Spitzer illustrates specific programs in order to give readers an idea of how these programs work, and examines his own practical suggestions in light of current theoretical perspectives. In Chapter 16, Kate Keifer, Stephen Reid, and Charles R. Smith, all of Colorado State University, provide essential information for those contemplating using another important computer tool: the style checkers or style-analysis programs. They argue that style checkers are not intended to be used independently by students. To be effective, the programs need to be part of a teacher's pedagogy and need to be intricately woven into the curriculum and syllabus.

The next three chapters describe further applications of computers in the English classroom. Chapter 17, by Frank Madden of Westchester

Community College, Valhalla, New York, examines the role of computers in the literature class, where they can help inexperienced students understand, appreciate, and write about literature. Madden suggests criteria for literature programs and discusses specific programs for literary analysis. Chapters 18 and 19 describe how teachers might use two additional computer-supported tools in the composition classroom: databases and networks. In Chapter 18, Stephen Marcus of the University of California at Santa Barbara explores how database programs can be used in the classroom. Marcus illustrates how database programs operate, describes several available programs, and explains how teachers can be trained to customize and use these programs in their classes. Next, in Chapter 19, Trent Batson of Gallaudet University provides advice on teaching in networked classrooms. With a networked classroom, Batson notes, comes the possibilities for computer-writing pedagogy to alter radically the classroom environment. Batson lucidly explains how and why teachers need to be trained to teach in these classrooms of the future.

The final chapters in this section address the central issues of pedagogical approach and evaluation. Chapter 20, "Computer-Supported Writing Classes: Lessons for Teachers" by Cynthia L. Selfe and Billie J. Wahlstrom of Michigan Technological University, offers insights into the way a new context—the computer classroom—dramatically alters pedagogy. Even if teachers will only meet infrequently in a lab with their students, they need to understand some of the peculiarities inherent in teaching in a lab. In Chapter 21, Raymond J. Rodrigues of Colorado State University concludes the book by offering advice on the evaluation of computer-writing curriculum projects. Rodrigues, an experienced consultant for public schools as well as a university professor and administrator, believes that such projects need to be evaluated carefully. He discusses solutions to such questions as, How do teachers and administrators know if their programs have been successful? How can teachers be actively involved in program evaluation? How can a school district develop guidelines for evaluating their projects?

Work Cited

Oates, William R., et al. 1985. "Leadership in Literacy for the Information Age." Report of the Committee on Instructional Technology, National Council of Teachers of English, Urbana, Ill.

Part I: Existing Teacher-Preparation Programs and Inservice Programs

1 A Computer-Training Program for English Teachers: Cuyahoga Community College and the Urban Initiatives Action Program

David Humphreys, Cuyahoga Community College

> Hence, could a machine be invented which would instantaneously arrange on paper each idea as it occurs to us, without any exertion on our part, how extremely useful would it be considered.
>
> Henry David Thoreau

The Program

Computers, those "extremely useful" machines, change not only what we teach in the English classroom, but how we teach as well. Learning to harness the power of the machine, however, has created a growing need for continuing education among local teachers who do not already have the necessary computer skills, and the problem of access to continuing education is a growing political issue in our profession. While courses at four-year institutions are costly and sometimes unavailable to teachers, free noncredit courses at the community college level can often provide both the hardware and the training needed to bring our profession knowledgeably into the computer age.

Why are community colleges often in a better position to answer our professional needs for teacher training in connection with computers? The all-out competition in the last decade among post-secondary schools for market share has come to blur the lines separating community and four-year colleges or universities. The community college, however, still tries to retain its emphasis on teaching rather than on research; traditionally, its English teachers concentrate on teaching composition and not on doing research for advanced literature classes. This makes community colleges a natural place for local teachers to find the training they need to keep up with the technology. Furthermore, community colleges are usually located right within the community and therefore are in a better position to respond directly to local needs. Fiscally, community colleges may also answer the needs of area teachers; programs at community colleges can be free or given for a nominal fee that is often much lower than what the four-year schools can offer. Finally, these courses are more available because teachers rarely need to go through lengthy admissions procedures or worry about degree-track requirements.

In September of 1984, Cuyahoga Community College, serving Cleveland, Ohio, and the Urban Initiatives Action Program created a program to train community teachers to use the computer in teaching writing. Major funding for this joint CCC–UI teacher program was provided by the Ohio Board of Regents. While the Urban Initiatives Program had several broad goals on our campus, we were most interested in its charge to "investigate and introduce teachers to ways that technology, particularly computer-based instruction, can be used to supplement or expand the learning of language skills" (Stewart, Kaul, and Murphy 1986). In an effort to address this charge, we designed a teacher-training program to meet the needs of local teachers from elementary through postsecondary schools. This teacher-training program is based on three important assumptions about learning to use computers in composition classes.

1. *Teachers learn a new technology best when they can take the machines home.* If computers are available, teachers are more likely to work with the machines when they have a few moments of spare time. Making time to go to a lab to practice always seems to take more time, and hence teachers are less likely to try. Most teachers cannot get into a school's computer lab until the end of the day, and then, of course, they are most anxious to go home. More important, perhaps, is that teachers be given a chance to try and to fail in private; many teachers do not like to expose their own vulnerability while students may be lurking about in the same room.

2. *The most effective training program does not begin with bits and bytes, the "BASICs" of data processing, but with applications.* When computers first appeared, the only people who could use them were people trained in programming; they had come up through traditional data-processing education programs or computer "literacy" projects learning BASIC, COBOL, FORTRAN, or one of the other computer languages. Unfortunately, these languages are like any other foreign language; in order to use them effectively, teachers need to work at them almost daily. Many of the teachers we have spoken with have dropped out of these traditional courses in pro-

gramming, discouraged about ever using computers with their students. The most effective computer-training programs, on the other hand, now bring teachers to computers through the variety of applications packages readily available commercially. Knowledge of bits and bytes comes only as the teachers find a need to know them or as their curiosity demands.

3. *Teachers need an opportunity to take the technology directly into their classrooms for a real chance to see how it will affect their own students and curricula.* Many of the teachers who come through our computers-in-composition class complain that while they may have become very excited about computers, they have no way to experiment with them in their classes. Some schools have no computer facilities at all; others have computer labs dominated by the data-processing, accounting, or math faculties. To remedy this shortage at least partially, Cuyahoga Community College and the Urban Initiatives Program purchased thirty-five portable computers to be loaned to one teacher each nine-week interval. Such an arrangement gives the teacher the freedom to work with his or her own students intensively to explore the impact of the technology on the curriculum.

The Course

In August of 1984, Cuyahoga Community College purchased fourteen Apple IIc computers, monitors, and printers and one Sony video projector to be used in the teacher-training program. Since then, the computers have been loaned out to English teachers from the college and from neighboring elementary and secondary schools for periods of eight to ten weeks. The teachers have taken them home to learn at their own pace the fundamentals of word processing and software evaluation. Many of the teachers have become comfortable enough even before the end of the course to take the machines into their own classrooms and to demonstrate principles of the writing process to their students.

The course itself consists of eight two-hour sessions held once a week at one of the campuses of Cuyahoga Community College, the offices of the Computer Consortium of Ohio, or the computer center of one of the local high schools. Because these sessions stress that most new users come to the computer not through traditional data-processing education but through applications of the computer to specific tasks, these sessions are devoted to three types of activities: basic instruction in word processing and its application in teaching writing; evaluation of existing language arts software; and presentations by participants illustrating ways the computer might be introduced into their own curricula. The session topics follow.

Session One	Introduction
Session Two	Word Processing
Session Three	Word Processing
Session Four	Applications of Word Processing in Teaching Writing
Session Five	Software Evaluation
Session Six	Software Evaluation and Other Considerations
Session Seven	Teacher Presentations
Session Eight	Teacher Presentations

Word Processing

The one application of the computer that will have by far the most profound impact on writing and the teaching of writing is word processing. The ability to make changes in the text nearly as fast as the writer can think of them suddenly makes "writing as process" more than just an abstraction (Daiute 1983, 137). Writers have known for many years that writing is a complex, reiterative process requiring multiple drafts. Unfortunately, the fullest realization of the goals of the writing process remained only for those committed to an arduous pursuit through recursive examinations and recopyings (Murray 1980, 7–8). The advent of computerized word processing, however, reduces the time and effort normally demanded by the process so that even the least experienced writers are willing to develop and refine ideas through successive drafts. As a result, teachers, with the aid of the word processor, can help students learn to write clearer, better developed, and more focused papers.

Many, if not the majority, of the teachers who enroll in our teacher-training program need to begin with the fundamentals of computer operation and the basics of word processing. Often they come to the course motivated by the inadequacy they feel as they watch their students or their own children operate computers with aplomb. Some come to the course at the urging of their department heads or colleagues; others come out of a fear that they are missing an opportunity to develop a skill they can use in their own writing. A few come out of plain fear: the school board is placing a computer in their classroom, and they must learn to do "something" with it. Occasionally, teachers already familiar with word processing enroll to explore ways to use word processing with their students. Whatever the motivation, however, the majority really need to begin by learning to find the on/off switch of the computer.

Given these various motivations, we devote the first class period to helping the teachers get acquainted with one another, reassuring them that they are in fact in the right place, and exploring their expectations for the class. After this initial discussion, the teachers see how to assemble the Apple IIc when they get the machine home. The Apple IIc is especially well suited for novices because each of the ports is unique and marked with an icon that matches one on the connecting cord. The Apple IIc was designed as a "portable" computer, but anyone trying to lug it around knows that what Apple meant was "transportable"—barely! Nevertheless, at the end of the first session, the teachers carry away the whole system—CPU, monitor, printer, mouse, software, and supply of paper—in one or two carloads and are prepared to reassemble the lot at home.

During the next two class meetings, the teachers learn the fundamentals of word processing in much the same way that we recommend teaching these skills to the students: within the context of the writing process as they work on real writing tasks. At this stage in the introduction of computers into the school curriculum, we cannot count on uniform skills among our students, and the early days of the semester must often be given over to instruction in basic keyboarding skills. These days, however, need not be counted as lost. Sessions two and three of our program provide teachers with a model for keyboarding lessons that teach development as they teach "insert," pruning as they teach "delete," organization as they teach "move," and editing as they teach "find." Teachers even discover how they can introduce students to concepts related to collaborative writing as they teach "save" and "merge." Indeed, if all of the various word-processing functions are taught in accordance with this model, teachers can provide students with a précis of the four stages of the writing process as an introduction to the entire course.

Teachers, like their students, usually learn best by doing; therefore, participants role-play as students to try their hands at a simple example of this model—one paragraph of ten to twelve sentences in scrambled order. We give the teachers a paper copy of the sentences and load a copy of it into each machine. First, we discuss the various kinds of organization an essay may take, and then we talk of logical indicators or transition words. Then the teachers "practice" dealing with organizational principles in the composition. Once they figure out the order of the sentences in the paragraph, they learn to "move" the sentences about on the computer screen. There is always at least one sentence that does not belong, so they learn the necessity of editing out what has already been written using the "erase" function. When the teachers have reformatted all of the remaining sentences into a single paragraph, we ask them to look through the text to find a place where one more detail would be appropriate and to "insert" a sentence. Several of the words in the paragraph have been left vague or abstract deliberately, and teachers may then use "find" or "find and replace" to make the language more precise.

When the teachers have completed this portion of the exercise, we load a copy of the reformatted paragraph into the computer driving the video projector, and we model a lesson in paragraph development. We again ask each teacher to play student and, in turn, to give the detail that he or she had added. We then insert these details into the text at the places indicated. Soon the paragraph grows to rather breathless proportions, and usually one of the teachers suggests that we now have too much for one paragraph. This expansion, the teachers discover, is a good way of teaching development of an idea, for the students can easily see how a simple idea can be exploited by the addition of detail. Having created a "monster paragraph," we now suggest ways of dividing the idea into smaller units, discuss the structure of these smaller units (i.e., topic sentences and supporting detail), and add a thesis sentence to provide control for the newly created entity. The teachers can now see that the computer can make the process of writing a dynamic one, letting students see the evolution of idea through manipulation of the text.

Once the teachers have become comfortable in manipulating the computers, they must learn to apply word processing in their curriculum as a tool for student writing. We are convinced that teacher-training programs fail if they do not train teachers to take the fullest advantage of those things that the computer is uniquely qualified to do. We cannot let teachers go back into the classroom thinking that the computer should be used merely to "beautify" a composition cosmetically, that it is somehow a substitute for oceans of whiteout on the final draft. In session four of our program, we demonstrate a number of these activities and ask teachers to try them out at home in preparing a document (typically a letter, a proposal, or a lesson plan) to be turned in at session five.

We begin this fourth session by demonstrating with sample essays how the teachers can help their students separate the various stages of the writing process in order to control the variables that often threaten to overwhelm them in writing. The activities of prewriting, drafting, revising, and editing can be separated, allowing students to concentrate on one element at a time. We feel that the teachers should learn that within each of these stages, too, the computer can help the student manipulate the variables to advantage. Once the first drafts of their essays have been safely stored on disk, the teachers are free to "play" with the copy that remains in the memory of the computer. They can fracture the text by inserting hard returns between sentences in order to treat the individual sentences of their own compositions as they would "exercises" in a grammar text. They can move whole paragraphs around within the body of the essay or switch the introduction and conclusion to try "what-if" games with organization. They can then discard the experimental copy, retrieve a fresh copy of the original, and add their discoveries to the essay.

But in addition to being an effective tool for writing, the computer can serve teachers as a marvelous tool for visually representing the writing process. The teachers in the CCC–UI program learn to use a computer hooked up to large-screen televisions or video projectors to demonstrate methods of drafting or revising for a classroom discussion. Lessons in which it is important to show several possibilities simultaneously—sentence-combining exercises, for example—are more graphic and compelling when done on the big screen. Perhaps the most miraculous application of this technology, however, is in the teacher's modeling of the writing process.

Teacher modeling of the writing process fills a gap in the students' experience that cannot be filled in any other way. In many traditional classes, the teacher tells the students how to write, prescribing in great detail the various steps to be followed, the many considerations to be made. The teacher may produce several published works or student essays as models and ask the students to produce their own work. Unfortunately, the students do not always understand the process involved in producing the essay because they have not successfully participated in that process. They often lack experience in solving the problems they encounter in the writing. Using the capabilities of the computer, however, the teacher can provide that experience by modeling his or her own style of solving the problems in invention, drafting, and revising.

In the CCC–UI program, we spend at least a full hour going through one complete writing assignment, carrying on a sort of stream-of-consciousness monologue to describe the decisions reached at every turn in the composing process. Some of the program participants enjoy experimenting with this strategy as part of their presentations during the last meetings of the class. All of the teachers, however, quickly see how to get their students to participate in the process in a controlled way, avoiding the risk of stalling or completely missing the goal of the writing assignment. Having participated in writing in such a controlled way, students are better able to go through the process on their own.

Software Evaluation and Other Considerations

While the emphasis of the class is clearly on word processing and its application to the writing process, we feel it is important for teachers to spend some time evaluating the various kinds of software that have been produced commercially for use in the composition classroom. We ask the teachers to examine the software in teams of two so that they can help each other through the documentation. Documentation for a good many programs is dismal at best, and the proverbial two heads are usually better than one. Trainers should also recognize that when novices work in pairs, they carry their chagrin more easily if a program just does not run. Trainers can minimize the number of such failures if they take advantage of the knowledge and confidence of the more experienced users by pairing them with novices. To guide teachers through these evaluations, we provide them with copies of the guidelines for software evaluation established by the National Council of Teachers of English (Guidelines 1984), reminding them that the real standard is whether the program brings the student into the writing process.

Because we believe computers best support a process-based writing class, we try to give participants an opportunity to try out a variety of programs that address each of the stages of the writing process. They begin by examining Hugh Burns's first attempt with *Aristotle* and *Topoi* and then move on to *Writer's Helper, Story Machine,* and some of the so-called interactive literature programs like *Story Tree* and *Eamon's Cave,* which can be used to create characters for story starters or to introduce elements of setting, plot, and character. The teachers also experiment with several different word-processing packages, including *Magic Slate* and *Homeword.* Software for the revising and editing stages of the writing process includes programs like *Ghost Writer.* The teachers also have the chance to try out the more comprehensive programs that cover all of the stages of the writing process, including Milliken's *The Writing Workshop* and the highly touted *HBJ Writer.* We also make available to the participants a number of programs like *Sentence Combining, Word Attack,* and a variety of the programs being marketed by the book publishing houses as incentives to adopt their wares (e.g., Houghton Mifflin's *Tri-Pac,* Little, Brown's *GrammarLab,* and Random House's *Borzoi College Writer).*

Another important aspect of our discussions in these classes is the preparation for change in the teachers' relationships with their colleagues. The introduction of any new element into the curriculum, and especially one involving technology, will inevitably raise a furor, especially among humanities scholars, who are often uncomfortable with technology and reluctant to accept these changes. One teacher, when faced with the introduction of computers, lamented that "there must be one avenue left open for the imagination"; another complained that "students need to develop the mind, not depend on a machine." More commonly, teachers report that their colleagues think of the computer as a "glamorous, high-tech typewriter." One teacher worried that computers were too hard to learn to use, observing that "learning to write is difficult; learning to write and learning to use a computer makes matters worse." Of course, computers are not the magic weapon in the fight for literacy, and some objections may be well founded. More often than not, however, the issues that critics raise really are not the point.

The point is change itself. Whether the innovation is the process approach, writing across the curriculum, or computers in composition, innovation means teachers are being asked to restructure those premises and relationships which they have already learned to master and with which they are comfortable. Confronted by change, they no longer find themselves in command of the vocabulary and ground rules. Power structures within the department must change to accommodate the new experts; novices will have to expend new energy in acquiring new skills. Performance may now be measured along unfamiliar lines. Each of these problems threatens the image that teachers have of themselves as competent, experienced teachers of others.

The CCC–UI course certainly does not offer foolproof strategies for winning over whole departments of English teachers. It does, however, prepare teachers, through discussion and a chance to share experiences, for the reception they sometimes find waiting for them in their own schools. They learn that they must work with their colleagues to give them time to get familiar with the new technology, to understand the real advantages it offers, and then to gain some ownership of this technology, which will eventually transform the way that we teach English. Above all, the participants in this workshop are encouraged to avoid being too defensive with their colleagues, to answer legitimate objections as well as they can, and to avoid personalizing the debate over issues that express only another's fear of change.

Applications for the Curriculum

An important part of any teacher-training program is the opportunity to bring newly acquired skills or theories into each teacher's own curriculum. Teachers still new to computer concepts are sometimes reluctant to take the first step in transferring the concepts to their own activities. Reserving a fair portion of class time for individual teachers to present their own experiences assures at least a beginning upon which to build.

The remaining two or three class periods in the CCC–UI course provide time for the teachers to show how what they have learned might apply in their own classes. Teachers can choose from several types of presentations.

1. We encourage most of the teachers to find one objective in their curriculum which can be presented effectively using a computer. They can then write a lesson plan and try it out on the other participants.
2. In lieu of such a model lesson, the teachers may also review two or three word-processing programs or other software packages. Apple systems are widely used by the school districts in this area, and the teachers have little difficulty in getting additional software since many of their schools have become members of the Minnesota Educational Computing Corporation (M.E.C.C.) or the Educational Computer Consortium of Ohio (E.C.C.O.).
3. Teachers may also review two or three books or magazines that they have found useful in learning to use computers in their classrooms.
4. At least one teacher found another option; she did a detailed survey of how other teachers in her district had solved the thorny management problems that come with having only one computer in the classroom.

The one requirement of the course, which is offered at no charge to teachers, is that the teachers write summaries of their presentations, the best of which are then photocopied, placed in a three-ring binder, and given to the next class of teachers who take the course.

This latter portion of the course has been especially valuable, given the inter-institutional makeup of the class. Teachers from all teaching levels have been able to exchange ideas not only about technology in the classroom, but also about a variety of problems or approaches to teaching. Technology, for example, does not exist apart from methodology; discussions of word processing inevitably lead to discussions of writing as process. Ultimately, these discussions present an opportunity for greater understanding and cooperation among the schools throughout the county. In the long run, such collaboration will suggest ways to improve the continuity of elementary through postsecondary instruction.

The NEC Loan Program

Unfortunately, many of the public school teachers who attend our teacher-training workshop face a serious handicap when they wish to try out what they have learned about computers. The computer labs in their schools, if they are lucky enough to have such luxuries, are often monopolized by the math, science, or computer science departments, leaving little opportunity for English classes to use the machines. To address this problem, we have purchased thirty-five NEC 8201A portable computers, which we began loaning out in the fall of 1986 to selected public school teachers from the CCC–UI training program for use with their students.

This element of the program is an extension of Cuyahoga Community College's own experience in using NEC portable computers to teach sections of developmental English and college composition. Students at CCC make a deposit of ten dollars and receive one of these laptop computers to take home for the quarter. While the memory is small and the text processor is limited, the NEC 8201A's are well suited for the job. It is easy to learn to operate them, permitting the teacher to spend less time teaching data processing and more time teaching English. Because these machines are portable, students can take them home or use them in class, an option that combines the public and private modes of composition. Students at all levels of our curriculum have responded well to these machines, often showing a better attitude toward writing as a result.

These same qualities made the NEC computers even more attractive for use with the CCC–UI program. Because the equipment would have to be moved every nine weeks from one school to another, we wanted machines that would give us the greatest portability with the most computing power, both for student writing and for teacher demonstration. The NEC 8201A has a 16K nonvolatile memory, a 40-column by 8-line LCD screen, and the ability to run either with an AC adapter or four "AA" alkaline batteries. The nonvolatile memory is especially important because it eliminates the need to teach younger students the intricacies of storage and retrieval on disks or tapes. When the students have finished writing, they merely turn the machine off, and the backup NiCad batteries preserve their files for up to thirty days. The ability to run on batteries also means that any classroom can be turned into a "computer lab" without completely rewiring the room with fifty or sixty outlets.

The machine reserved for the teacher is equipped with several enhancements. First, it has a disk drive. Teachers need to be at least a day or two ahead of their students in creating lessons; but the 16K memory, unfortunately, is too small to keep more than a couple of lessons in memory at one time. The more usual data recorder is often unreliable and much too slow for loading thirty-five student machines with the day's lessons. Therefore, the teacher's machine comes with the optional 3½-inch disk drive. Second, the teacher's machine also includes a special CRT adapter that enables the teacher to project the lesson on a large-screen television or video projector. The regular LCD screen makes classroom demonstration difficult, if not impossible. These enhancements, unfortunately, further erode the amount of memory available for writing, but they are essential in the classroom.

Under the CCC–UI program, a teacher has the machines for one nine-week interval. Both of the sixth-grade teachers involved in the first loan program were quite enthusiastic about having the computers in their classes. They found that students were more willing to edit, print, and reprint using the computers. Students and teachers alike loved the computers and did more writing using them. Indeed, the variety of their writing assignments (several types of poems, personal narratives, autobiographies, and a short research project) suggests that they were quite productive in the short time that they had the machines. Most important, perhaps, is the teachers' observation that writing was again "exciting to teach."

There are, of course, demons to wrestle in such a loan program. The greatest of these is time. Most school curricula are regulated by a district syllabus with more than enough material to fill each day of the school year. Adding computers to this already-busy schedule means that both teacher and syllabus have to make accommodations for the computer. Time is also a demon in the practical workings of the class day. Our program, for instance, could only provide one printer, hardly enough for all twenty-four students to print out their work by the end of the fifty-minute period. The teachers reported, "since students did not have access to computers or printers outside of the classroom, time was precious and always rushed. It was difficult to provide individualization." For the most part, though, the demons were manageable, and the teachers were able to build upon the enthusiasm for the computer, which one sixth-grade student said made him feel like he was "a professional writer."

As these "extremely useful" machines move closer to the center of the school curriculum, the role of the community college in continuing education for local teachers will grow accordingly. The two-year college must provide the best of resources and training programs to help teachers move into the computer age. We believe that the Cuyahoga Community College–Urban Initiatives program is a significant step in that direction, providing affordable workshops at convenient times and places. Teachers who have participated in these workshops have returned to their classrooms with "useful" skills and renewed enthusiasm for teaching writing.

Works Cited

Daiute, Colette A. 1983. "The Computer as Stylus and Audience." *College Composition and Communication* 34: 134–45.

Guidelines for Review and Evaluation of English Language Arts Software. 1984. Urbana, Ill.: National Council of Teachers of English.

Murray, Donald M. 1980. "Writing as Process: How Writing Finds Its Own Meaning." In *Eight Approaches to Teaching Composition,* edited by Timothy R. Donovan and Ben W. McClelland, 3–20. Urbana, Ill.: National Council of Teachers of English.

Stewart, Mac, Theodore Kaul, and Gratia Murphy. 1986. *External Evaluation Report on the Urban Initiatives Action Programs.* Columbus: Ohio Board of Regents.

2 Integrating Computers into the Language Arts Curriculum at Lesley College

Joan Dunfey, Lesley College

Introduction

"Integrating Computers into the Language Arts Curriculum" is a three-credit graduate-level class in the Computers in Education master's degree program at Lesley College in Cambridge, Massachusetts. The focus is on learning how to use computers as an effective tool in an educational setting. Lesley was the first college in the country to offer this specialized degree, which fits into its philosophy of offering quality teacher-training programs using adult learning models. Unlike most teacher-training programs, which are limited to reaching teachers within defined geographical bounds, Lesley College offers this class in one of two settings:

1. On campus at the Lesley College computer lab in Cambridge on a semester basis. Here we serve primarily the greater Boston and New England area.
2. In an "Outreach" setting away from the school. We meet a real need by taking the program "on the road" to various cities across the country to teachers who cannot come on campus. It has been taught in Boulder, Denver, and Colorado Springs, Colorado; Omaha, Nebraska; St. Louis, Missouri; Casper, Wyoming; Albuquerque, New Mexico; and Boston and Fall River, Massachusetts.

Most teachers in the class are involved in the Lesley program on a part-time basis, taking two courses a semester and holding full-time teaching jobs. A few teachers are on sabbatical, and this course is part of their full-time class load.

Teaching this class on campus is quite different from teaching it off campus in an outreach setting, where the course meets in a wide variety of places: school computer labs, adult education centers, libraries, or anywhere a number of computers are available. The facilities range from labs extensively supplied with software to small rooms with a few computers. The outreach setting also demands a classroom-centered approach. Because there is no campus as traditionally defined, the teachers create a unique group identity. The space belongs to them, and the instructor is the visitor. It is crucial for us to be aware of the group's identity and needs and to adapt the course to their level of experience and their goals as much as possible.

Because meeting teachers' real needs is our goal, either version of this course can be taken as part of a master's program or simply for personal enrichment. This concept is especially important for English and language arts teachers who do not want to be computer experts, but rather who are looking for training only in this one area.

Course Design

When we designed this course, we decided to use a traditional language arts curriculum model and to arrange the syllabus around the subject areas of reading, writing, and language study. Each class begins with a discussion of the current research and effective teaching methodology in each area. With this discussion as a background, the computer is introduced as a tool. The course is as much about effective ways of teaching language arts as it is about computer implementation.

The goals of the course are threefold. First, we want teachers to begin to see that the computer can be a useful tool for the teaching of language arts. Second, we want to offer teachers a valid language arts curriculum course which provides them with a theoretically sound background in the pedagogy for teaching the different areas of language arts. Third, we hope to use the computer to revitalize experienced teachers who are looking for new ways to teach language arts.

Because we use an adult learning model, we are concerned that the students, practicing classroom teachers, be thoroughly involved in the class. Wherever possible, we make sure that the topics discussed in the course relate to actual classroom settings. Similarly, we make sure that the projects in the course utilize a sound theoretical base yet deal with implementation issues that could relate to the realities of teachers' classrooms.

Also central to our course is allotting time for sharing of experiences about classroom implementations that work. As much as possible, we strive to make the teachers and their concerns the focus of the class.

The reality of this varies drastically from class to class. Some classes have a number of teachers with a depth of knowledge about language arts, but no actual experience using a computer in a language arts setting. When this occurs, we step in and offer ideas and share projects from other classes. When the class has rich experiences, these experiences become the center of discussion.

Given our perspective, the computer represents a "neat phenomenon" (Lawler 1982), one in which the student and teacher are caught up in the magic of the power of the computer's ability. We hope this new tool can help transform ineffectual teaching methods by offering teachers a new and creative way to teach language skills. Language arts teachers need to be free of their fears of machines and also need to learn enough about computers to understand how they work.

The Structure of the Course

To understand how the class functions, it is necessary to investigate the different settings of the meetings, the activities, the readings, and the projects. The structure of "Integrating Computers into the Language Arts Curriculum" varies according to the setting in which it is offered. On campus, the course takes a standard graduate-level format by meeting once a week for fifteen weeks. Each three-hour class is divided into a combination of lecture, software demonstration, group discussion, and hands-on time in the computer lab. In an outreach setting, the course is offered in an intensive weekend format. Students meet Friday evening and all day Saturday and Sunday. Two weekends, separated by a month, fulfill the time requirements for a three-hour graduate-level course. Students complete part of their written work in the intervening weeks and then have a month after the last weekend to submit their final projects.

In-class activities include the following:

1. A lecture or discussion
2. A demonstration of software
3. A critical discussion of the software in a large or small group
4. Hands-on time
5. Group discussion of implementation issues
6. Examples of classroom materials
7. Guest speakers

The lecture generally reviews the research on the methodology of teaching that particular subject area—writing, reading, or language arts. Discussions center around teachers' experiences in teaching the particular topic. Often the demonstration of software models a classroom implementation. Teachers try out the software in the role of students to explore all of its possibilities. Occasionally we plan a structured activity in which teachers are grouped into teams by grade levels or play a game against another group. After this session the class meets as a whole and discusses classroom implementation issues: management, how the software fits into an existing curriculum, appropriate grade levels, and how to modify it for different age levels. On campus, guest speakers often share their expertise. Software developers demonstrate a program in progress, or experienced teachers share their curricular ideas with the class.

The assigned readings provide the necessary theoretical background and suggestions for computer implementation. For some teachers, they act as a review; for others, they serve as an introduction to research.

The focus of the teachers' projects is intentionally diverse. Our goal in this adult learning model is to have projects meet the needs of individual teachers. Most teachers do classroom-specific projects. Others, however, write research papers or evaluate software, and some create programs specifically for their own classes. Still other teachers choose to learn tool programs, word processors, or databases. Some teachers collaborate and do a joint project. We devote considerable class time for discussion of projects before the teachers begin, and they often use each other as resources for materials and ideas. After trying out their ideas with their own classes, teachers present their projects to the entire class.

Course Topics

"Integrating Computers into the Language Arts Curriculum" deals specifically with six major topics: language arts issues and software evaluation; the process approach to writing, including prewriting, word processing, revision, and publication; reading; adventure games; language and LOGO; and databases.

1. Language Arts Issues and Software Evaluation

The first major topic we cover in "Integrating Computers into the Language Arts Curriculum" is the role of the computer in a language arts setting and an evaluation of software. We begin by raising the issue of melding the complex nature of English as a subject with the literal nature of computers. Some knowledge of how computers work and how programs function helps in understanding the kind of programs available to teachers. Teachers often want programs which check students' answers for correctness. But English is a complex language, and computer systems as yet cannot know all the possible "right" answers. Using Carol Chomsky's (1984) evaluative criteria, we focus specifically on language arts issues by asking such questions as:

> Is the program interesting to you?
>
> Does the thinking that the program requires seem worthwhile?
>
> Is the emphasis on thinking rather than on repetitive practice?
>
> Does the program involve two or more students at a time?
>
> Does the program introduce an activity or thought that is different from that provided by books or paper and pencil?
>
> Does the program allow the user to customize material?
>
> Can the program be used many times by a student and remain interesting and worthwhile?
>
> Does the program allow time for reflection?
>
> Does satisfaction in using the program come from the content itself?

This list differs dramatically from the standard software evaluative criteria in its focus on language arts issues.

2. The Process Approach to Writing

The second major topic covered in "Integrating Computers into the Language Arts Curriculum" is the process approach to writing and valid computer implementations at each stage. The discussion of word processing begins with a demonstration of the word processor's simplest capabilities, the ability to type in words. We then examine our list of issues and concerns surrounding writing: students' lack of motivation, their unwillingness to revise, their fear of making mistakes, their focusing on superficial errors.

Because the students in the teachers' classes are young, the issues for teachers in choosing a word-processing system tend to be practical. Ease of use, compatibility with adjunct software (such as a spelling checker and a thesaurus), and availability are the features seen as most important. Most teachers of elementary children particularly like the systems which offer large letters and speech synthesis because they so readily meet immediate curricular needs.

Once they learn how to select a word-processing system, teachers are most concerned with management issues: teaching a system, using a lab versus a single computer, pairing students, creating classroom experts, and group writing assignments. We discuss research findings on word processing (Daiute 1985) and successful strategies for implementation.

We then focus on prewriting by brainstorming what teachers would like a computer to do for them in the area of prewriting. After a hands-on period in which we look at several prewriting programs, we use a word processor to model different prewriting strategies.

We begin the discussion of revision and editing by evaluating various revision strategies that are theoretically sound: teacher conferencing, small group responding, and peer editing. We discuss the research findings which suggest that although word processing makes revision much easier, it lends itself to superficial corrections (Daiute 1985). We demonstrate how a readability formula works, and we try out different kinds of passages. We type in random letters, and the teachers are surprised to see that nonsense can be given a high readability while a passage from Hemingway merits only a fourth-grade reading level. The goal is for teachers to see the mechanics of how style-analysis programs work and to be able to use them wisely. We evaluate spelling checkers, and we discuss how to use their capabilities, word frequency, and word flagging in a writing conference.

Embedded in the discussions of writing are illustrations of successful publishing techniques using computer printouts. We show teachers how they can creatively combine word-processed writing with student illustrations to produce professional-appearing newspapers, pamphlets, and bound books. A simple beginning project for young children is to have them write a short story with the text printed at the bottom of the page. Each child illustrates his or her story with various media, ranging from watercolors to markers to crayons. The stories are collected into a single class book, which can be added to the school library.

After teachers learn how to use a word processor as a writing tool, we explore the different ways that a word processor can be used as a tool for creating language arts activities (Dunfey 1985; Wresch 1987; Rodrigues and Rodrigues 1986). Prewriting prompts based on particular works of fiction can be created by the teacher and stored for later use as outlines for papers. Reading activities for sequencing can be easily created. In this class we demonstrate how teachers can enter the lines of a story out of order and ask students to use the "move" command to put the story back in order. This system dramatically improves on the old paper-and-pencil technique of drawing arrows or renumbering the sentences in a passage. Students can literally see the passage in the correct order.

3. Reading

When we move to the next topic, reading, we begin by defining our goals. Then we ask teachers to express their expectations. Some teachers have high hopes for programs that reputedly diagnose strengths and weaknesses and keep track of kinds of errors. Other teachers hope to give students practice in skill work in a motivating format, but find only electronic workbooks. Another hope is that the computer can create activities to teach reading skills on the computer that can then be transferred to reading away from the computer.

We first evaluate software that represents trends in beginning-reading programs. Some programs teach sight words by combining a limited vocabulary with computer animation. These programs give young children power over words and put the youngsters in the active role of seeing how words work, rather than in the passive role of merely reading them. We then move to evaluating software that uses the cloze procedure, which offers teachers editing opportunities. These programs are based on verifiable research on the nature of reading and deal with reading skills holistically. Each of these programs promotes using context and language clues to help the reader supply the missing word or parts of words. For example, with *M-ss-ng L-nks,* students must use a variety of kinds of clues—their knowledge of spelling, grammatical constructions, common word patterns, usage, and the source of the passage—to solve the game.

Because most of the reading software on the market takes the form of workbooks, we focus discussions around a few quality pieces of software that are not electronic workbooks. Each of the software programs we choose uses the computer to do an activity which cannot be done otherwise, and each works with reading skills but not in a conventional way.

We model the use of a controversial piece of software called *The Puzzler* in a brainstorming session. Using the skills of predicting, confirming, and integrating based on research in these areas, this program asks the student to use his or her own experience in life as clues to reading. We read one of the passages, "Unusual Friend," a page at a time. As we proceed, the teachers make some predictions about who or what the friend could be. The group interaction provides a wealth of responses. The more we read, the closer we get to determining who the friend is, and we modify our predictions by using vocabulary, context, and categorization skills. When the class examines the kind of feedback produced, controversy arises. The program never tells readers the one "right" answer; instead, it offers the opportunity to see and evaluate previous players' decisions. When played in a group format, the game is a thought-provoking and wonderful opportunity for shared testing of different hypotheses.

Another thought-provoking reading activity that we play in class involves using *Suspect Sentences* in groups. Because the computer is best used for collaborative learning, the class of teachers is divided into teams. Each team reads a paragraph, writes a sentence which imitates the tone and style of the paragraph, and then decides where in the paragraph to hide it. We save our new paragraph on a disk, and the other team must try to find the inserted sentence. Each team becomes deeply involved in tricking the other one. This game deals with higher-level thinking and with reading and writing skills in a motivating game format.

4. *Adventure Games*

The next major topic we cover is using adventure games to teach language and reading skills. Adventure games use a format similar to choose-your-own-adventure books; the student tries to achieve a goal, but meets with various misfortunes along the way. Programs range from simple branching stories to complex quests. The time needed to solve each can range from an hour to hundreds of hours. Students, especially low-level readers, love these games. A helpful exercise for teachers is to play one game and then to make a list of all of the reading skills used along the way. Teachers soon realize that to survive they must take notes, make a map, make predictions, test out hypotheses, and learn new vocabulary words. Adventure games give students practice with reading skills in a totally new way.

5. *Language Learning*

After reviewing the research on our next topic—language learning—we discuss the distinction between language knowledge and language use. To illustrate this distinction, we evaluate a number of programs. The first is a popular program in which students shoot down words according to their parts of speech, using a key on the keyboard. The next program asks students to identify parts of speech in a sentence written by someone else. Finally, we write a cinquain poem by using a computer program which asks for words by parts of speech. Here we are using language in a real setting for a real purpose. We have progressed from knowledge of grammatical facts to using language for a real purpose. We next evaluate commercially available programs which deal with grammar and language and put them into either category, language learning or language use. Because the majority of programs are grammar drill and practice, teachers see how few actually deal with language use.

Another unique way that we suggest for teaching language skills with a computer is to use the programming language LOGO. A minimal knowledge of LOGO's list-processing capabilities lets students explore language in a totally new way. LOGO is often viewed as the computer language for young children who want to draw pictures. In reality, it is a dialect of LISP, a high-level language used in artificial intelligence. By using programs which use the list-processing capabilities of LOGO, students can enter and categorize lists of words. To illustrate this capability, teachers use a simple program called *MAKEWORD*, which asks users to type in a list of prefixes, such as *un-*, *sub-*, *pre-*, *re-*, and *post-*, and a list of root words, such as *amble*, *mix*, *judge*, *read*, and *sound*. The computer then randomly generates new words: *prejudge*, *postamble*, *submix*, *subsound*, *preread*, *unmix*, *unjudge*, *unsound*, and so on. We then brainstorm language activities which use these new words, such as finding the real words, determining the definition of a prefix by seeing how it changes the meaning of words in the same way, defining the new words by our knowledge of both parts, or compiling a dictionary of these new words and defining them. We use the *GRAM* program (Sharples 1983) to explore how a sentence works by rearranging the order of parts of speech and letting the computer generate sentences for us. The unique ability of the computer to manipulate language offers a change from the worksheet approach to language learning.

6. Databases for Research

The final topic explored in "Integrating Computers into the Language Arts Curriculum" is the use of databases of information as tools for research. A research assignment can be drastically reshaped by using a database which transforms "dead facts" into living knowledge.

Conclusion

We feel that our course provides a sound way to retrain teachers in the current research and methodology of teaching writing, reading, and language, as well as computer implementation. Also, this kind of a course provides an ideal method of revitalizing teachers. Teachers like the option of doing classroom-specific projects and sharing ideas and successful teaching strategies.

"Integrating Computers into the Language Arts Curriculum" has evolved over a three-year time period and has improved substantially for a variety of reasons. More and better software exists today, and the storehouse of materials and curricula that we can share only increases. The idea of computer use in a language arts setting, especially in the area of word processing, has become accepted by the educational community. The state of computer education has shifted from programming to curriculum implementation. Moreover, as computer labs sit vacant, schools systems are beginning to recognize the need for courses designed to help teachers see the connection between their existing curriculum and computer use.

Using a computer to teach language arts offers an exciting new path for innovative teachers. For teachers who are eager to try out new and creative ideas, the computer offers new possiblities. Many teachers find that the work they do using a computer is the most creative and energizing of their careers.

As computer technology increases and as the price of computers comes down, computers will be more accessible to all. In the not-far future, every child may have his or her own word-processing machine as a personal writing tool. Classes like ours meet a real need in our profession today by helping teachers prepare for the future.

Works Cited

Chomsky, Carol. 1984. "Finding the Best Language Arts Software." *Classroom Computer Learning* (January): 61–63.

Daiute, Colette. 1985. *Writing and Computers*. Reading, Mass.: Addison-Wesley.

Dunfey, Joan. 1985. "Writer's Dozen." *Teaching and Computers* (April): 20–24.

Lawlor, Joseph, ed. 1982. *Computers in Composition Instruction*. Los Alamitos, Calif.: SWRL Education Research and Development.

Rodrigues, Dawn, and Raymond J. Rodrigues. 1986. *Teaching Writing with a Word Processor, Grades 7–13*. Urbana, Ill.: National Council of Teachers of English.

Sharples, Michael. 1983. "A Construction Kit for Language." In *Exploring English with Microcomputers*, edited by D. Chandler, 51–58. London: Council for Educational Technology.

Wresch, William. 1987. *A Practical Guide to Computer Uses in the English Language Arts Classroom*. Englewood Cliffs, N.J.: Prentice-Hall.

3 English Teachers and the Potential of Microcomputers as Instructional Resources at the State University of New York at Buffalo

Elizabeth A. Sommers, Boston University

James L. Collins, State University of New York at Buffalo

Introduction

In this chapter we discuss the English education graduate course we developed at SUNY at Buffalo to teach educators how to integrate microcomputers into their language arts programs. We begin by discussing our approach to using microcomputers as instructional resources in the English language arts, and we describe our goals and audiences for the course. Next, we present the theoretical framework for our computer-assisted language instruction program as we explain specific activities and practices. Finally, we evaluate the strengths and weaknesses of our program.

Microcomputers as Instructional Resources

Our approach to using microcomputers in the English language arts holds that they should be used as instructional resources, as a means of teaching and learning rather than as an end in themselves. Sound pedagogical theory and practice must shape the use of microcomputers in English language arts classrooms, and we must not allow computers to determine what teachers and students do. Computer skills, we believe, are not an appropriate focus of instruction for English and language arts teachers; instead, we advocate keeping the focus on language skills and on using the computer as an instrument to enhance the learning of language, writing, and literature. The microcomputer in this approach is not the subject being studied but, rather, a resource or tool for teaching and learning.

Teachers of English and language arts looking for ways to use microcomputers in writing instruction, for example, will benefit from holding firmly to the principle that the heart of the matter is to teach writing, not word processing. Too often we have seen and heard the assumption that word processing by itself has an effect on writing abilities. This assumption probably comes from being overly enthusiastic about the power of computers to influence writing abilities, as in the case of the teacher who recently told us that a dissertation is easier to write on a word processor than by any other means. We disagree; perhaps the dissertation would be easier to type, but the writing would still be a major project. No other tool by itself improves skill, whether it is the writer's craft or any other. Computers by themselves might increase motivation for writing and make certain aspects of writing easier, but we doubt if computers by themselves can improve writing abilities, no more than electric screwdrivers, by themselves, can improve woodworking abilities.

Our course is designed to help teachers become sensitive to how microcomputers and word-processing software can combine with the best possible instructional theory and practice. The course has two primary goals: to improve writing instruction through intensive study of theory and practice, and to give teachers access to the potentials of microcomputers as teaching and writing resources in their classrooms. We also have two primary audiences: English teachers and teachers of content courses. The teachers of English, writing, and language arts come to the course from area schools as well as from graduate courses in English education and reading education, and their interests are mainly in using computers to teach writing, reading, and literature. The teachers of other subjects take our course as an elective in a graduate program called Microcomputers in Education, and their predominant interests are many, ranging, for example, across science and math education, computer programming, software design and development, and computer applications in a variety of disciplines.

While we eventually discovered how to make this heterogeneous audience an advantage, in the planning stages it created baffling problems for us. In the same course, we somehow had to serve the needs of classroom teachers of language arts with extensive teaching experience but no microcomputer experience; doctoral candidates in English education with a firm theoretical grounding in composition and some college teaching experience but no computer backgrounds; master's students in English education who sometimes had neither classroom nor computer experience; and content-course teachers with varying degrees of computer experience but no experience as writing teachers. These teachers, moreover, came from every educational level and teaching situation. How were we to accommodate such diverse needs?

We knew it was imperative that we incorporate the basics in composition theory, teaching practices, and educational computing uses, introducing novices to each strand while reinforcing and refining for more experienced teachers. We also knew our attempts to disseminate information through readings, discussions, and lectures, while important, were insufficient tools for such ambitious purposes. Our solution became the true strength of our "Computers and Composition" course: while addressing theory, practices, and computer uses, we take the opportunity to model an integrative writing course.

Theory and Practice

We find our approach is most effective when separate rooms are used and two teachers (or a teacher and a skillful student facilitator) can lead separate activities. Because we have dual instructional intentions, these logistics are important.

In our plan, we methodically present a common theoretical framework for the teaching of writing on-line throughout the semester, discussing selected readings in small groups. Most importantly, we want teachers in our course to understand that writing is best taught as a problem-solving process in decentralized, student-centered classrooms. This means informing teachers about composing processes, response to student writing, assignment making, and the teacher's classroom roles. It also means informing teachers about the vocabulary, uses, and evaluation of microcomputer uses in the English classroom.

Simultaneously, we supplement the theoretical discussions with a full semester's participation in an integrative writing course. The decentralized, student-centered writing classroom which we model is a vital illustration of the meaning of the theories for teaching language and writing. Both theoretical principles and teaching practices are discussed fully below.

First, we introduce the concept of writing as a process, new to many of our students and viewed too simplistically by many others. Rejecting a linear model in which writers prewrite, write, and perhaps revise, we discuss text production as a complex, recursive, and idiosyncratic activity, only partially understood. We make our students aware of conflicting theories of discourse production, including a cognitive deficit model (Lunsford 1979) and Flower and Hayes's (1981) four-phase cognitive process model, based upon the four distinct but concurrent thinking processes of planning, translating, reviewing, and monitoring.

We especially attempt to help writers grasp the intricacies of revision, often misconstrued as error remediation by both teachers and students. To this end, we draw from selected readings about revision. For example, Murray (1978) distinguishes between two kinds of revision. Internal revision is the process of making meaning through language, and the writer serves as primary audience here. External revision, in contrast, involves transformation of a text for an outside audience through such work as editorial corrections and stylistic reshaping. Flower's (1979) discussion of writer-based prose, or discourse written primarily for the writer as audience, suggests that students must be taught revision as a meaning-making process, transforming writer-based prose by considering the audience and its purpose. In a third revision model, Faigley and Witte (1981) divide revisions into two broad categories of surface and meaning changes. They further subdivide surface changes into formal and meaning-preserving changes. Meaning changes, depending upon whether they affect the text on a local or holistic level, are subdivided into microstructure and macrostructure changes. While different, all of these approaches recognize the importance of higher-level writing concerns: for example, content development, rhetorical considerations, and discourse structure.

We also draw from research on the differences between successful and unsuccessful student composing strategies. Such studies show that unskilled writers overedit prematurely, revise largely at surface and word levels, and are unaware of or unable to cope with larger, holistic textual concerns. Lack of confidence and little sense of an audience outside of themselves further handicap unskilled writers (Perl 1979; Sommers 1980). Successful student writers, in contrast, tend to perceive meaningful revision as vital, the means through which the discourse framework is built. These writers have also internalized a sense of audience (Sommers 1980).

In our classroom, teachers new to these ideas often write as unskilled basic writers themselves, using the same composing strategies as other basic writers; we help them toward more productive strategies and higher-order discourse concerns. To this end, from the onset we ask teachers to become writers themselves for the entire course, and we teach them about writing by making writing a primary concern. Teachers compose self-sponsored texts of various types: journals, short essays, and midterm and final projects. These texts prove important in many ways. Daily journal writing is valuable both as a record of thought and as an instrument of further thinking. Our students discover their journals are fertile ground for small group discussions, for grappling with concepts related to the course, and for final projects. And writing immediately helps teachers become aware of their own writing processes as well as those of other students, making theoretical constructs more comprehensible (if sometimes less credible).

Our theoretical stance is that writing is best taught one-on-one in writing conferences, and we introduce our students to this often-new concept early in the course. In our approach, teachers and writers explore subsequent drafts of a text in order to solve problems and to learn both process and subskills. We advocate textual intervention in the hierarchical pattern in which first content, then organization, and finally sentence and word problems are the primary concerns (Beach 1980; Garrison 1981; Murray 1980). We try to be certain that teachers make connections between the readings about conferences and the studies we present on student revision practices. They need to know that they can help students learn more successful writing processes through skillful conferring, by helping writers recognize and solve higher-level writing problems.

As we provide this background, we require that teachers learn how to confer with writers by conferring regularly with each other and with us. Here, too, writers' own texts—more often, the short essays about various aspects of computing and composing—prove beneficial in illustrating theories. Our teachers genuinely care about this writing and have a vested interest in working through their ideas. As they grapple with their texts, revision quickly becomes far more than simple error correction. They realize and appreciate the complexity of any writer's attempts to make meaning with language. Playing the student's role, teachers soon understand how much their texts can be improved by discussion with concerned and helpful readers. This discussion includes readers' responding and also writers' clarifying meaning by talking it through with readers (David 1986). If they experience flat, meaningless, or incomprehensible responses, this may not be bad. It illustrates the confusion or frustration student writers can feel as a result of fruitless writing conferences. Playing the teacher's role, our students gain experience in response and begin to master the difficult art of expert response. Finally, in conferring with every class member, our teachers encounter a wide range of possible conference styles.

Rather than use our limited time to develop a comprehensive base for the evaluation of writing, we refer teachers to primary sources which elaborate upon measurement and summative evaluation of writing quality (Cooper and Odell 1977; Diederich 1974). Instead, in discussion we stress the importance of formative evaluation, or ongoing response to texts in progress. This ties in well with our ongoing work with writing and conferring. Teachers experience formative evaluation firsthand in writing conferences with one another and with us. Expert response to unfinished work, they also realize, can appreciably improve writing quality in a way final evaluations seldom do. Students infer our primary message about effective evaluation: valuable response is specific and informative, not judgmental.

Assignment making and sequencing are the next important theoretical concerns we address. Here we introduce readings which suggest writers most profitably benefit from a wide range of rhetorical contexts and writing forms (Judy 1980; Lauer 1980) rather than typically writing for the teacher as examiner (Britton et al. 1975). But teachers often present writers with tasks which are too restrictive, both in subject and rhetorical context (Jenkins 1980; Larson 1970; Throckmorton 1980).

We make teachers aware of how difficult and critical it is to design effective writing assignments. Suitable writing assignments are designed with writers' skill levels, experiences, and concerns in mind and are meant both to challenge and to intrigue. Without unduly restricting writers, assignments should provide guidelines for content and organization. Good assignments also encourage writers to explore a range of voices and audiences. Ideally, sequential writing assignments become increasingly intricate and demanding, connecting past knowledge to present capabilities while opening future possibilities (Brick 1981; Hoffman and Schifsky 1977; Jordan 1967; Larson 1970; Simon, Hawley, and Britton 1973; Throckmorton 1980).

We supplement this theoretical base by asking teachers to write assignments for their students, experimenting with different audiences and purposes as well as different forms and content expectations. Teachers share, discuss, and revise these assignments, which we then compile into a master list at the end of the semester.

The writing teacher's role in a decentralized classroom, we believe, is that of collaborator and facilitator, but still the teacher needs to structure the class for success, to create a positive environment for writing, to plan meaningful activities and assignments, and to respond effectively to writing. Here "decentralized" means many carefully planned and orchestrated individual and group learning experiences; it does not mean simply trusting students to their own designs or having students do individually what they could do just as well as a class. Thus, a visitor to our classroom would see many activities in a typical class period:

1. An opening round of journal writing and voluntary reading from journal entries.
2. A round of sharing problems and possibilities encountered while writing and word processing, with the whole class or a special-interest group, such as teachers interested in writing in math classrooms, taking part in the discussion.
3. Individual and coauthored writing at computers and tables: some writers working on papers for the course or other projects, two writers collaborating on a paper on teacher utilities software, two others transcribing interviews for the class newspaper, and so on.
4. Writer conferences between partners and among members of small groups.
5. A closing round of somewhat more formal discussions, led by one of us and involving half the class at a time, on topics and readings from our syllabus.

We also act as expert consultants during the course. The diversity of our students means, of course, that many special needs must be addressed. Our decentralized classroom makes it possible for us to work with individual teachers to find the best uses of computers in their own teaching situations. We provide a thorough bibliography on the teaching of writing and research on microcomputers as language arts tools, and since research is still limited at this point, we help teachers answer their questions by returning again and again to the theoretical underpinnings described earlier.

Our students, too, practice the role of expert consultants. Early in the semester, teachers begin work on a final project, which can take a variety of forms. For example, students can take a close look at some of the issues raised in small group discussions or in the class readings, or they can hold outside discussions or locate other readings, or they can do outside research. They can also explore their own computer-assisted writing processes, evaluate software in their fields, or set up a computer-assisted language arts program for their own instructional situations. Often, teachers in similar situations are able to provide their colleagues with more informative response than we can, and they form student-initiated small groups to help one another with projects.

Consistent with our decentralized and student-centered approach, we strongly encourage this collaboration.

Small groups, in fact, have a vital function throughout our course. We believe that all students learn best when actively involved, and that both oral and written language skills facilitate learning. We make practical use of these beliefs by using regular small group meetings in which theory and practice are introduced, written about in journals, discussed, and debated. We also require an oral presentation of the final project in small groups. Acting as facilitators in these sessions far more often than lecturers, we give our students ample opportunities to learn by talking, writing, and responding. Teachers debate such diverse questions as the best model for writing processes, appropriate use of spelling checkers, conference priorities with developmental writers, the value of various prewriting and editing programs, strategies to facilitate revision, and the use, if any, for automatic error-remediation software.

Integrating Microcomputers

Where does the microcomputer fit into all of this? Everywhere, but within distinct boundaries: the microcomputer in this approach is not the subject being studied, not the focus of instruction. The microcomputer and its software are tools to help us get on with our work. Having established these boundaries, we explore microcomputer uses throughout the course.

We teach the language of computing and word processing by teaching vocabulary from the technical jargon known as computerese, and we do so early in the semester. Here again, though, we are teaching a language skill; we are not teaching the computer in isolation from the real work of the course. Language underlies and supports all teaching and learning; indeed, learning a subject is in many ways equivalent to learning the language of a subject. And computers are no exception, at least not in D. B. Smith's recent formulation: "Rather than being not technology, language is metatechnology—technology that enables other technology. Presumably, nearly all of the sociocultural innovations that have made humanity a successful species have been disseminated through language. Even today, when we teach a technology, we first teach its vocabulary" (1986, 573).

A major goal of our course is to teach our students to recognize sound and unsound microcomputer uses. To this end, we provide three types of background readings on computer-assisted language instruction. First, we offer classroom models for teachers in secondary writing classrooms (Lindemann and Willert 1985), middle school literature classrooms (Bickel 1985), and college literature classrooms (Evans 1985). Each of these models is different, but they share some critical characteristics. They integrate sound teaching theory in writing, reading, and literature; and the computer plays an important but secondary role in language instruction.

Second, we introduce research studies on computers as composing tools. We try to give our teachers a full and realistic sense of the realities of computer-assisted instruction, and so we include studies which quell any naive beliefs in the supernatural powers of computers. Collier's (1983) study, for example, shows that writers who used word processing without receiving revision help did not revise more effectively than other writers. Selfe's (1985) survey shows that students writing on-line sometimes find disadvantages, including such problems as the inability to view an entire page of text, eye fatigue, and overcrowded laboratory conditions. In addition, Selfe shows that writers working on-line have different composing styles, only some of which are enhanced by the computer. These studies and others also report highly positive benefits, particularly in ease of text production, revision, and writer enthusiasm (Bean 1983; Womble 1985). We discuss both advantages and disadvantages of computer-assisted writing with our teachers, especially trying to help them understand a basic but often ignored fact: simply because computers make revision easier does not mean writers know how to revise. They need to be taught, not just placed in front of machines (Sommers 1986).

Third, we select readings which help teachers take a critical stance regarding language arts software. The most helpful evaluative guidelines we have found come directly from Petersen, Selfe, and Wahlstrom (1984). They suggest teachers use seven criteria for assessing software, determining whether: (1) the writing concern addressed by the software is significant; (2) it is process-oriented; (3) it recognizes and provides practice with shifting rhetorical parameters (such as audience and purpose); (4) actual writing is required; (5) it meets the needs of diverse writers; (6) it is authored by both composition and software design experts; and (7) the program is proven through field testing. In addition, this article provides guidelines for gauging the effects of a given program on student users and for designing comprehensive evaluative instruments for computer-assisted language instruction programs to determine their effects on writing processes and products.

Our students also read Spitzer's guidelines for selecting word-processing software. He discusses the basic functions of any word-processing program—text manipulation, storage, and printing—as well as more advanced features. Eighteen word-processing features, including, for example, 80-column display, cursor movement, and format ease, are rated on a scale of 1 to 5 on their importance to beginning, intermediate, and advanced writing students (Spitzer 1985, 35).

Finally, we make teachers aware of our own stance, widely shared by other scholars, that language arts software should be integrative, interactive, user-friendly, and individualized. Here, too, we believe it is best to explore thoroughly the meaning behind these terms, which are often used as catchwords by software manufacturers. While we define an "integrative" program as one which is based upon sound writing theory and teaching principles, we have often seen it bandied about in publishers' advertisements for drill-and-practice programs. Presumably students "integrate" missing words into blanks left in sentences, or the software is "integrated" into lessons isolating grammar and usage from writing practice, but this is inappropriate and misinformed language instruction.

As we present and discuss these evaluative guidelines, teachers learn to use word processing for their own real writing. We concentrate on word-processing software because we believe this is the most useful software to date for writers. Teachers are able to select programs to try out from about two dozen that we borrow from SUNY at Buffalo's Software Evaluation Project. We discovered this method has several advantages. First, not only do the advantages and disadvantages of a word-processing program become evident through actual use, but also the virtue of word processing—the ease of revising and editing—becomes apparent to new and experienced teachers alike. Second, we believe teachers learn faster and more efficiently by using word processing to write meaningful pieces of writing. Rather than running through tutorials and practicing exercises, teachers learn word-processing commands as they are required by a writing task, adding the commands on the spot. We make teachers active learners of the writer's craft, and we place word processing in a proper subordinate role.

In addition to word-processing software, teachers are able to survey a wide range of software available for their particular grade level and interests. This software includes prewriting, error-remediation, post-writing, and text-analysis programs. We ask our students to critique this software based upon principles of writing instruction and software evaluation. Each teacher, in other words, must find a way to integrate theory into practice. When teaching literature, for example, we should have students read and should help them make careful inferences about their reading, and when computer programs can help with the processes of reading and inferring, such as by analyzing style or by comparing different texts, we should have students use computer programs. What we should not do is teach the computer for its own sake, as if technology has some worth beyond service to human needs.

This continuous sampling has several purposes. First, teachers gain experience in using a wide variety of language arts software. Second, they learn to apply the evaluative framework presented above to each program, reinforcing it again and again. Third, teachers gain confidence in their own evaluative expertise as they review many programs. We want them to rely on their own judgments because of the sheer volume of weak software being manufactured.

Next time we teach the course, in fact, we plan to remove a caveat we have thus far used. Instead of selecting software from the Software Evaluation Project to bring to class, we will send our teachers to the project to examine the wide array of reading, writing, language arts, and English software available. Our original intention was to protect our teachers from mindless drill-and-practice software, but our revised thinking is that teachers need to learn to fend for themselves. Indeed, this is the reason for the Software Evaluation Project's existence: software is expensive, and it is easy to make mistakes when purchasing unfamiliar programs.

Evaluation of Our Course

At the conclusion of "Composition and Computers," we use several methods to evaluate our course. First, teachers respond to an anonymous course evaluation at the end of the semester. Second, our administrative roles allow us to observe some curricula as they develop; we sometimes also serve as consultants to other teachers who work with us. Third, we ourselves evaluate the strengths and weaknesses of our program, trying for a difficult-to-manage objectivity.

Course evaluations indicate that our students generally leave our course informed about writing principles and practices, knowledgeable about integrative computer-assisted language arts methods and software, and confident about their own teaching and evaluative skills. Perhaps more persuasively, the curricula we have observed firsthand are right on target. Our teachers use microcomputers integratively and are not deluded into believing technology to be a panacea. They recognize and reject unsound practices and software, and for good reasons. They know from extensive readings what is theoretically sound, and they know from firsthand experience what helps them as writers. Just filling in the blanks is not beneficial. Especially rewarding to us are those teachers of science, social studies, and other content areas who learn to value writing as a learning tool, and who integrate writing into their computer-assisted instruction programs.

Our own evaluation, perhaps inevitably, is the most critical. First, as professional writing teachers and researchers, we know the complexity of the ideas with which we grapple within a limited time span. Catch phrases such as "the writing process" and "revision" are potentially misleading terms for intricate and only partially understood cognitive processes. Can one course even begin to do justice to them?

Second, we are aware of the pressures schools face to computerize classrooms, sometimes regardless of the pedagogical appropriateness. We have visited a classroom, for example, with thirty microcomputers attached to thirty printers and so many wires running back and forth that it literally was impossible to find a sheet of paper on any of the tables. It appeared that class size, the administrator's magic number thirty, had determined much of what was happening instructionally. How can English be taught if we cannot write on paper? We are leery of contributing to this unjustified technological mania, and we worry about doing so inadvertently.

Third, we know our course has an inherent, if unavoidable, weakness: research on computer-assisted language instruction is so new that we really cannot claim unequivocally at this point that we know the best ways to integrate computers into the English language arts classroom. Research to date shows clearly that word processing has not proven to be a panacea, nor do writers inevitably improve when they write with the help of the glowing screen. It is highly possible that the best instructional methods for using computers have yet to evolve. All we can do is make this clear to our students and make sure our present uses are pedagogically sound.

Nevertheless, we believe our work really does make a positive impact on computer-assisted language instruction. After all, we argue, computers are becoming the writing tools of choice by increasing numbers of student writers, and we offer an exemplary instructional model to their teachers. We teach sound theory, model excellent practices, and insist upon discerning evaluation. This is high-caliber language instruction, and educators who work with us learn its value.

We believe these fine results mean we have accomplished our purposes as English educators.

Works Cited

Beach, Richard. 1980. "The Effects of Between-Draft Teacher Evaluation Versus Self-Evaluation on High School Students' Revising of Rough Drafts." *Research in the Teaching of English* 13: 111–19.

Bean, John C. 1983. "Computerized Word Processing as an Aid to Revision." *College Composition and Communication* 34: 146–48.

Bickel, Linda L. 1985. "Word Processing and the Integration of Reading and Writing Instruction." In *Writing On-Line: Using Computers in the Teaching of Writing*, edited by James L. Collins and Elizabeth A. Sommers, 39–45. Upper Montclair, N.J.: Boynton/Cook.

Brick, Allan. 1986. "First Person Singular, First Person Plural, and Exposition." *College English* 43: 508–15.

Britton, James, Tony Burgess, Nancy Martin, Alex McLeod, and Harold Rosen. 1975. *The Development of Writing Abilities (11–18)*. London: Macmillan Education.

Collier, Richard M. 1983. "The Word Processor and Revision Strategies." *College Composition and Communication* 34: 149–55.

Cooper, Charles R., and Lee Odell, eds. 1977. *Evaluating Writing: Describing, Measuring, Judging*. Urbana, Ill.: National Council of Teachers of English.

David, Denise L. 1986. "An Ethnographic Investigation of the Uses of Peer Talk in Small Group Writing Workshops in a College Classroom." Ph.D. diss., State University of New York at Buffalo.

Diederich, Paul B. 1974. *Measuring Growth in English*. Urbana, Ill.: National Council of Teachers of English.

Evans, John R. 1985. "Teaching Literature Using Word Processing." In *Writing On-Line: Using Computers in the Teaching of Writing*, edited by James L. Collins and Elizabeth A. Sommers, 83–88. Upper Montclair, N.J.: Boynton/Cook.

Faigley, Lester, and Stephen Witte. 1981. "Analyzing Revision." *College Composition and Communication* 32: 400–14.

Flower, Linda S. 1979. "Writer-Based Prose: A Cognitive Basis for Problems in Writing." *College English* 41: 19–37.

Flower, Linda S., and J. R. Hayes. 1981. "A Cognitive Process Theory of Writing." *College Composition and Communication* 32: 365–87.

Garrison, Roger. 1981. *How a Writer Works*. New York: Harper and Row.

Hoffman, Eleanor M., and John P. Schifsky. 1977. "Designing Writing Assignments." *English Journal* 66(9): 41–45.

Jenkins, Cheryl Sandford. 1980. "Writing Assignment: An Obstacle or a Vehicle?" *English Journal* 69(9): 66–69.

Jordan, John E. 1967. "Theme Assignments: Servants or Masters?" In *Teaching Freshman Composition*, edited by Gary Tate and Edward P. J. Corbett, 227–30. New York: Oxford University Press.

Judy, Stephen. 1980. "The Experiential Approach: Inner Worlds to Outer Worlds." In *Eight Approaches to Teaching Composition*, edited by Timothy R. Donovan and Ben W. McClelland, 37–51. Urbana, Ill.: National Council of Teachers of English.

Larson, Richard L. 1970. "Teaching Before We Judge: Planning Assignments in Composition." In *Teaching High School English*, edited by Gary Tate and Edward P. J. Corbett, 207–18. New York: Oxford University Press.

Lauer, Janice M. 1980. "The Rhetorical Approach: Stages of Writing and Strategies for Writers." In *Eight Approaches to Teaching Composition*, edited by Timothy R. Donovan and Ben W. McClelland, 53–64. Urbana, Ill.: National Council of Teachers of English.

Lindemann, Shirlee, and Jeanette Willert. 1985. "Word Processing in High School Writing Classes." In *Writing On-Line: Using Computers in the Teaching of Writing*, edited by James L. Collins and Elizabeth A. Sommers, 47–53. Upper Montclair, N.J.: Boynton/Cook.

Lunsford, Andrea A. 1979. "Cognitive Development and the Basic Writer." *College English* 41: 39–46.

Murray, Donald M. 1978. "Internal Revision: A Process of Discovery." In *Research on Composing: Points of Departure*, edited by Charles R. Cooper and Lee Odell, 85–103. Urbana, Ill.: National Council of Teachers of English.

———. 1980. "Writing as Process: How Writing Finds Its Own Meaning." In *Eight Approaches to Teaching Composition*, edited by Timothy R. Donovan and Ben W. McClelland, 3–20. Urbana, Ill.: National Council of Teachers of English.

Perl, Sondra. 1979. "The Composing Processes of Unskilled College Writers." *Research in the Teaching of English* 13: 317–36.

Petersen, Bruce T., Cynthia L. Selfe, and Billie J. Wahlstrom. 1984. "Computer-Assisted Instruction and the Writing Process: Questions for Research and Evaluation." *College Composition and Communication* 35: 98–101.

Selfe, Cynthia L. 1985. "The Electronic Pen: Computers and the Composing Process." In *Writing On-Line: Using Computers in the Teaching of Writing*, edited by James L. Collins and Elizabeth A. Sommers, 55–66. Upper Montclair, N.J.: Boynton/Cook.

Simon, S. B., R. C. Hawley, and D. D. Britton. 1973. *Composition for Personal Growth*. New York: Hart Publishing Company.

Smith, D. B. 1986. "Axioms for English in a Technical Age," *College English* 48: 573.

Sommers, Elizabeth A. 1986. "The Effects of Word Processing and Writing Instruction on the Writing Processes and Projects of College Writers." Ph.D. diss., State University of New York at Buffalo.

Sommers, Nancy. 1980. "Revision Strategies of Student Writers and Experienced Adult Writers." *College Composition and Communication* 31: 378–88.

Spitzer, Michael. 1985. "Selecting Word Processing Software." In *Writing On-Line: Using Computers in the Teaching of Writing*, edited by James L. Collins and Elizabeth A. Sommers, 29–36. Upper Montclair, N.J.: Boynton/Cook.

Throckmorton, Helen J. 1980. "Do Your Writing Assignments Work?" *English Journal* 69(8): 56–59.

Womble, Gail G. 1985. "Revising and Computing." In *Writing On-Line: Using Computers in the Teaching of Writing*, edited by James L. Collins and Elizabeth A. Sommers, 75–82. Upper Montclair, N.J.: Boynton/Cook.

4 Interactive Computer Tools for Teachers of Writing at All Instructional Levels at Columbia University's Teachers College

Amy L. Heebner, Teachers College, Columbia University

Introduction

Should we bring the computer to English teachers, or should we bring English teachers to the computer? At Columbia University's Teachers College we are investigating both alternatives. While teachers and teachers-in-training study the uses of computers in course offerings at the college, teachers in selected public schools receive support for their efforts to make computers a part of school life.

These activities are part of Writing with Interactive Tools (WIT), a new teacher education project sponsored by the Teachers College Center for Intelligent Tools in Education (CITE) in cooperation with the Teachers College Writing Project. WIT draws on both the technological expertise of CITE and the expertise of the Writing Project in the teaching of writing. Our approach to teacher training integrates practical experience with the broader perspectives provided by current research on writing and educational computing.

Now is an appropriate time for collaboration between public school teachers and university-based researchers with regard to the uses of computers in education. In the early 1980s, classroom practice in computers and writing developed with minimal guidance from research. Many teachers used computer tools in their classrooms, but they found few forums for learning about similar classrooms in other parts of the country. Now we can draw upon several years of research conducted both in and out of the classroom (Bridwell et al. 1985; Daiute 1985; and others). Research contributes multiple viewpoints, offering teachers a glimpse at other classrooms, other teachers, and other students. If researchers and teachers communicate with each other, the teaching practice will be enriched now and in the future.

Background of Writing with Interactive Tools

The original idea for the Center for Intelligent Tools in Education (CITE), one of the parents of the Writing with Interactive Tools (WIT) project, grew from extended discussions among Teachers College faculty regarding the role of computer-based technology in educational settings. Meetings with the University Relations group at IBM led to the formation of the center in autumn 1985. Funding from IBM, offered for a three-year period, included $645,000 for faculty and student support and $550,000 worth of equipment. The purpose of the grant is to produce research, teacher education models, and educational software that contribute to an assessment of the future of computing in education. CITE projects focus on teacher education and software development in four areas: language arts instruction, social studies instruction, special education, and educational administration.

WIT's other parent, the Writing Project, is a development project at Teachers College that sends teacher trainers into classrooms throughout the New York City public school system. These trainers, selected by the director of the Writing Project, serve as consultants to individual teachers, helping to transform classrooms into "writing workshops." The concept of the writing workshop is grounded in classroom-based research concerning the teaching and learning of writing (Graves 1983; Calkins 1986). The one-on-one work between trainer and classroom teacher is the focus of the Writing Project's work. The Writing Project, which began in 1983, is funded by the New York City Board of Education and several private foundations.

The idea to create a link between CITE and the Writing Project grew from faculty discussions about the importance of computers in language arts instruction. In September 1985, two CITE faculty members and the director of the Writing Project, also a Teachers College faculty member, initiated a collaborative project to focus on writing with computer tools.

The WIT project combines a process-based approach to teaching writing with current developments in educational computing. As the project title suggests, the concerns of WIT are not limited to applications of word-processing and database software, although these are useful and important implements in many English classrooms.

WIT has three components:

1. A "Computers and Writing" course.
2. Case-study research in writing classrooms.
3. Software-development projects. Teacher education in the WIT project focuses on inservice training because Teachers College is strictly a graduate institution. Therefore, the following discussion focuses on the training of practicing teachers; some observations, however, will be applicable to preservice programs as well.

Description of the "Computers and Writing" Course

The "Computers and Writing" course is the heart of teacher training at the WIT project, although case studies and software-development projects, conducted by the same individuals who teach "Computers and Writing," expand the resource base for the course. The class thus becomes a prism that absorbs and reflects information generated by the research and development projects.

"Computers and Writing," offered for three credits, is held in the teaching lab containing twenty-one IBM XTs. Most of the students in the course are, or plan to be, teachers of language arts or computing in elementary, secondary, or college settings. The goals of the class include the following:

1. To present a process-oriented approach to the teaching of writing with computers. In fulfilling this objective, the class draws on case studies conducted as part of the WIT project, in addition to other research.
2. To enable students to gain competence with word-processing software.
3. To provide a historical perspective on the development of computer-writing instruments and a vision of the future of writing technologies. This phase of the class draws on WIT's software-development projects.

The course meets for fourteen sessions of approximately two hours each, with one class session scheduled for each week of the semester. Novice computer users are required to attend four additional hours of basic instruction in word processing. Many students who take the class have already taken "Computer Applications in Education," a three-credit class that introduces word-processing, database, and spreadsheet software. All students are expected to spend at least one hour per week working with computers outside of class time. Teachers College has equipped two "computer libraries" for student use. One of these facilities contains a combination of IBM PCs, XTs, and ATs, Macintoshes, and assorted printers, including two laser printers; the other facility is equipped with IBM PCjrs and printers.

Class meetings begin with a short lecture or software demonstration. A workshop session follows, with opportunities for individual and small group conferences about writing or software use. Each session concludes with a discussion of issues related to writing with computers, and often with readings of works-in-progress. This structure reflects the Writing Project's conception of the writing workshop, which begins with a mini-lesson, is followed by a workshop, and concludes with a sharing session (Calkins 1986). As students gain competence with word-processing software and become familiar with the process approach to the teaching of writing, they are introduced to research literature on computers and writing classrooms. Findings from WIT case studies fuel these discussions.

The last five sessions of the course are reserved for discussion of the impact of computers on writing habits in our culture. New computer-writing tools from software-development projects are demonstrated and discussed in class. Student presentations also contribute to this discussion. Recent student presentations have included such topics as "Computer Education in Barbados," "Word Processing in a Special Education Classroom," and "Technology in the Third World."

In the following sections, each of the main components of the "Computers and Writing" course will be discussed in more detail. The discussion reflects the kinds of classroom structures we model for teachers, as well as the information and skills we want to impart.

Process-Based Approach to Teaching Writing

"Computers and Writing" is informed by a process-based approach to the teaching of writing. Because research on writing processes is too voluminous to discuss as a single topic, class discussions focus on those studies that relate primarily to the teaching and learning of writing, drawing heavily on the descriptive research of Graves (1983) and Calkins (1986), among others. These studies describe writing workshops in which each writer has a large margin of autonomy in pursuing the work of drafting, revising, and editing. This structure is ideal for a computer-writing environment.

In this class, we try to show prospective teachers that the computer offers new capabilities to writers, and not only in the areas of revision and editing. Freewriting and loop writing, two strategies for generating ideas and composing text that are elaborated by Elbow (1981), are new experiences with a word processor. Some teachers-in-training discover that they are able to engage in freewriting for the first time, creating text continuously without censoring. For these teachers, the light touch of the computer keyboard and the fact that they can look away from the screen while writing enable them to write more freely than they have ever experienced with pencil and paper.

We also try to show prospective teachers how to take individual writing processes into account in the use of computer writing tools.

Researchers have shown that while the writing process seems to have multiple phases, each individual writer follows a unique journey toward the final product. Some writers seem to plan, draft, and revise all at once, while others go through a long initial planning process before they begin to compose. We help teachers see that changing writing implements often catalyzes a change in writing process. For instance, many writers find that they write more drafts with a word processor than with traditional writing implements. The computer seems to help these writers play with ideas in a more experimental fashion, so that they plan as they write.

We outline patterns of change that researchers have discovered in the writing habits of writers who use computers. Some teachers in the class experience a similar change in personal writing habits as they write the course assignments with a word processor, and discuss their experiences in class. For all of our teachers-in-training, writing conferences and response groups become a central component of the "Computers and Writing" class. During the first half of the semester, all participants keep a journal about their experiences with the computer, using a word-processing program as the principal writing tool. Our assumption is that the journal is a relatively straightforward form, and that novice computer users need simple writing tasks like the journal at first, in order to integrate the new writing tool with their personal writing habits. The teachers bring selections from their journals to class, sharing their concerns and discoveries with others in their response groups. Later, teachers begin reflective writing focused on specific topics of their own choosing.

Word-Processing Instruction

In structuring the word-processing phase of "Computers and Writing," we have assumed that learning by doing is the best method of learning to write with a computer. Writers and teachers of writing need to experience word processing in order to understand its benefits and to decide whether the computer will be the writing tool of choice. The essential teaching task here is a balancing act. The teacher needs to provide enough technical information for the writer to have some independence, while still keeping the writing impulse alive.

Another principle that informs our "Computers and Writing" class rests on our assumption that computer writers, particularly novices, need information presented in small bits and ample time for practice. This approach developed from the Writing Project's method of teaching writing. Writing Project trainers present a small amount of instruction and then give teachers a chance to put new information into practice. After the teacher has made the new information part of his or her repertoire, the trainer offers more instruction.

Similarly, "Computers and Writing" offers word-processing instruction in small doses because this interdisciplinary class involves prospective teachers from the Teachers College programs in English education, linguistics, and computing in education. One of the course's aims is to create ways in which differences among these teachers enhance their learning. The key is small group work, assigned in small doses. Early in the semester, we have in-class word-processing instruction. In each of several small groups, a computing major coaches a few individuals who are trying to master word processing. In these small groups, each writer gets personal attention from the leader at the time when it is most needed. One prospective teacher commented:

> I noticed immediately after the group exercises that the class had come together as a whole. All of the students felt a real camaraderie that resulted from a shared experience—the struggle for competency on the machine.

The group leaders learn about the vicissitudes of running a computer workshop and appreciate firsthand the importance of individualized instruction. In scheduling the small group work early in the semester, we achieve two purposes. We provide a model for a student-centered computer writing workshop, while simultaneously allowing for the different needs of individuals in the class. The small group work is continued in response groups in which language teachers and computing teachers share their writing and their different kinds of expertise with each other.

Perspectives on Computer Writing Instruments

In order to help teachers identify the unique properties of electronic writing implements, we initiate thinking about writing processes and tools in historical perspective. We begin by asking prospective teachers to write personal histories of themselves as writers and users of computers. Student journals chronicle the processes of struggle and eventual mastery over the computer as writing instrument. Breakthroughs happen at all stages of computer learning, but the first breakthrough is often uniquely exciting. This breakthrough point is a time when people want to talk more about their experiences. They begin a process of understanding their own experiences in relation to others in the class and in relation to other professionals who have studied computer technology. After this breakthrough, a more reflective phase of learning begins.

This is the right time to introduce the results of recent research on educational computing and English teaching and to encourage the process of reflective writing on topics that arise from class discussion of reading. The works of Taylor (1980), Turkle (1984), and Papert (1980), among others, stimulate discussion of the human side of computer technology. English education and linguistics majors, in particular, seem fascinated by the psychological implications of computing. Some find that writing with the computer is a highly interactive process:

> When I write on a computer, I feel that writing is more like a conversation with the computer rather than isolating myself from the rest of the world. With a computer, I don't feel that I am writing. It's like talking to somebody. I don't feel any kind of isolation at all. On the contrary, what I see on the screen—my voice, neatly formatted—is not exactly the same as, but is very similar to, the kind of feedback I can get from a person I am talking to.

Other teachers are more cautious about attributing "interactivity," which may be considered an intrinsically human quality, to a machine. One language teacher wrote:

> I do not think that it is possible to communicate with a machine. Communication is an inherently creative act, and computers are inherently uncommunicative. Rather, computers facilitate . . . communication with oneself and with others.

As prospective teachers reflect on the computer's capabilities, they naturally begin to apply their newfound knowledge in their own professional work. Some teachers have written about their own problems and successes in introducing computers into their school environments. Their concerns include a wide range of issues, such as problems of software and hardware selection and ways to involve teachers in ongoing staff development. Each of these topics is an important concern in teacher education because each points to factors that may enhance, or prevent, the integration of computers into classrooms.

Additional WIT Resources

Other components of the WIT program generate information that feeds into the "Computers and Writing" course, enriching class discussion and expanding the sense of possibilities. The two principal sources of information are case-study research in public schools and software-development projects. These two activities provide knowledge of inservice training that is useful in English classrooms where computers are used.

Case-Study Research in Writing Classrooms

Classroom-based research is of immediate interest to students in the "Computers and Writing" class. Many of them use computers in their teaching or plan to do so. In the class, as part of our survey of literature on the teaching of writing with computers, we discuss artifacts and findings from case studies conducted through WIT. Because we work with a large amount of information within a single semester, teachers are not required to conduct case studies themselves as part of the class. However, some teachers begin to view their own classrooms as possible sites for research to be conducted after completion of the class.

The entire class looks closely at student texts, following the patterns of revision and editing made on computers. In addition, we use videotapes to study images of computer writing classrooms. In viewing these videotapes, teachers learn how to structure classroom environments in which students write independently, both on and off the computer, and in which equipment resources are utilized fully for the entire class. A few minutes of videotape sometimes yield more clarity than volumes of literature. The videotapes selected for the class show that children learn word processing collaboratively before they can write alone with the computer, and reveal this collective word-processing knowledge much more convincingly than a verbal description could. The videotapes also illustrate that children like to move back and forth between writing on the screen and on paper. This is a practical strategy for stretching the available computer time in a classroom. At first, students often write on paper and use the computer as a glorified typewriter. Gradually they learn to use the screen as their writing surface.

Case studies of teachers are important, too. Some of the class participants in "Computers and Writing" are teacher trainers; some are school computer specialists; others are English teachers with a relatively new interest in computing. They have much to learn from each other, and the experiences recounted by individual teachers contribute to our discussions of teacher training. Each teacher's story is a window into a whole world of complex issues and motives. For example, we often use the story of a first-grade teacher, Lynn, to illustrate the importance of long-term planning in staff development.

Lynn's exposure to computers began in 1983 when she taught herself to use LOGO on the first computer purchased by her school. The following year she participated in a series of word-processing workshops. During the spring semester of 1986, a WIT instructor served as a participant-observer in her classroom. Lynn did several tutorial sessions in word processing with the WIT instructor and then introduced word processing to some of her students. Yet she maintained an uneasy relationship with the "computer corner." Often she commented that she thought the children benefited from the word processing, but she seldom came over to watch or confer with the children writing with the computers. When visits to Lynn's classroom came to an end, the children were highly enthusiastic about writing with the computer, while the teacher still seemed uncertain.

But Lynn did a surprising thing the following fall. She took on the responsibility of teaching LOGO to children in an after-school program. Then she began to introduce the other first-grade teachers to the computer in weekly training sessions. Now she plans to bring three computers into her classroom and to introduce her new crop of first graders to word processing. She says, "I like knowing about computers. Not many women do. I like that!" She speculates about becoming a home-computer consultant and, after her retirement from teaching, adopting a new career in the computing field.

This teacher's story confirms two points that are central to our training outlook: (1) staff development programs need to be conceived in terms of years, rather than weeks or months; and (2) computing expertise has multiple levels of appeal, including its pragmatic value in the world outside the schools.

Software-Development Projects

We also believe that teachers benefit from a look at the future of computer writing tools, and therefore we demonstrate exciting software-development projects underway at Teachers College. These new projects give a rich context to the more mundane tasks of computer learning, such as the mechanics of MS DOS and word-processing software. Three software-development projects have a direct connection with writing, reading, and multimedia composition, the concerns of the WIT project.

First is the Academic Networking Facility, which includes the teaching lab, the site of the "Computers and Writing" class. This facility houses twenty-one IBM XT computers that are connected, via a growing, collegewide local area network, with other XTs and ATs used for educational software development. Two other classrooms with networked systems are about to become operational. One lecture hall is linked to the network with a system set for large-screen display of computer-controlled text and video. All together, these facilities comprise the Academic Networking Facility. We spend at least one or two sessions of "Computers and Writing" on the network so that teachers can experience the process of accessing software through the network and the use of electronic mail. We plan further investigation of the uses of the network within the content of the class.

A second software-development project, the Multimedia Development Lab, offers teachers an array of equipment for composing educational materials that integrate text, video, graphics, and sound. At present, this lab is equipped with an IVIS videodisk system and a work station for HANDY, the experimental language for multimedia composition designed by Don Nix of IBM. In past "Computers and Writing" classes, teachers have watched demonstrations of this facility and have enthusiastically discussed its implications for their students. In the future, we would like the class to explore the medium of computer-controlled video, a medium that expands the concept of "writing" to include imagery as well as text.

Teachers have also witnessed demonstrations of the early stages of the CD-ROM Development Facility, currently being installed, which will contain an optical scanner for digitizing text and a CD-ROM emulation system run from an IBM AT. This facility will allow teachers to create and test curriculum resources through the use of large databases transferred to CD-ROM disks (McClintock 1986). Many teachers are fascinated by the possibilities of this system, which makes large quantities of information available through associative access patterns.

These three facilities, which serve as resources for the WIT project, exemplify diversification in educational technology. This kind of arrangement is inappropriate for most elementary and secondary schools. Still, we believe that teachers who train in a varied electronic environment will have an awareness of "coming attractions" in educational technology and a heightened sense of the rapidity of technological change.

Conclusion

The WIT project aims to mediate between teaching practice and research in educational technology. A particularly strong aspect of the

WIT project is the excellence of its two parent projects, which feed the "Computers and Writing" class, conferences, and workshops in a variety of ways, both direct and indirect. For example, the individuals who instruct teachers in the "Computers and Writing" class are also the individuals who conduct case-study research and software-development projects that produce instructional material as feedback for the class. It must be noted that CITE and the Writing Project maintain different emphases. CITE projects center on the development and use of computer tools, with a primary emphasis on the tools themselves. In contrast, the Writing Project is focused strongly on individual teachers and on the development of the art and craft of teaching writing. This range of expertise is both a challenge to teacher training and an opportunity. WIT aims to achieve a creative balance between the concerns of the Writing Project and those of CITE, between human factors and current developments in technology. This potential for diversity and comprehensiveness is a very positive aspect of WIT.

Works Cited

Bridwell, Lillian, Donald Ross, Cynthia L. Selfe, and Kathleen E. Keifer, eds. 1985. *Computers and Composition: New Directions in Teaching and Research.* Fort Collins, Colo., and Houghton, Mich.: Colorado State University and Michigan Technological University.

Calkins, Lucy McCormick. 1986. *The Art of Teaching Writing.* Portsmouth, N.H.: Heinemann.

Daiute, Colette. 1985. "Issues in Using Computers to Socialize the Writing Process." *Educational Communication and Technology: A Journal of Theory, Research, and Development* 33(1): 41–50.

Elbow, Peter. 1981. *Writing with Power.* New York: Oxford University Press.

Graves, Donald H. 1983. *Writing: Teachers and Children at Work.* Portsmouth, N.H.: Heinemann.

McClintock, Robert O. 1986. "On Computing and the Curriculum." *Outlook: A Publication of the Special Interest Group on Computer Uses in Education* (Association for Computing Machinery) 19(1/2): 25–40.

Papert, Seymour. 1980. *Mindstorms: Children, Computers, and Powerful Ideas.* New York: Basic Books.

Taylor, Robert P. 1980. *The Computer in the School: Tutor, Tool, Tutee.* New York: Teachers College Press.

Turkle, Sherry. 1984. *The Second Self: Computers and the Human Spirit.* New York: Simon and Schuster.

5 The Gateway Writing Project: Staff Development and Computers in St. Louis

Jane Zeni Flinn, University of Missouri–St. Louis

Chris Madigan, Albuquerque, New Mexico

Introduction

When the Gateway Writing Project (GWP) began working with computers in 1984, we decided to bring to the university our strongest writing project graduates, introduce these teacher-consultants to the computer, and then follow them back to their classrooms to observe, question, coach, and study how they actually used computers in a process-oriented writing curriculum. In subsequent years, we would apply the insights of this collaborative research to training additional teachers.

Based at the University of Missouri–St. Louis and at Harris-Stowe State College, GWP is an affiliate of the National Writing Project (NWP). With an established network of successful writing teachers and a solid base in the writing project tradition, we began in 1984 to develop our training model for teaching writing with computers.

Our model features four main kinds of activities: teacher training in the writing process and computer applications; support for instructional change; action research in the classrooms of trained teachers; and dissemination both of curriculum and of exemplary school programs. We are finding that this multifaceted approach allows us to respond to the short-term need for training as well as the longer-term need for assistance in applying that training in actual school situations. In addition, classroom-based research and dissemination provide constant feedback to keep our training in tune with the best current practice in a rapidly developing field. We believe each of these components is essential for an effective program of ongoing professional development.

Our first component, teacher training, was based on typical practice at the NWP sites. We provided intensive summer institutes for experienced teachers, university courses open also to preservice teachers, and shorter inservice workshops led by our teacher-consultants in local school districts. Like many English teachers around the country, Gateway staff knew computers as powerful writing tools, but feared the public might embrace a too-narrowly defined technology. In our work with teachers, we sought to counter the computer-driven basics while applying the technology to real writing tasks. We would keep language in the foreground and technology in the background.

The second feature of our teacher-training project was support for instructional change. We provided monthly support meetings for teachers, seminars for administrators, and leadership training for school writing-improvement teams. The need for this component was evident in our writing project before we ever worked with computers. We saw well-trained and enthusiastic teacher-consultants losing momentum when they returned to schools with supervisors who did not understand a process approach to writing instruction. When the computer became part of our training in the writing process, the need for ongoing support was intensified. A lone teacher could not deal with instructional change, technological change, and the whole range of administrative decisions, such as purchasing software, computer access, and writing-lab design. We saw that we needed to educate building leaders.

The third component, action research, was our response to rapidly changing technology and growing instructional sophistication. Initially the university staff observed in the classrooms of skilled project-trained writing teachers and worked with them during the year when they began using computers as writing tools. More recently, our school visits have been an opportunity to observe writing-improvement teams of teachers and administrators as they plan, critique, and evaluate their own computer-equipped writing programs. What we learn each year from this practical, ethnographic research becomes part of what we teach the next summer's teachers.

Dissemination, our fourth component, draws on all three of the previously mentioned areas. We sponsor a series of curriculum guides authored by teachers during and after the summer institutes. We help maintain teacher momentum through publications and presentations. We support the development of new writing programs in schools and universities modeled on excellent writing centers and on the Gateway site itself. We learn how to apply our research findings through networking with professional groups and through computer teleconferencing.

In response to our proposal outlining these four components, the Department of Education's Fund for the Improvement of Post-Secondary Education awarded GWP a grant exceeding $100,000 for the years 1984 to 1987. That grant funded the computer-related activities described in this chapter.

Goals and Questions

Since 1984, the Gateway Writing Project's primary goal has been to improve writing instruction by integrating computers into a training model based on the National Writing Project. While the goal was clear, this computer-assisted writing project has taken shape gradually as we worked with the new technology and reflected on that experience. Since many of the answers were not yet available in the professional literature when we began the project in 1984, we relied on a process of teaching, inquiry, and feedback to lead us to a working model. We began by investigating three aspects of the computer—as a tool, a cultural artifact, and a medium of instruction.

1. As a tool, how would the computer differ from pen or pencil? Would using a new tool reshape writers' composing habits (Madigan 1984)? Could students learn to choose different tools for different purposes?
2. As a cultural artifact, how would the computer change the climate of writing project institutes and of the writing classes taught by their graduates? Could the presence of computers in a school building serve as a catalyst for writing across the curriculum?
3. As a medium of instruction, could the computer stay out of the limelight? Could we empower teachers with knowledge about teaching writing with computers while letting machines play a rather small role in teacher training? The National Writing Project traditionally emphasizes doing writing rather than talking about methods.

The next sections describe in detail the major components of the model that emerged: teacher training, support for instructional change, research, and distribution.

Summer Institutes

In the years 1984 to 1987, the Gateway Writing Project conducted intensive summer institutes on "Teaching Writing with Computers."

Offered for five hours of graduate credit, such institutes provide a cadre of teacher-consultants with the training and confidence to staff the shorter inservice workshops offered during the school year. Each summer, our institute's teacher applicants were more computer literate, the lab facilities better, and the staff more experienced, so each year the climate of the institute changed.

We began, for example, with the conviction that our focus would be on writing, not on technology. We saw the computer as an add-on, a new tool incorporated into our accustomed schedule of activities. In practice, this approach meant that we spent mornings in a seminar room, with lectures, teaching demonstrations, and informal writing—we used no computers, but mentioned their applications along with prewriting (invention software), revising (word processing), or mechanics (spelling checkers). Each afternoon, during our usual writing group, library, and conference time, teachers got a turn in the computer lab. This first institute divorced the writing workshop from the computers. During the next summers, we integrated the technology more fully in our curriculum and in our classroom design.

We soon learned that physical and temporal arrangements could subtly control the institute's climate. In the first year, computers were isolated in a lab down the hall which each writer visited for an hour per day; the machines sat in straight rows, leaving little room for discussion. By 1986, the institute spent the entire day in a large resource center with computers arranged about the periphery and movable seminar tables in the middle for writing groups; a large monitor made it easy to demonstrate relevant software during the morning's presentations. Such a flexible setting for electronic composing tools can help build communities of writers.

Based on what we have learned through four summers, we can now sketch our preferred practice in a teacher-training institute. Core staff, a university professor and a project-trained teacher-consultant from the public schools, lead the four-week summer program. Support staff may include a student aide, guest teacher-consultants, graduate interns, and faculty researchers. We find that such staffing shows teachers the importance of collaboration among educators in diverse roles.

Planning for the summer institute aims for high visibility and high commitment. In February, staff members circulate promotional fliers and personal letters to public and private school administrators seeking nominations of exemplary writing teachers. In April, staff members select about twenty-five elementary, secondary, and college teachers. Candidates receive a welcome letter and an assignment to read and respond to in a journal before the institute starts in late June.

They also buy one book on the writing process (Murray 1985) and one on writing with computers (Rodrigues and Rodrigues 1986).

Our computer-aided summer institute still follows a plan quite typical of the National Writing Project. It runs four weeks, 9:00 a.m. to 3:00 p.m., Monday through Friday. The topics are still organized on the basis of the writing process, but the computer is woven into each part of the syllabus:

Week One
Introduction to the writing process
Introduction to word processing
Prewriting and data-gathering strategies
Demonstrating composing with a large-screen monitor
Drafting a personal experience essay

Week Two
Teaching the writing process
Advanced word-processing techniques
Peer response, conferencing
Collaboration, teleconferencing
Primary trait system of instructional design
Drafting a curriculum paper

Week Three
Sentence combining, expansion, modeling
Editing and standard English usage
Software and hardware for teaching writing
Evaluating writing
Handling the paperload

Week Four
Publishing student writing
School publishing houses, young authors' conferences
Writing labs and centers
Teacher research and publication
Planning inservice workshops
School and district dissemination

Morning is still primarily class time; afternoon is writing time. In the morning, groups meet to share reading responses. Teachers discuss their students' and their own writing processes, present model lessons, see software and teaching demonstrations on a large monitor, and do writing exercises (brainstorming, guided meditation, multiple leads, revision agendas) for the assigned papers—sometimes by hand, sometimes by machine. They also respond to each other's writing in pairs and small groups, discuss how to adapt their experiences to their classrooms, eat donuts, and drink gallons of coffee.

In the afternoon, teachers read and write. At first, they may get comfortable with the computer through collaborative writing (e.g., inventing cartoon dialogue). Later, while half the writers use the computers, the other half kibitz, confer with peers or teachers on their drafts, browse through the GWP reserve collection in the library, or read the next day's handouts. Depending on need, one or both core staff may be helping at the computers or conferring at the tables.

The second assignment is to create a unit of classroom-ready curriculum. That might be three days of lesson plans, complete with transparencies, feedback sheets, workshop instructions, and evaluation checklists for students, or it might be an extended writing assignment with an evaluation rubric and sample papers. The curriculum paper takes about two weeks. Because rough and final copies must be composed on the computer, institute staff make a point of introducing activities for generating ideas, critiquing, and revising drafts on the machine. The completed guide will be sold to schools, so participants must learn advanced commands for professional layout.

The most successful first assignment—"Re-create for the rest of the class an experience you had (good or bad) with a machine"—takes a week, ventilates feelings about technology (usually cars), and mimics personal experience assignments that teachers often give to their own students. Most people compose first drafts on paper; then they enter, revise, and print later drafts with the computer. They save their final copies onto a class disk, from which institute staff prepare a letter-quality anthology for distribution to the group. As faculty, we write and publish the same assignment.

Except for the first day, when we talk about working memory and how to handle a floppy disk, the focus is writing, and computers are taught only at need-to-know points. For example, when writers ask how to return the cursor to the beginning of the next line, faculty explain word wrap. When writers are ready to go home, they learn to save files.

Our institute goes beyond helping teachers write with computers: we also try to teach them to manage a computer-supported classroom through setting up multiple sources of help. Participants learn, for example, to consult one another or check wallposters that list steps for deleting, adding, retrieving, saving, and printing. One poster stresses self-help: "Ask three, then ask me" (i.e., the teacher). Untrained tutors may do too much for computer novices (Michaels 1986), so we encourage peers and staff to teach first things first, giving basic examples rather than multiple solutions. We do try to protect learners from disastrous mistakes, encourage experimentation, help novices develop problem-solving strategies, and debug aloud. The following dialogue illustrates a typical "help exchange":

Writer: How do I get rid of this word?

Tutor: Well, your cursor's right at the end of the word. Hold down the "delete" key and see what happens. [Word processors delete words several ways, but on the first day, or for a frustrated user, we would not explain how to jump to the beginning of the word and use the "word-delete" function. We do not teach alternatives until users are ready.]

Writer: Can I change this *an* to *the* with a global replace?

Tutor: Save your file first. Then try the replace and see. [The tutor prevents the writer from ruining the file, but encourages the experiment. Afterwards, the writer will never replace a single word with a global command.]

Writer: The computer lost my file! I saved it yesterday as "DRAFT," and now the computer doesn't have it!

Tutor: How do you find what you've saved to your disk?

Writer: I don't know.

Tutor: Display the directory.

Writer: How do I do that?

Tutor: From the main menu. How do you get there? [Writer presses "escape," and the main menu appears.] Now which option do you want? [Writer types "D" but does not press "return."] Why hasn't the directory come up?

Writer: Oh, I didn't press "return." [Presses "return." The directory appears.] Oh, I see. I misspelled it. I saved it as "Daft"!

To encourage problem solving, at "stuck points" the tutor verbalizes a competent user's questions. Whenever possible, the tutor avoids taking control of the keyboard. We model this approach to peer tutoring and self-help so that teachers can later apply it with their own students.

This approach, like our summer institute curriculum, has evolved over the years. In 1984, few teachers had ever used computers, one instructor was barely familiar with the hardware, and the other was barely familiar with the software. That year, three experienced participants quickly emerged as tutors and were asked for help as often as the staff. Participants at each succeeding summer institute have been more computer literate; we now see more widespread informal help and less reliance on designated "experts."

District Inservice Programs

Ideally, we believe that an intensive, graduate-credit institute on writing and computers would benefit every English teacher. In practice, of course, just a small percent of this population is trained.

When school officials contact the Gateway Writing Project to request teacher training, most often they are thinking of a brief introduction to word-processing software with a few techniques for teaching writing. Our first task is to convince this audience that teachers really need a more thorough, more integrated experience. Next we must provide a workshop that compresses the key features of the summer institute into a shorter, yet meaningful, training period.

"An Introduction to Writing with Computers" is a ten-hour noncredit inservice workshop that we have given for teachers from all disciplines. Led by Gateway graduates, it introduces teachers to process-based approaches for teaching writing and to their district's standard word-processing package. Though all our inservice workshops cover such basics as how to handle files and how to respond helpfully to papers, leaders of each workshop choose their own assignments, activities, and handouts.

Rather than full training experiences, we regard these brief workshops as appetite-whetters and consciousness-raisers. We also use them to recruit some teachers for the summer institute. Nevertheless, most teachers receive no further training. The workshops alone seem adequate for teachers who have previous knowledge of the writing process but are new to computer applications, and also for teachers who are returning to school buildings where there are strong, project-trained teachers available to help them.

Supporting Instructional Change

When computers enter writing programs, administrative leadership becomes absolutely necessary. Teachers cannot normally purchase software, set up labs, or schedule classes without such support. Since the summer of 1985, GWP has sponsored one-day seminars for administrators on "Computers, Writing, and Effective Leadership" in which a teacher-consultant gives a presentation on the writing process with computers, a computer coordinator talks about planning labs and facilities, a principal discusses leadership in writing and in computers, and the GWP director explains the project's writing-improvement teams.

Research suggests that the most crucial focus of staff development is not the teacher, administrator, or school district, but the individual school (Berman and McLaughlin 1975; see also Neale, Bailey, and Ross 1981). Thus our project has worked with individual pilot schools to build writing-improvement teams—in-house cadres of computer-and-writing specialists. A writing-improvement team requires one or more administrators who have attended GWP seminars, two or more project-trained teachers, resource staff (e.g., a librarian, computer director, lab assistant), access to new knowledge (e.g., through a university or technical consortium), regular planning and meeting time at the school site, and power to make decisions about writing and computers.

After the teachers' summer institute and the administrators' seminar, all team members attend a two-day leadership training program. There the team assesses their school's staff, equipment, and organizational climate and then writes an action plan for integrating computers into the writing curriculum. For the two years during which we developed this program, GWP university staff visited pilot schools regularly to observe teachers and students, meet with the writing-improvement teams, and offer feedback.

Our four pilot sites represent inner-city and affluent suburban secondary schools, creating a natural laboratory for studying computer-rich writing programs. At one high school, the writing-improvement team, with the support of an energetic new administrator, arranged an inservice course for the whole English department, a schoolwide assessment of writing samples, and a more equitable schedule for access to the writing lab; future plans include pairing teachers to observe one another's writing classes and to share feedback on key features of writing-process instruction. At a city middle school, another writing-improvement team (two writing lab teachers and an instructional coordinator paid through desegregation funds) worked with a local public relations firm to help students produce a computer-printed newspaper, school publicity, and radio scripts. In both these examples, the presence of administrators as well as teachers and the creative use of outside resources have led to effective integration of computers in the writing curriculum.

Research on Writing with Computers

Our project is rooted in the tradition of "action research"—studies in which the practical needs of participants generate the research questions—using descriptive ethnography (McCall 1984; Smith 1979). Action research has been endorsed by such National Writing Project leaders as Miles Myers (1985) and Sondra Perl (1986) because it provides a focus for teachers to continue learning, growing, inquiring, and publishing after they leave the intensive summer course. We find this blend of training and research especially well suited to a computer-oriented writing project. We are working with teachers in a rapidly changing technological field where researchers cannot pretend to have all the answers and where even the right questions may become apparent only in the classroom.

Our first study, "Collaborative Research on Teaching and Learning, Grades 3–12," asked how highly skilled teachers of writing would restructure their classes to make use of the computer. We were not interested in randomly selected teachers or in a rigidly imposed curriculum, either in text or on disk. Instead, we collaborated with our strongest Gateway graduates as they made decisions, changed decisions, tried new techniques, tried old techniques, and revised what almost worked until it did work (Flinn 1985a).

During 1984 to 1985, a grant from the National Writing Project provided small fellowships for ten such teacher-researchers. To analyze what happened as their students began writing with computers, each teacher logged noteworthy events, quotes, successes, and disasters. Each kept writing folders for a target class, including handwritten drafts and computer printouts. In the writing project tradition, the experience of collaborative research helped build a "new professionalism" among teachers (Nelms 1979). School and university researchers shared their observations at the project meetings and disseminated the results (Flinn 1985b).

Teacher-researchers identified and summarized ways in which the computer changed their approaches to instruction and classroom management (Wright 1988). The research team also identified four settings in which computers could assist writing instruction:

1. A traditional classroom may use a single computer, connected to a large monitor, to demonstrate writing processes. For example, the whole class can propose revisions to a displayed text and see how those changes affect style, tone, and meaning (Wright 1985).
2. A classroom with learning centers can use computers as a writing center. For example, one middle school classroom held two computers, two typewriters, racks of paperbacks, and areas for group and individual work. Sometimes children collaborated at the keyboard. At other times, children drafted papers individually,

by hand or by machine. Peers responded with pencil on hard copy before writers revised and a final printout was made.

3. A tutorial writing center may support writing across the school's curriculum. In the St. Louis area, long before computers, several GWP teacher-consultants founded writing centers for conferences and individual coaching. Because of early successes, those centers obtained funds for computers, resulting in some unusually well-staffed, well-equipped facilities (Wright 1986).
4. Finally, a computer lab, usually staffed by an aide, can serve many classes. Small labs cannot accommodate whole writing classes, so most teachers send a dozen students to work on their own, with mixed success. Larger labs can allow a project-trained teacher to assist an entire class while students write, providing essential support during the writing process.

Distribution

As we develop new models for instruction, support, and research on writing with computers, we share them with others in the field. Vehicles for distribution include the various training programs already described as well as publications, comments in computer conferences, and convention speeches.

We have found that good programs in writing with computers spread information by word of mouth and by imitation as much as by direct teaching. In the past four years, dozens of high schools in St. Louis and its suburbs have established writing centers, most staffed or led by Gateway teacher-consultants. For example, the center founded by a GWP codirector at a suburban high school includes two labs, large tables for writing conferences, a book and software collection for teachers, and twenty-five computers. The National Council of Teachers of English named this facility a Center of Excellence in 1986, and many other schools have modeled their own labs after it (Wright 1987).

Just as good school writing programs have become models for others, good university teacher-training programs can become models for other campuses. Harris-Stowe State College, which prepares most of the inner-city elementary teachers in St. Louis, has now joined with the University of Missouri–St. Louis to create a joint Gateway site funded by the National Writing Project. Legislators have long urged partnerships between state institutions, but the recent emphasis on computer training for teachers, coupled with the need for pooling resources, has implemented this partnership.

Another university site took root when one of the authors of this chapter left St. Louis for the University of New Mexico. He soon revamped their Writing Institute to reflect NWP principles and Gateway practices. The UNM Writing Institute will soon seek NWP affiliation.

Conclusion

During the past four years, we have revised our training model much as writers revise papers: through collaboration, feedback, recursion, and successive approximation. We feel that such evolution is characteristic of most successful teacher-training programs involving computers.

As a tool, the computer was first simply a technological add-on to our writing project institutes. With each summer's experience, however, we learned to integrate it more fully into the writing process. Teachers who go through our project now routinely use computers, pencils, pens, markers, chalk, and occasionally fingerpaint as writing tools. Some tasks, such as notetaking on a field trip, clearly call for pen and paper. Others, especially those requiring revision, work better at the computer. If rhetoric is the art of making linguistic choices, we hope to help teachers develop a rhetoric of writing tools as we experiment and discuss such alternatives (Flinn 1987).

As a cultural artifact, the computer has changed the climate of our teacher-training workshops. There is a new sense of the immediacy of participants' writing because so many texts are generated directly on computers and open to public view. There is also a new tension and excitement linked to the use of these powerful new writing tools. Finally, there is a greater awareness of collaboration and revision, and computers seem to support and highlight these values.

As a medium of instruction, the computer has paradoxically become both more and less focal in our project. The first year, instructors and teachers struggled with barely familiar equipment and a setting isolated from the writers. Today, we have pulled together the computer strand and the writing-process strand of our training. Word processing has become such an integral part of our institute—and the instructors have become so comfortable teaching with computers—that by midsummer it seems almost transparent.

At the same time, we have become more sophisticated in our approach to computer applications. We now demonstrate networks, modems, databases for research writing, prewriting computer-assisted instruction (CAI), spelling checkers, and style feedback. These applications are still attention-getting techniques, but in time they too may become transparent to the experience of the writing workshop.

Our work with computers in the Gateway Writing Project leaves us both encouraged and realistic about the role of technology. Computers cannot of themselves create better schools, better teachers, or even better writers. But they can provide the motivation for educators to work together toward these goals.

Works Cited

Berman, Paul, and Milbrey Wallin McLaughlin. 1975. *Federal Programs Supporting Educational Change.* Vol. 4, *The Findings in Review.* Santa Monica, Calif.: Rand Corporation.

Flinn, Jane Zeni. 1985a. "Collaborative Research as a Writing Project Goal." Paper presented at the National Council of Teachers of English "Models for Excellence" Conference on Writing Projects, Cedar Rapids, Iowa, 30 May.

———. 1985b. "Tales from Twelve Classrooms: Teaching Writing with Computers." University of Missouri–St. Louis. Unpublished report.

———. 1987. "Computers in the Writing Process: A Rhetoric of Tools." *Quarterly of the National Writing Project and the Center for the Study of Writing* 9(2): 24.

McCall, George. 1984. "Systematic Field Observation." *Annual Review of Sociology* 10: 263–82.

Madigan, Chris. 1984. "The Tools That Shape Us: Composing by Hand vs. Composing by Machine." *English Education* 16: 143–50.

Michaels, Sarah. 1986. "The Computer as a Dependent Variable." Graduate School of Education, Harvard University, Cambridge, Mass. Unpublished essay.

Murray, Donald. 1985. *A Writer Teaches Writing,* 2d. ed. Boston: Houghton-Mifflin.

Myers, Miles. 1985. *The Teacher-Researcher: How to Study Writing in the Classroom.* Urbana, Ill.: National Council of Teachers of English and ERIC Clearinghouse on Reading and Communication Skills.

Neale, Daniel, William Bailey, and Billy Ross. 1981. *Strategies for School Improvement: Cooperative Planning and Organizational Development.* Boston: Allyn and Bacon.

Nelms, Ben. 1979. "Writing Projects: Toward a New Professionalism." *English Education* 10: 131–33.

Perl, Sondra. 1986. *Through Teachers' Eyes: Portraits of Writing Teachers at Work.* Portsmouth, N.H.: Heinemann.

Rodrigues, Dawn, and Raymond J. Rodrigues. 1986. *Teaching Writing with a Word Processor, Grades 7–13.* Urbana, Ill.: ERIC Clearinghouse on Reading and Communication Skills and National Council of Teachers of English.

Smith, Louis M. 1979. "An Evolving Logic of Participant Observation, Educational Ethnography, and Other Case Studies." In *Review of Research in Education*, vol. 6, edited by L. Shulman, 316–77. Chicago: Peacock.

Wright, Anne. 1985. "Revising with an Apple or an Apple Orchard." Paper presented at the National Council of Teachers of English "Models for Excellence" Conference on Writing Projects, Cedar Rapids, Iowa, 30 May.

———. 1986. "Hazelwood West Writing Lab: A Center of Excellence." *Quarterly of the National Writing Project and the Center for the Study of Writing* 8(3): 10–11. Reprinted in Phi Delta Kappan *Writing* (Exemplary Practice Series). Bloomington, Ind.: Center on Evaluation, Development, and Research, 1987.

———. 1987. "Terminal Writing in the Writing Lab." *Writing Center Journal* 3(1): 21–28.

———. 1988. "Teaching English While Jumping through New Technological Hoops." *English Journal* 77(7): 33–38.

6 Linking Secondary School and College Writing Teachers: CAI Staff Development That Works in Indianapolis

Barbara L. Cambridge, Indiana University–Purdue University at Indianapolis

Ulla Connor, Indiana University–Purdue University at Indianapolis

Overcoming Obstacles in School-College Collaborations

School-college collaborative programs offer academic institutions and school corporations opportunities to learn from each other. Unfortunately, such attempted liaisons are often plagued by a lack of understanding about mutual needs and goals, which can breed unfounded surmises: "Why don't the high schools teach writing, not just grammar?" "Why don't universities make clear what they want from high school graduates?" "University professors don't understand the constraints of large classes, disciplinary problems, and lack of student motivation." "Because high school teachers can't keep up with current research in writing, their teaching suffers." High school teachers and college instructors may regard each other as diabolical, deficient, or simply ignorant about the other's circumstances. Both faculty and students suffer from such misrepresentations or misunderstandings.

A second obstacle to school and college collaborations on writing instruction involves a concern with focus. How do we go about addressing all the areas of concern in writing? Should we talk about theory, about heuristics, about revising strategies, about peer responding, about classroom management? Can we tackle all our concerns and really effect change, or should we deal with one focused area? These questions may cause the problems of collaboration to seem so numerous that useful cooperative ventures are doomed before they start.

Yet a third obstacle to cooperation involves funding. How do we get time away from the classroom to interact? Should the university and the school corporation share equally in providing resources? If a grant is secured, who administers it? Will that unit usurp power over the direction of the venture? As with all educational projects, funding decisions are crucial: with universities and school corporations whose mechanisms and priorities may be very different, hammering out costs and expenditures may override the educational value of a cooperative endeavor.

Fortunately, however, more and more colleges and school corporations are overcoming these obstacles. For instance, the Educational Equality Project Models Program for School-College Collaboration of the College Board has established a network of fifty-seven school systems or individual high schools and fifty-five institutions of higher education located in eighteen different states. In School-College Collaborative Programs in English, the Modern Language Association provides models of successful cooperative programs of all kinds between high school and college English teachers. Programs involve teacher exchanges, early admission testing, summer seminars, and writing festivals. None of these models, however, centers primarily on the integration of computers into the teaching of writing. Our school-college linkage may, therefore, interest corporations and universities searching for a way to begin their work together.

Establishing a Base

Mutuality in our university-school linkage project was a major concern. Both partners wished to bring to the union experience and expertise. Fortunately, two exciting changes in the teaching of writing enabled this mutuality: our profession's changing vision of writing as a process, a pedagogy which was thoroughly incorporated into the Writing Program at Indiana University–Purdue University at Indianapolis (IUPUI), and our profession's recent interest in teaching writing with computers, a movement underway in every junior high and high school of the Indianapolis Public Schools (IPS). If our writing philosophy and goals were similar, we reasoned, we could learn together how to use most effectively computer-aided instruction (CAI) in writing. In the grant proposal our concise statement of purpose thus read:

> The purpose of the project is to develop an innovative and comprehensive model of CAI in writing that best meets the needs of students and teachers of writing in public schools and in university settings. In order to share technological advances in CAI and to develop teaching strategies accordingly, the project will provide

> inservice training for public school teachers and university instructors. Through mutual evaluations of the goals of both programs' curricula, the project will promote motivation for innovative ways to prewrite, compose and revise using the microcomputer. The main components of the project are curriculum analysis, software evaluation and adoption, and dissemination of project results within and beyond IUPUI and IPS.

Thus our faculty development model was designed to link teachers so that they could prepare themselves for using computers to teach the process of writing in their language arts and composition classrooms.

In the remainder of this chapter we will discuss the three major phases of our school-college collaborative program: (1) exploring common pedagogical concerns, (2) reviewing existing software, and (3) writing software.

Exploring Common Pedagogical Concerns

An integral part of the project was reflection on previous teaching and curricula as well as changes suggested by the use of computers in the classrooms. Our first step, therefore, was generating a philosophy of writing instruction and identifying some common goals in teaching writing.

During the first month the school-college collaboration project met five times. During those meetings, we shared syllabuses and curriculum guides to educate each other about current goals and practices. One afternoon of collaborative writing led to a mutually acceptable philosophy of writing:

> Writing is the process of discovering ideas and making a responsible commitment to express those thoughts to an audience, oneself or others, through a presentation appropriate to the communicator's purpose.

Another day we fashioned a list of goals applicable to all levels of writing instruction:

1. To create a positive writing attitude
2. To make available processes and strategies necessary to discover and present what writers are thinking and feeling
3. To show that writing serves a variety of purposes depending upon audience and situation
4. To make available instructors as readers and writers

5. To show that students evolve as writers based on their cumulative writing experience

At another early meeting each core teacher involved the whole group in a strategy for teaching writing that might be enhanced by being incorporated into a computer program. These activities included cubing, tagmemic analysis, generation of detail through impetus of a tactile object, and an innovative method for checking coherence. The first and last activities, cubing and coherence, were later chosen as software-development projects.

We also developed an evaluation form for screening existing software which supported the teaching of writing as a process. The evaluation form posed the following questions:

1. Does the software work to enhance the student-teacher-computer triad and not isolate those elements? Why or why not?
2. Does the software accurately identify its purpose? Why or why not?
3. Does the software use the student's name and provide appropriate praise and appropriate response to error? In what way(s) is positive or negative response appropriate or not appropriate?
4. Does the software provide activities keyed to the particular stages of the writing process being taught, i.e., prewriting, composing, or revising and editing? How are they keyed or not keyed?
5. Is the software easy to operate? Are the directions to the student clear? Are the directions accessible when needed? Can the student operate the program independently? Is the student prevented from getting lost in the program, with no way out? Is the student provided with options to quit or continue at any time? What other features add to or subtract from the ease of operation?
6. Does the program use graphics? If yes, does the software use graphics only when appropriate for the purpose of the program? If no, were graphics necessary or advisable for the purpose of the program?
7. Does the software appear to be intrinsically fun to use more than once? Why or why not?
8. Do you recommend testing and/or purchase of this software? Why or why not?

Because we believed that the choice of software implies a teaching-learning model as well as a theory of composition, we included on the form our philosophy of writing and our definition of the goals of instruction in composing. Building on forms shared by other teachers through the National Council of Teachers of English, we fashioned our form to ask the questions that we thought were most crucial for our own purposes. Question 1 emphasizes our insistence that the computer not be regarded as a separate teaching device but as an integral part of the student-teacher learning team. In questions 2 and 4 we responded to advertising on some programs which bill themselves as contributing to parts of the process but which provide only drill and practice. Because some programs are only negligibly interactive, in question 3 we asked about student-directed praise and advice. In questions 5–7 we focused on the user-friendliness of the programs, including elements which might generate positive student reaction. Lastly, in question 8 we provided aid for each other in asking for an opinion about future reviewing or possible purchase. Working together to construct the questions on the form assured that we knew exactly what we sought in the software programs to be reviewed.

In addition to generating philosophy and goals, deciding on activities for computer instruction, and developing an evaluation form, we placed our work in the context of current theory about writing instruction and what other institutions were doing in the area of computer-aided instruction. For example, at the annual Indiana Teachers of Writing Conference, we attended sessions presented by instructors using computers, and three of us attended a session on authoring programs. At one of our meetings, an outside consultant lectured about a major text-analysis program, an event to which we invited other faculty at our institutions. During the planning stage we refined our understanding of our current practices and goals for the future.

Reviewing Existing Software

Having developed an evaluation tool, we reviewed software which we hoped would support our goals. Because the university and the school system had already purchased some software, our first assignment was to review these programs in view of our own goals. We reviewed programs both for the Apples in the junior high schools and for the IBM PCs in the high schools and in the university's computer classroom. Recurring responses were "The presentation is rather blah," "The activities have no direct relationship to the composing process," "The teacher is bookkeeper of the student's independent work, but neither knows what the student has done correctly or what he has missed," and "I do not recommend." We felt that our objectives in teaching writing extended beyond the rote exercises and programmed writing reinforced by the existing software. As Cynthia L. Selfe (1986) notes, two problems dominated these programs: the CAI in writing either mimicked audiovisual materials from other media or focused only on surface features, not the composing process.

Because this software had been purchased without knowledge of the work of Hugh Burns, the *WANDAH* team, or William Wresch, we were reviewing software best forgotten. We concurred with Donald Ross and Lillian Bridwell that the two kinds of useful software that existed were (1) programs that aid invention and (2) programs that analyze existing text. For example, university students in a junior-level "Writing and Study of Language" class reviewed Hugh Burns's invention program and used it in their own composing process. Students in four first-year composition classes used and discussed the relative merits of three text-analysis programs—*Grammatik, Right Writer,* and *Punctuation and Style.* Despite these two uses, we felt a need to generate more prewriting and composing software to accentuate our commitment to teaching writing as a process.

Writing Software

Undaunted by our ignorance about authoring a program, we contracted with a linguist computer specialist to teach us to write scripts, flow charts, and pseudocode. Although intuitively we went through stages that Selfe (1986, 15) has formalized, the order of our stages differed:

1. Choosing a topic in a CAI lesson
2. Determining how the CAI lesson would fit in the current writing program
3. Adjusting the focus of the CAI lesson
4. Completing a task analysis of the lesson
5. Creating a lesson-overview flow chart
6. Writing a script for the CAI lesson

These activities forced us to assess and reassess the advantage and applicability of using a computer for a particular activity in the process of writing. We had to answer numerous questions: "What is the advantage of doing cubing on a computer rather than on a chalkboard?" "Will students prewriting about a persuasive letter on a computer be more effective than prewriting in a classroom?" "What are the benefits of teaching students to check for coherence in their writing on a computer rather than in a classroom?" "Are these programs an integral part of a larger instructional plan?"

In scripting the CAI lessons, teachers sometimes worked alone and sometimes in collaborative groups, much as our students work in classrooms. The programs produced were about writing persuasive and descriptive letters, cubing a topic, and checking for coherence. Although the junior and senior high school programs were targeted for specific levels, instructors were able to help each other by reacting to each others' programs screen by screen.

After teachers had helped a programmer iron out any problems, we were ready for field-testing. This stage provided a good opportunity for the core team to work with seventeen additional teachers from the school system and nine additional teachers from the university to collaborate on refining the software and accompanying teacher materials. As teachers used the software, they reported to its writers any bugs in the programs. Students also found difficulties that teachers had not foreseen. On levels ranging from word choice to which keys to press, we modified and modified some more the details of the programs. In addition, mutual agreement emerged at this stage about the roles of CAI software in general and in the writing curricula in the school system and at the university.

Benefits of the Teacher-Training Program

By the end of the first year, every participant in this project identified substantial benefits. Five major categories of benefits include improved student attitude, improved self-perception by teachers, mutual admiration between school and college instructors, practice and modeling of collaborative writing, and teachers training teachers. Positive efforts marked both students and teachers.

Improved Student Attitude

Teachers noticed changes in student attitude. Students' increased enthusiasm for writing was capsulized in a teacher's comment that her students "were simply ecstatic" about their work on computers. According to different instructors, that enthusiasm evolved from at least three sources: an elevated sense of the importance of writing ("The technological nature of the lab environment elevated the importance of writing"), improved grades ("My computer composition class earned higher grades than my non-computer sections''), and an increased sense of student teamwork (students reviewed software with the instructor). Students discovered that teachers themselves are writers, a fact many instructors have been emphasizing by sharing their own work-in-progress, and also that teachers are learners, a status that instructors new to computer composition instruction inevitably displayed in the classroom. Parson rightly labels the computer as equalizer and suggests that teachers learning about computers are modeling a ''positive attitude toward lifetime learning'' (1985, 97).

One teacher enthusiastically predicted that ''if the software and accompanying materials—now designed and planned—become available to all IPS language arts teachers at the secondary level, I believe their students would experience positive results in their writing.'' If ''positive results in their writing'' means not only attention to the finished products, but focus on the process of writing, this instructor's statement correlates with one conclusion of the Johns Hopkins University Center for Social Organization of Schools, which surveyed 2,029 schools on school uses of microcomputers.

Teachers say the greatest impact of microcomputers has been social. For the most part, microcomputer-using teachers find that the effects of microcomputers have been more on the social organization of learning than on increased student achievement per se. Substantial numbers of microcomputer-using teachers believe that micros have led to ''increased student enthusiasm for schooling; to students working more independently without assistance from teachers; to students helping one another and answering each other's questions and to students being assigned to do work more appropriate to their achievement level'' (Parson 1985, 91).

Improved Self-Perception by Teachers

The second set of benefits from teachers' participation in a faculty development program for CAI in composition centers around teachers' perception of themselves as teachers. Besides noting an increase in positive student evaluations (''My teacher evaluations are noticeably improved over last semester''), one instructor evaluated her own future as a teacher: ''Being able to use my knowledge for programming helped me to understand that I will not become obsolete as a teacher.'' Another teacher found herself reassessing the goals of her teaching: ''I had to test my assumptions about what I was teaching. What did I value and why?'' Yet another instructor relished an increase in her own sense of ability: ''As an individual teacher I am a better teacher of writing as a result of my participation with the team.'' This last comment leads to a third set of benefits arising when teachers work together on CAI in writing.

Mutual Admiration between School and College Instructors

Cooperation among public school teachers and university instructors brought mutual admiration. For instance, one teacher concluded, "I have thoroughly enjoyed working with the other teachers in the program. They are all very creative, hard working, and professional." Recognizing mutual problems about lack of time to develop programs, domination of computer classrooms by other departments, and uneasiness about lack of experience, teachers commiserated but then worked to discover solutions. Our experience corroborated that of Linda Bischoff, who writes that "teachers going through this should have meetings, like we did, even if once a month, get together in workshops, share ideas. It gets your confidence up, and your energy level up, and that's important. After a while we need all the boosts you can get. We needed to talk to each other" (Parson 1985, 118). The constant interaction at meetings and through correspondence also increased productivity. As one instructor put it, "Reporting our work to each other made me more productive than I would have been alone."

Practice and Modeling of Collaborative Writing

A fourth set of benefits builds on cooperation leading to mutual admiration. In coauthoring programs, teachers practiced what Andrea Lunsford and Lisa Ede see as a more widespread practice than we typically model in our classrooms. Although writers tend to think of themselves as writing "alone," they often collaborate on "the mental and procedural activities which precede and co-occur with the act of writing, as well as on the construction of text" (Lunsford and Ede 1986, 73). If we are preparing students to write in their workplaces, where Lunsford and Ede's early findings indicate 87 percent of employees write as part of a team or group (1986, 76), our practical experience in the dynamics of group authorship makes us better able to teach the processes involved when several people must produce a finished project. One teacher lauded this collegial effort: "The expertise of the other teachers has been of great help. We needed each other's strategies to succeed as a group."

Teachers Training Teachers

A fifth set of benefits affects teachers joining the project during its second year. Two different teachers during the first year foresaw their work as important for others beyond the initial participants. In a statement focusing both inwardly on herself and outwardly on others, one instructor praised the project for providing "a satisfaction of working on computer programs that should help other teachers with the composition process." Another predicted that "this program being designed by concerned teachers will be an inspiration for other teachers." If faculty members are well trained themselves, they seem naturally to look beyond their classrooms to how they can influence others positively.

Recommendations

These five sets of benefits speak to the positive consequences of our project. We learned many other things in our project, however, that may be useful for future training projects in CAI. Although certain activities and attitudes went well throughout the project, some aspects related to participant characteristics and administrative details needed to be considered on a continuing basis. Anyone planning faculty development should consider the following six recommendations.

Recommendation 1: Adjust to Learning Styles

All teacher trainers should be aware of and adjust to "technology learning styles." Marybeth Darrow and Gail Parson (1985) explain how what they call "technology learning styles" differ from learning styles for non–technology-related material. We found that some teachers were less verbal in expressing their needs, likes, and dislikes when talking about computer-related concerns than when describing classroom teaching techniques, for example. To reduce this kind of anxiety, we found that a nonthreatening workshop environment to review programs and CAI lessons was helpful.

We also discovered that our teachers fit into three distinct styles of training models posited by Darrow and Parson.

1. The word-processing pro is most directed and most sequenced. Training for this individual needs to be challenging and enriching.
2. The word-processing coach displays moderate skills, is less structured, and learns with students.
3. The word-processing booster encourages students to learn even if he or she does not know all about computers.

Faculty development programs need to provide a variety of materials with detailed instructional sequence. Structured and unstructured time with the computer is needed, including formal workshops and practice at one's own pace.

These learning styles emerged in our project during the planning and composing stages. Although we learned to adjust to these different learning styles, it would be better if teachers would identify their learning styles and predict ways in which they might best learn. We also found that a certain amount of conflict related to individual learning styles was necessary. For example, two classic word-processing coaches needed the challenge of organizing a computer workshop for the teachers at their schools as encouragement to become more active in their own use of CAI.

Recommendation 2: Encourage Feedback

Teacher trainers should plan to develop substantial follow-up activities and feedback opportunities. No matter what learning styles our members had, follow-up activities for each initial activity helped the team work productively. In the cases where the members of our team reported back in sufficient detail about specific advantages and disadvantages of particular software, the whole team benefited. Written evaluations and group observations of programs, such as we did in evaluating the *HBJ Writer* and *The Writer's Helper*, led to better decision making.

Recommendation 3: Meet Regularly

In a long-term project, teacher trainers and teachers need to meet regularly to discuss progress. We found that we gained self-confidence from frequent contact. Even if individual subteams meet regularly, either routine general meetings should be held or representative members of the various subteams should convene. Conflict among core participants occurred only twice, each after a span of individual meetings with no general meeting to emphasize continuity of the whole group.

Recommendation 4: Encourage Self-Direction

All teacher trainers should provide opportunities for self-direction and leadership. Every participant should be an expert and a leader to provide self-direction. For instance, core teachers in our project tended to look to writers of the grant for each next step in the process. When they initiated activities after learning that their expertise was valued, more productive work ensued.

Recommendation 5: Anticipate Change

Teacher trainers and teachers should be ready for change. Participants may change due to reassignment of schools, a shift in responsibilities or positions, or a change in commitment to the project. For instance, among our nine initial participants, three of our university instructors took new jobs, one public school administrator resigned, and two public school teachers were assigned to new schools. Adjusting to change in availability of computer labs and new teaching assignments affected the kind of participation by each team member. Another example of change in our project which necessitated an addition of core personnel was our decision to write our own software. Although we had included in our original plan computer experts from both the school system and the university, we needed an instructional media specialist and a programmer. Because most long-term projects evolve over time, built-in opportunities for flexibility in personnel and funding are an excellent idea.

Recommendation 6: Acknowledge Limitations

Teacher trainers and teachers need to be realistic about how much can be accomplished in a certain time period. Even though we were adequately advised by Ralph Lundgren of Lilly Endowment, Inc., about careful selection of the number of accomplishments predicted in our two-year project, our enthusiasm, nonetheless, at times caused us to overestimate our capabilities. For instance, when we decided on the specific programs which we would write, we did not realize the amount of time involved in programming and debugging programs. During our second year, therefore, we were able to field-test in the classrooms fewer programs than we had hoped. These considerations of our beginning years are helping us now as we plan for our future.

Planning for the Future

As the grant which fostered our mutual development of CAI in writing comes to a close, we think of it in terms of commencement. Our teacher-training program has enabled us to accomplish many goals in the teaching of writing. First of all, we are graduating from our two-ear experience with greater mutual admiration and more knowledge bout CAI. In the school system, each junior high and high school now as a teacher who is knowledgeable about programs and practices of AI. At the university, we now have a computer-writing classroom vith writing classes scheduled all day long. Both first-year English vriting classes and several more advanced writing classes regularly se the computer classroom. Altogether, nineteen teachers hold a class n the computer classroom using a number of available commercial omputer programs in addition to our locally made programs and xercises.

Our project was enhanced by our ability to author our own software. No longer are we constrained or limited when we identify ctivities which can best be done on computers but which cannot be ound in commercial software. With our new knowledge and resources we can develop our own software.

Thanks to our grant, we were able to purchase software and conduct vorkshops as we needed them. Yet, we feel that school systems and niversities could accomplish similar results if resources were pooled. or instance, schools could use regularly scheduled inservice days for AI workshops and programs, and many software packages could be btained for preview. Because two educational units are contributing, osts are shared in a way that benefits both the schools and the niversity.

Commencement means beginning as well as finishing. We will ontinue our liaison between Indiana University–Purdue University at ndianapolis and the Indianapolis Public Schools to achieve our commitment of producing the best instruction possible for writers in our lassrooms. More and more emphasis on CAI in writing, we know, igures in that future instruction.

Vorks Cited

)arrow, Marybeth, and Gail Parson. 1985. "Training Teachers and Students to Use Word Processing: It's Simply a Matter of Style." In *Hand-in-Hand: The Writing Process and the Microcomputer*, edited by Gail Parson, 67–73. Juneau: Alaska Department of Education.

unsford, Andrea, and Lisa Ede. 1986. "Why Write . . . Together: A Research Update." *Rhetoric Review* 5: 71–77.

'arson, Gail, ed. 1985. *Hand-in-Hand: The Writing Process and the Microcomputer*. Juneau: Alaska Department of Education.

elfe, Cynthia L. 1986. *Computer-Assisted Instruction in Composition: Create Your Own!* Urbana, Ill.: National Council of Teachers of English.

7 Captain Jacobsen and the Apple Jocks: Computers and English Teachers at Glendora High School

Sandra Hooven, Glendora High School, Glendora, California

Introduction: "Closing the Generation Gap"

Sometimes public education is so busy moving forward that it ends up being backward. By this cryptic statement, I mean simply that we are so zealously moving our students into the future that we fail to appreciate the obvious. Our students are more in and of the future than we are; and on a day-to-day basis we can move into the future faster and farther with their help than we can under our own power.

The day the first of my ninth-grade honors students walked into my classroom with a paper prepared not on a typewriter but on a word processor, I realized with a vague sense of unease, if not downright inferiority, that my omnipotence (shaky omnipotence at its strongest) was being threatened. The year was 1983, and only two of my students had their own computers, printers, and word-processing outfits, so I relaxed and put my vague sense of an impending computer-induced doom on standby.

So it must be in schools across the land for teachers everywhere. There comes a moment when our bastion of special knowledge becomes vulnerable and assailable, and not in expected ways or by expected intellectual enemies, such as scholars, scientists, or the media. Our students, who are living behind us in years, are beyond us in timely knowledge of computers. It is our challenge as English educators that when the inevitable moment of relativity strikes our discipline (the moment when the past and the future collide), we respond with all the open-minded strengths given to us by our educational backgrounds and specializations, and we say yes to the future.

This chapter describes one school's solution to the problem of training English teachers to integrate computers into their language arts classes. To accomplish this task, we turned to the real computer specialists in our school for help and developed a program wherein our own students taught a group of English teachers to become comfortable with computers. We called this program Captain Jacobsen and the Apple Jocks.

Background of the Program: What, Why, and How We Did What We Did

I said yes to the future of the computer in English education by accident. Had someone offered me computer knowledge like pheasant under glass, I probably would have said, "No, thank you. I like my verbal knowledge just as it stands—pure and untainted by machines."

Instead, computers sneaked up on me with assistance from a friend and teacher aide, whose name was John. John arrived on the scene in early May, just after the editor of the literary magazine had informed me that he would be too busy to put out the final issue that year.

After a minimum of pleading on my part, John—who relished computers like baseball fans relish cheap hot dogs, and who, like the baby Hercules, had strangled two computer languages in the crib—agreed to take on the project. He produced possibly the finest publication distributed on our campus. From that moment on I was a captive of the computer future, and events just seemed to fall into place without any effort on my part. It occurred to me that John could teach me and other teachers in the department to become computer literate on the four Apple IIe computers that would be arriving in our department in a few days.

With a colleague who supported the idea, I proposed to the district administrator in charge of curriculum that John be hired at a certain small hourly wage to teach the teachers in the English department at our school about computers. The program was a cheap, informal, and interesting educational experiment in role reversal that was bound to have educationally significant results.

In fact, the mere thought of specialized knowledge being passed from student to teacher instead of vice versa made the top ten tidbits of campus gossip. As soon as the math and science departments heard about the program, they set about trying to get pay for the student assistants in their computer lab. (I always get a cheap secret thrill when the English department conducts the first experiment in something.)

Even before it began, the Apple Jock program had every component of a winning team. Such a winning formula is easily within the grasp of almost any high school in the nation. Needed are simply the following components:

An expert coach who will work for low pay

A team of players who are eager to learn to play and who have much potential but not a lot of confidence (too much confidence would undermine the role reversal from the start)

A district administration that is ready to stand by and support the experiment, but that will not be too judgmental about the trial run

Grab a floppy disk now, bench press it a few times, and begin to create your own winning program as I present the basic outline of our basic Apple Jock workout. Wish I had a video version!

Program Description: The Apple Jocks Do Daily Calisthenics

The goals of the Apple Jock program were twofold and very basic. The first was to introduce the entire staff of the English department in our high school to the computer as a teaching machine and as a potentially revolutionary catalyst for education. The other goal was to excite the staff by these possibilities so that word processing as a new language art would begin to make its appearance in a traditional curriculum where it had, theretofore, played no part whatsoever.

It was an accidental benefit of our on-the-job training by a senior student, not a critical expert, that a trendy new fashion (computers) would be introduced in a cozy old environment (our own campus) with a maximum amount of attention to our personal needs for immediate access and a nonthreatening environment.

The broad instructional assumption upon which our program was based was as simple as the plan itself. During the last period of the day, two days per week for as long as it took, the English staff who were willing (no one was forced, tied, gagged, or bound in an effort for full participation) would be introduced to the computer as tool and as word processor via *Bank Street Writer*. This software had been ordered because we did not know any better; serendipitously, the 40-column program proved wondrously elemental and perfectly matched our needs and skills.

Due to its primitive nature, the instructional site itself was also crucial to the success of the project. Our four brand-new Apples and printers were housed in a leftover office with a sink, a couple of old cans of cleanser, three gray walls, and a door that resisted closing. The informal, cramped quarters, while a source of much humor, also made us all feel more like daring adventurers (Ben Franklins flying our kites at night) than like teachers entering into a new brand of knowledge for which, after many years of education, multiple degrees, and numerous years of teaching experience, we were totally unprepared.

Our teacher education project met for hourly sessions twice a week for nearly the entire year and reached twenty teachers as well as two classified employees. As one group of two or three English teachers graduated, floppy disk in hand, a new group took its place. Teachers were eager to sign up, and almost every teacher in the department completed at least some training.

During the sessions, I had the foresight to keep a journal in which I described the confusion, pleasure, humor, and pathos involved in acquiring computer literacy. Excerpts from this journal recount some of our experiences.

A Journal: Living through a Course in Computer Training

October 8, 1984: The Prelude

Agenda: setting up the computers, identifying the parts, allowing the students to voice some insecurities

The computer room was ready. The gray monoliths, possible Stonehenges of the future, lined the cracked walls poised on tidy little tables with master switches so that the computers could be operated from a single punch of a switch. The switches glowed red in the dark—a symbol of our eagerness to begin the project.

The teacher, Coach John Jacobsen, had his master plan prepared for the first lesson, and his team, the unknown quantity, were ready, willing, and able to begin their training.

A diverse group at best, they represented all facets of the English staff: Jane, age 59, a total professional devoted to quality education and grammatical excellence for 20 years; Arlan, gentle teacher of the successful and unsuccessful alike, basketball coach and saver of lost souls; Sandra, experimentalist par excellence, but a bit of a sentence fragment.

To play on a computer team they began the regimen totally unfit. A coach's dream or nightmare, depending on how one looks upon it.

Day one the flab was evident. I looked at the setup of the monitor, disk drive, printer, and keyboard and asked, "Where's the computer?"

Jane kept muttering, "I'll never be able to understand this stuff. And if I do I'll never have time to practice it."

Arlan, the Department Chair, said quietly, "I think this might be very interesting if I could stay for the entire session, but I have a meeting in one half hour."

So much for our auspicious beginnings.

October 9, 1984

Agenda: an overview of educational potential that includes the on and off switches

The first lesson took place, really. After Monday's lecture on computer parts and column cards, etc., we got down to the business of what a computer can do for us.

We were amazed at the breadth and depth of the educational possibilities that ranged from the testing of reading, to SAT review, to skill building through rote memory activities, to the crème de la crème of computer possibilities—word processing.

We decided to do double duty and double days for awhile just to get the program moving more rapidly and at the same time satisfy the intellectual curiosity that had just added incredible vistas to our lesson plan of the future.

Calisthenics for this day included learning where all the plugs went, how to double-check a faulty function, and all about turning our Apples on and off.

We were beaming confidence and expertise by the end of the session. Sort of like swimmers who just completed a successful dive and don't know that they are about to drown.

October 10, 1984

Agenda: brainstorming possible educational goals for ourselves and our use of computers

At this point, yesterday's excitement still burns in our memories, but we flounder a bit at the start for we are unsure of how fast we might advance and whether or not our progress will be rapid enough to invite all the humanities faculty to join us in our computer calisthenics.

My personal goal is to use the computer in the classroom for writing tasks of every description, from paragraph to essay, and to use the computer's power to help students critique the technical errors as well as the style of their papers. Such a computer-assisted critique would enable the teacher to save discussion and teaching time for the more philosophic and less technical aspects of teaching language mastery.

Once I attain expertise, my imagination soars into the possibility of writing my own programs.

A secondary goal is to teach the editors and contributors of the literary magazine all about computer-assisted publishing: arranging, saving and printing their contributions on disk as well as using *Print Shop* graphics and fancy tampering with the print options to create expanded titles and stylistic variations that are pleasing to the eye as well as the intellect. John did it last year, so I am sure that other students will be entranced by the possibilities. Creating at the computer could become a byword for our group of young writers.

I sharply curtail my dreaming and bring my attention to the expertise with which our "student teacher" handles the class. Granted there are only three of us, but the organized, logical and patient way he presents the material is impressive.

I notice that I am totally unable to visualize what is written in explanations about using computers and am learning strictly by taking notes, watching carefully and then applying what I have learned using the keyboard, monitor and disks.

I continue to be excited by the possibility of learning right on campus, the individualized instruction that we are receiving and how effective it can be, and the way this student-to-teacher instruction will strengthen my role in the classroom and bring it in step with technology.

Math and science teachers can talk at lunch eternally about their own experiences in the computer lab teaching whatever they teach, and I will have a clear vision of what might be going on.

When students discuss the lessons in business classes that relate to computers, I can nod sagely when they mention BASIC and Pascal and then insert my own comments about word processing.

Everywhere I see computers being used—from the gas company to NASA, I feel powerfully a part of the computer age.

Wow! My computer muscles are bulging today!!

October 15, 1984

Agenda: discussing disks—DOS, Apple Presents Apple, and blank

The coach had prepared a tidy little list of dos and don'ts for the computer disks which will be hung in the room. Grand idea. These disks have private parts that must not be touched or invaded. Grab 'em by the labels only. Also, if you leave them lying around without their little jackets, Coach Jacobsen snarls at you. Overall treat the disks like newborn babies—don't maul 'em and keep 'em covered when they're exposed to the elements. This last item will be very important for computer training the students.

How to treat a disk was the easy part of the lesson. Other important facts about disks—always put the disk in before you switch the on button on and do not (I repeat), do not remove the disk while the red light is on. Causes a meltdown—to the core.

Well, so much for everything you always wanted to know about disks. I haven't got the slightest idea what the relationship between the disk and the computer is (hopefully not illicit). That will come with time no doubt.

Today we play with the DOS disk and the Apple Presents Apple Introduction Disk. As I understand it right now, the DOS disk is good for only copy purposes. Apple Presents Apple is fun. I am already feeling like a computer jock even though I can't type a lick. I understand there are computer programs that teach you how to type on the spot—timed writings and all and only the computer knows how slow and inaccurate you are. I'll have to get one for the other students (my own) who can't type. They can learn to type at the same time they learn word processing.

Ah! Computers! Where were you when I was rubbing holes in my term papers with ink erasers? Computers, with their instant correction and easy save and easy print, have made writing miraculously easy. I'll have to tell my students a little story about the "bad ol' days" when I teach them the *Back Street Writer*.

October 17, 1984

Agenda: practicing our skills, dealing with cuts

I withhold judgment on exactly what we learned. At the end of the session, the coach reassured us by telling us that someday soon we too would be able to play the computer game, but I could not help wondering whether or not it would be in this lifetime.

The Department Chair was once again driven to absenteeism by a busy schedule and former commitments, so Jane and I carried on alone. The fewer the better where basic instruction is concerned.

We were feeling so computer fit because we could tell the computer from the monitor from the disk, and then we got inundated with incredible quantities of senseless terminology like "boot up, initializing, passwords and labels." We labeled our disks and little cases, and were informed that disks have a little notch on the right-hand side that, if touched, shuts down forever. The Rape of the Disk!

The specialized vocabulary really threw me because it was piled on top of a bunch of other new things, and I planned to present computers to my students with translations into the vernacular of all the fancy terms so they wouldn't have to learn a whole new language right away.

Jane and I spent two lunches in the computer room playing with our disks, eating salads stacked into Tupperware containers, and doing homework. Students, too, we decided, must have quiet access to the computers outside of classroom hours to practice their new knowledge.

Jane and I feel as though we are a winning team in spite of feeling totally frustrated upon occasion and incredibly ignorant at least once a day. The best part of computers is what they have to teach us about how to get out of a bad situation—push "escape!"

October 22, 1984

Agenda: menus

All three computer fledglings were present for today's lesson. We are feeling like a real team who is unafraid to admit that our skills are weak and who can wait patiently for the instructor to answer our thousand questions and attend to our many needs.

Computers, in simplest form, are very demanding. Even when the coach tells us to play with our *Bank Street Writer* disks and print whatever we are moved to type, we get stumped. Finally we wrote something inane—Jane typed a fairy tale, Arlan, Shakespeare (what do you expect from the Department Chair), and I (being on a diet) described a gourmet meal.

For sure, when I present computer assignments to my own students (who are slightly less mature than I), I will have had them write something in advance.

The word "Menu" probably triggered my whole sense of inadequacy all over again as I thought about attempting to distinguish between the main menu, the transfer menu, and the Weight Watcher menu currently in my vocabulary.

The three of us typed, deleted, played and played, and were taught never to forget to save what we wanted to print else we might score zero points for the day. Big red signs around the classroom saying SAVE YOUR INPUT might be just the ticket to inspire students to do just that.

Tomorrow and tomorrow is hanging very heavily upon Arlan because he is so far behind while Jane and I are almost ready to graduate. A typical classroom.

October 24, 1984

Agenda: computer costs, deleting of students as well as errors

The teacher was slightly unprepared and discovered the fine old art of "winging it." It was a winning day anyway. We set our first round as experimental and the following rounds as firm and fair.

The projected time line sees us finished with our basic program (no pun intended) by October 31. The coach deserves a week's respite before the new team descends for basic training.

Perhaps it would be wise to allow some lapse time when teaching computers to students as well. Computer maintenance and repair are as essential to a program as lesson plans, so allowing time for inspection of the equipment between learning sessions might be wise.

Just keeping a class in floppy disks could be expensive. Not to mention teaching them the finer points like options and the gentle art of deleting without destroying entire files.

Jane plans on staying in training for the whole year, not just a few weeks. She's just like that student who hangs around the teacher's neck for an entire year just begging for that one extra crumb of learning.

Arlan's truancy will allow him to be a rerun, so I will be the only professional on the first team.

If two teachers don't graduate the first time around, I know I will need to have very flexible expectations for my students.

October 31, 1984

Agenda: memory banks and ASCII codes (Eeeeek)

The group assembles at odd moments, as usual. We come into the room, sit at the machine and proceed with remarkable diligence to test our memories about what we have learned so far and how much there is yet to go.

Like a true team, we discuss the large gaps in our computer knowledge but agree to allow the four hopefuls knocking on Coach Jacobsen's door access by November 19.

We decide that whoever goes next needs to make a firm commitment to be present on lesson days. Ahem! Arlan has been the worst offender and frankly admits it.

The local paper is interested in doing an article on this experiment in role reversal in education.

The lesson on printing and ASCII codes ensues and though parts of it are boring and parts beyond us, we plug away because we know, better than most, how all the material stored in our very own memory banks can be of value later on.

November 7, 1984

Agenda: The light at the end of the tunnel!!

Almost a month has passed since we first sat at the computer and many great things have happened in our lives.

We have become computer fit. By bytes and bits, by hit and miss, by being brave enough to say "I don't understand" and foolish enough to keep trying to, we are now the Apple Jocks of our department. Anyway, two of us are.

Certainly we are not to be confused with the A-Team. We get lost. We forget things. We can't yet change printer codes. But starting from nowhere we have ended up somewhere that we wanted to be and somewhere that we recognize.

In a few short hours we will take our final exam—open book, of course. Hopefully we will pass.

The last session (boo-hoo—learning is fun) was just an ordinary mouth bite size. We learned that:

> The life of a disk is much longer than that of a human if treated properly.
>
> Every disk must be initialized (formatted) before it can be used. (That would be a useful invention for humans too.)
>
> Entire portions of disks or only specific segments can be copied and saved as backups for important material.

I was so ecstatically fit on this day that I made a new file, printed the file, and then lost the file and saved it twice.

I am working hard on creating a file that contains one poem per page and looks on the screen exactly as it will look in print. Each of my classes could put an entire poetry portfolio on computer disk when we do our creative writing in the spring.

Coach John sneers slightly when you admit that you don't remember something he said one month ago. Give me a break! It's easy to be perfect when you know it all. I think of how easy spelling is for me and how hard for some very bright students and imagine hooking up a spelling checker on the computer so that they can perfect their spelling without thumbing through thousands of dictionary pages.

I plan to study hard for the test. Here is a sample question the coach gave us to work on: What does "Getting inside the RAM mean?" Could it be sacking an LA Quarterback? Escaping from the cave of the Cyclops? Cracking the computer main memory barrier? All of the above?

I could go anywhere and play on a computer team because I know that the answer to that question is answer 3!!!!!! Just call me Apple Jock.

Conclusion: "We Learned to Be Intellectual Athletes"

Our student-led teacher-training project was an indubitable success. We played a game that we had never played before and lost a few self-confidences, a few preconceived ideas, and a lot of fears.

The strengths of the project were threefold: being introduced to an uncharted territory in a nonthreatening manner, seeing ourselves playing the role of student, from which we understood more about ourselves as teachers, and writing follow-up projects that have secured us countless computer benefices.

Wherever possible, except in cases where an entire English staff is already composed of computer aficionados, it is best to choose a setting right on campus during school hours for a teacher-training project. Dedicated paper-grading English teachers are more readily enticed into a computer experience when that experience will not detract too ostensibly from their precious preparation time.

Being the student instead of the teacher was a marvelous psychological experiment in role reversal that could have been a seminar in and of itself. Our student-turned teacher, John, was patient, organized, knowledgeable, and witty. He never put us down for asking stupid questions, and he readily handled all of our eager pesterings (sometimes three of us talking at once) without losing his temper. His temperament as a teacher was as much an unknown quantity as our aptitudes as students. And yet all of us acquitted ourselves well and were proud of our accomplishments.

Our successful follow-up to the project included a fine article in the local paper picturing Coach John teaching his third set of faculty, an $8,000 computer grant that befell us thanks to one of the original students, and an ongoing interest in computer education in our English department, which recently began loaning materials to the math and science departments.

We now have several instructional manuals written by the teachers that cover *AppleWorks* and *Bank Street Writer*, and we are busy building a software library for our sixteen-computer lab.

We are truly flexing our Apple Jock muscles. Yet, our program also had weaknesses because it was nearsighted rather than farsighted, and we, like countless other English departments across the country, are now faced with the task of finding ways to fit twenty-five teenage bodies into a lab and teach them word processing. It is assuredly a two-person job, and most classrooms in most districts are staffed at ratios of twenty-five or thirty to one.

Actual numbers may pose the smallest threat to integrating computers into our language arts curriculum, 9–12. What can be best and most appropriately done by each teacher at each grade level is still being hotly debated in our department. We also need to decide philosophically whether the broadest computer education might not go forth with two or three computers placed in each English classroom rather than a single lab. We may yet defeat ourselves!

Last but not least, where once again the past and the future lock horns, we must, along with the rest of our profession, decide in what ways computers can be used to educate students into their own eras. Many of us fear that a computer that can correct faculty spelling or grammar will create lazy students of weak intellect. Others know that such technology is just another tool created to make humankind simultaneously freer and more backward.

Our project, in its essence, was a single-faceted educational diamond—to show us the shining beauty of computers as a possible aid to verbal communication.

The next chapter in this story is being written right now—by a student—on a computer.

8 Computers: Catalysts for Change at Springfield High School

W. Edward Bureau, Springfield School District, Delaware County, Pennsylvania

Introduction

Computers can assume an active role as change agents in any school's language arts program. With them, a controlled change process can begin as English teachers realize the potential and the excitement of teaching writing with computers. To fuel such a change process, however, other factors must also converge in a timely fashion: teachers' curiosity, supervisors' knowledge and experience, central office support, funding, and creation of a carefully planned staff development project.

This chapter describes the second year of a three-year plan to integrate computers into language arts instruction at Springfield High School, Springfield (Delaware County), Pennsylvania. At the heart of this project rested our belief that the computer is only an extremely sophisticated tool, but one which has power that can be judiciously used to effect changes in written language, in teaching, and in curriculum. We also believed that simply making computers available to our language arts teachers would not guarantee that the machines would be effectively integrated into instruction; those sophisticated tools had to become part of an evolutionary process in which teachers were given training, time to learn, and support for their efforts. To begin the process, we had to help our teachers learn on a personal level to value the computer as a sophisticated writing tool; we continue to believe that this change in attitude is an essential precursor to teaching writing with word processing.

During the entire staff development project, we wanted to be certain teachers understood, and could apply to instruction, three fundamental concepts. First, through their own writing and initial explorations of how to teach writing with a word processor, we wanted teachers to develop an understanding of the close correlation between a word processor's editing functions and the essential activities of language manipulation: adding, removing, moving, and substituting (ARMS). Second, we wanted teachers to learn that computers could most effectively be used to teach writing by integrating them into the writing process. Finally, as they began teaching in our computer lab, we wanted teachers to validate a third major project concept, our notion that combining computers and writing process is best achieved in an "on/off" machine strategy, where students must come "off" the computer with a printed draft in order to revise effectively. From an understanding of these three fundamental concepts, our teachers moved toward teaching writing by computer and process.

The role of the computer in our staff development project and its effects on teaching, curriculum, and writing should be of interest to anyone trying to integrate computers into language arts—teachers, administrators, or teacher educators. More particularly, the success described should hearten those who believe that a successful marriage between technology and humanities can occur and those who know that teacher growth occurs with training, time, support, and developing senses of ownership.

An Overview of the Project

Who were we who used computers to change a language arts program? As language arts supervisor, I worked with six teachers, half of Springfield High School's language arts department, who volunteered to participate in the project. Before our project began, the teachers had been trained in word processing as part of a district computer literacy effort. Most had been exposed to the methods of writing process; four had made initial attempts to teach writing on four available computers housed in a tiny room. Together we worked with approximately a third of the school's student body, distributed across the spectrum of grade and ability levels, by teaching them word processing and then using it to teach writing.

Our year-long project was designed to effect changes in teachers' methods, the curriculum, and students' writing and had two major goals: (1) developing teachers' understanding of and methodologies for teaching writing by process and computer, and (2) radical revamping of the writing thread of the language arts curriculum to include both computers and process. Of equal importance, though not central to this discussion, was enhancing students' writing performance.

To work toward these goals, we formed a year-long project consisting of ten monthly day-long meetings, curriculum development and teacher-training workshops, and a network to offer support and assistance during and after teaching in the computer lab. As will be described throughout the chapter, activities were carefully planned based on project goals as well as on teacher needs. A time line for accomplishing the activities was established and followed. Rather than merely making computers available to teachers, we set out on a highly structured project guided by clearly defined goals. It was this foresight that ensured our project's eventual success.

How Our Project Originated

Several of the factors which combined to form the original impetus for our project are common to public schools and should be familiar to readers. Staff development and curriculum needs, as well as district goals for infusing computers into instruction, gave us the first indications that such a program was needed. They set the stage for developing our project. Our teachers had received limited training in teaching writing by the process approach and were, as noted, curious about teaching writing with computers. Their interest had been so piqued that six readily volunteered to participate in the project and to receive additional training.

A formal curriculum review also indicated the need to increase time spent on writing instruction, to include the writing-process approach, and to integrate computers as a writing tool. One of the critical needs we identified was building a writing curriculum that specified consistency of writing experiences in each of five major types of writing defined by purpose—to inform, to create, to persuade, to learn, and for fluency. Additionally, we found the need to adopt a standard device for determining student writing competency.

Beyond the context of our language arts curriculum existed a district goal to bring technology, especially computers, into classrooms in a controlled process which included training teachers how to use the equipment effectively in teaching. Consequently, we developed a three-year plan to integrate computers into the high school language arts program. Comprehensive in nature, the plan's components included curriculum, staff development, procedures for selecting software and hardware, and equipping a facility adequately for instruction. First-year activities in the three-year project centered on increasing teacher awareness of the word processor and its connection to writing process. Although computer use was tentative during that initial year, teachers' interest level grew, setting the stage for dramatic developments during the second year.

Calling for expanded staff development activities, computer facilities, and hardware availability, plans for the second year of the three-year project were radically expanded through federal Chapter 2 grant funds ($33,500). With the funding, we established the second-year phase by forming the grant project called "Computers: Catalysts to Change in a School's Language Arts Program." It is this second-year project that is described in this chapter.

Project components for this second-year effort were directly based upon elements of our original three-year plan. Two of the three components described in this chapter, staff development and curriculum revision, are at the heart of changes we made in the language arts program. Both were based on our fundamental assumptions about the interrelationship of computers, staff education, and curriculum.

Project Components and Activities

To meet the broad district goal of integrating computers into language arts, we chose the arena of writing instruction as the natural, broadest path to success. Though kept distinct for management purposes, the staff development and curriculum components of our project were inexorably intertwined. Development of a computer/process-based writing curriculum occurred formally in a workshop but also informally throughout the year as teachers learned how to teach by process and machine. That on-the-job staff development was combined with formal training, sharing with colleagues, and the act of writing the curriculum itself. Though very convoluted, these two project components can be separated, described, and evaluated.

Learning to Teach with Computers

Each component of the project to integrate computers and writing process into a curriculum was educative in nature. Our teachers found firsthand that the computer was the keystone in their own learning process, just as they came to value the machine as a sophisticated writing tool. As they worked with computers and writing-process techniques, teachers developed an understanding of and a commitment to the connections and potential of the two. That goal was achieved by using time and resources to give teachers support, staff development activities, and the latitude to change their own and students' roles in the writing class.

Teaching Each Other: Informal Instructional Support

Teachers received both formal and informal support during the project—the former through planned activities and the latter through mutual problem solving, critiquing, and encouragement. Nearly all formal support occurred during the ten monthly project meetings and was specifically aimed at teaching teachers the "how's and why's" of teaching by process and computers. Informal support came during those meetings and during times when teachers helped each other with students in the computer lab.

Project meetings were held monthly for a full school day throughout the ten-month duration of the second-year project. (Grant funds paid the wages of substitute teachers hired to cover the teachers' classes.) With a concentrated block of time, teachers had the latitude to learn, apply, and reflect on techniques and theories presented. To a person, they felt that the large blocks of time were essential to their own growth and to the project's success. Project meetings consisted of three supportive components—solving logistical problems, ensuring project continuity, and educating staff.

Both formal and informal support flowed as logistical problems and project continuity matters were addressed. Because teaching writing in a computer lab was a novel experience, teachers addressed problems ranging from security to room arrangement and from booting up machines to giving enough lead time to end class in an orderly fashion. Talking through problems together was not just educative, it built in us a sense of cohesiveness as a staff.

To help each other succeed in teaching writing with computers and to guarantee project success, we also set aside time to maintain project continuity—to complete activities essential for meeting project goals. Each of the following activities, spread throughout the year, became a learning experience for us:

- planning for taking samples of student writing
- creation of an activity bank of sample assignments
- review of professional and student materials
- completion of teacher assessments of project success
- informing administrators about the project

ensuring distribution of writings by purpose

making plans for extending the grant

An added feature in each project meeting was the "Open Forum" in which teachers could address each other's concerns, questions, and needs. Issues they needed to address determined the course of our discussion. Often we sought each other's advice on such problems as protecting against lost student files, helping nonparticipating teachers understand the project, or balancing time taken for writing instruction against time needed for other aspects of the curriculum.

Learning Together: Formal Instructional Support

More formalized staff development was conducted during project meetings by providing inservice education and by disseminating professional materials. At each monthly meeting we learned about at least one aspect of computers and writing. Planned presentations included the following:

class management strategies

group writing activities

designing and using templates for prewriting and revision

theories behind distributing writings by purpose

design and use of writing-competency scales

off-machine revision strategies

use of non–word-processing software

review of CAI software at a computer resource center at West Chester University of Pennsylvania

The Pennsylvania Writing Project (PAWP), regional center of the National Writing Project, gave us support for this inservice education. PAWP teacher trainers were chosen for their expertise in addressing many of the topics cited above. Each inservice topic was identified as a result of teacher needs or was planned in advance after consultation with the director of the PAWP. To be sure that we understood and could apply ideas and techniques presented, we planned follow-up activities; for example, after learning how to use templates during revision, teachers compiled a disk of writing-assignment response templates which became a resource during writing classes that followed.

As a further supplement to staff education, we selected and purchased professional materials, using an allocation from the grant budget to cover costs incurred. As project director, I purchased a number of books that I knew teachers would find helpful. Acting as a large committee, we collectively chose all other books, periodical subscriptions, and reprinted materials. Resources that came in single copies, such as a subscription to *Classroom Computer Learning,* were circulated among us with routing slips.

Changing Our Roles in the Writing Class

As had been indicated in the curriculum needs-assessment that preceded our project, writing instruction in our school tended to be teacher-centered and product-oriented. The project, as we planned it, would reorient instruction to be more student-centered and process-oriented. Besides changes in curriculum and instructional practices, the teachers' and, consequently, the students' roles in the writing class had to change. Changing the teachers' roles was seen as challenging, not just because of old roles entrenched after years of teaching, but because of ingrained attitudes toward writers.

Several teachers participating in the project had already begun adopting the process model for writing instruction and were switching toward a more student-centered classroom, yet a catalyst was needed to demonstrate dramatically the consequences of changing teacher and student roles: the computer served as that catalyst. By the nature of process-based computer-writing tasks and the demands of teaching in the computer lab, teachers had direct and repeated reinforcing experiences for a process-based model of teaching. Teaching writing with computers and process helped us adopt roles typified by several characteristics:

more coaching of writers and less "editing" of writing

permitting freedom so that writers could move as needed from one writing process stage to another, both on and off the computer

encouraging peer assistance among students

managing a flow of varied student writing activities rather than asserting control by keeping writers in a lockstep progression

To identify teachers' and students' changing roles, we completed on the computer midyear and year-end personal assessment templates which asked us to reflect on how roles had changed. Time was taken to discuss results of those assessments, just as time was taken during our Open Forum sessions to discuss how roles in the writing class were changing. A recurring reflection during our dialogues was of the need for, pleasures of, and consequences of the shifting role of the teacher toward one of less dominance and more facilitating of student writing—caused by teaching with both computers and writing process.

We found a direct, natural shift in students' roles as teachers' roles changed. Initially, students adept at word processing became invaluable aides in helping those learning the software and unable to wait for teachers who were besieged with innumerable frantic questions. Teachers found it not only expedient but also rewarding to give students the latitude and encouragement to help each other. This change in role spilled over into writing instruction itself as students helping each other with writing freed the teacher to work with writers who needed more concentrated help or advice.

Students' enthusiasm about working with computers in language arts was matched by their willingness to assist each other. In fact, teachers realized that students were more adept at helping each other than had been anticipated. At one particular Open Forum, we concluded that when students were allowed to assist each other and to move freely between activities, they became forgiving of difficulties caused by themselves or the teacher in a new learning situation—especially if the teacher conveyed the importance of learning together about writing with a computer.

Changing student and teacher roles was directly attributable to the class dynamics of teaching writing in the computer lab and to adopting the instructional techniques of writing process. Without the formal and informal support given each other and without planned staff development activities, roles would not have been altered. Teachers, too, were given time and latitude to try new roles, to seek support for difficulties, and to reflect on how they had changed. What teachers understood about their altered roles as writing teachers had a direct impact on their ability to construct a new writing curriculum.

Developing a New Curriculum with Computers and Writing Process

As shown in our curriculum needs-assessment, writing assignments given before the advent of our project tended to be expository in nature, often written about literature or topics related to it. Curricula for each grade level reflected aspects of writing process but were not wholly process-oriented in structure or intent. Thus, a central goal of the second-year project was to create a curriculum integrating process and computers. We also wanted to choose a standard device for evaluating student writing competency so that teachers could readily identify a writer's level of competence in writing. To build the curriculum we wanted, we learned and refined instructional techniques, revised curriculum guides, and evaluated the writing of students participating in the project.

Teaching with Process and Computer

As a participant in the project, each teacher was learning how to teach with process and computer, not just through inservice education but also by teaching in the computer lab. In a nutshell, each of them planned a year's sequence of process-based compositions (approximately eight), six of which were to be developed on computers.

Writing tasks typically were defined in terms of audience, purpose, and writing-process activities (prewriting through publishing). Students kept their writings in folders which were periodically reviewed during project meetings. On a standard template, teachers kept information about each assignment (e.g., process lessons, computer procedures, audience); this information and copies of sample student writings were assembled in an activity bank, which became a source of model assignments for teachers as they taught and as they wrote the new curriculum during a summer workshop.

Hand in hand with the writing process was development of methods for using the computer in the "off/on" machine strategy. Students, for example, might have done prewriting off of the machine, written a draft on the machine and printed a hard copy, gone off the machine to a response group for comments on the draft, returned to the computer to revise and print another copy, and published the piece off of the machine, perhaps by reading it aloud in class. We spent a large chunk of staff development time discussing the need for and ways to have students look critically at drafts off the machine in printed form because we found that students who simply revised at the machine made surface-level, if any, revisions. Discussing and evaluating the effectiveness of activities and strategies such as these gave us a wealth of information to build into the written curriculum.

Changing the Written Curriculum

From the outset of the project, our aim was to produce a curriculum, 9–12, of sequential, process-based writing tasks that utilized the power of the computer. With the generation of sample lessons during the year and with the wealth of instructional techniques tried, teachers had no trouble developing the curricula during a paid summer workshop. Working within a broad district format for curriculum guides, we agreed upon a uniform structure that would ensure a commonality of writing experiences while giving latitude for topics, for accompanying lessons in content, form, and mechanics, and for use of computers.

Using that format, teachers wrote a curriculum calling for consistent experiences in two types of non–process-based writing (to learn and for fluency) and three types of process-based writing (to inform, to persuade, and to create). Computer use, appropriate software, and instruction in writing-process strategies accompanied each writing task in the three process-based types of writing. For example, an eleventh grader is asked to do persuasive writing in the form of a college application essay. Simultaneously, she might receive instruction in a prewriting activity such as mapping, instruction in a computer-based ARMS revision activity, and language lessons in using the subjunctive, clarity of expression, or creating a convincing tone.

Following our district's procedure for curriculum management, we are now implementing the new curriculum. All department teachers, including those from the project, have received copies and explanations of the curriculum. As we implement it, we monitor progress by reviewing student papers, by addressing difficulties, and by supporting one another in use of computers and process.

Learning to Use a Writing-Competency Scale

Evaluation was planned as an essential ingredient involved in integrating computers and writing process into language arts instruction during the project—the first to build into the curriculum a procedure for determining levels of student writing competency, and the second to measure the effect that computers and process-based writing instruction have on writing. Working toward each evaluation goal was another dimension in staff education.

To model and to institute a device for measuring changes in levels of student writing competency, timed writing samples were taken, at the beginning and the end of the school year in which we ran the project. Students wrote from a choice of topics and followed a procedure for assuring anonymity of papers. These papers were collected and kept safe for scoring during a summer workshop. In the spring of the project year, we trained the project teachers in using a writing-competency scale patterned after the McCaig scale from Grosse Pointe, Michigan. With their training and the sample papers, we conducted a holistic scoring workshop and scored all preproject writing samples and then all postproject samples. The data we gathered by comparing results not only helped us evaluate the effectiveness of the project, but also taught teachers lessons in how to evaluate writing and to use the results in the classroom.

We have now adopted the scale as part of our curriculum and are introducing all department teachers to its use. In keeping with our goal of more student-centered writing classes, we are learning how to use the scale to identify students' writing-competency levels and to plan instruction accordingly. One tangible document produced during the holistic scoring workshop was a set of representative student papers at each competency level and a set of recommendations for moving students to the next higher competency level. Teachers learned how to use the recommendations to tailor instruction so that young writers can grow in competence.

What the Project Taught Us

From the outset of our project, we sought not just change but an understanding of why change would occur—or not occur—in instructional practices, curriculum, teacher roles, and student writing. We believed that the computer, the sophisticated tool, could be a catalyst for the changes we sought, but we were uncertain of the type and depth of changes that would result. From the start, devices were built into the project to give us data to evaluate—student writing samples and surveys, teacher questionnaires, analysis of student writings, and gathering of anecdotal data during the Open Forum time at monthly project meetings. All of this data was gathered and prepared for a two-day, paid project-evaluation workshop. Together we reviewed and discussed data and compiled our observations into a set of "lessons learned" about primary project goals.

Lesson 1: Role of Structured Activities and Available Time

Teachers felt that the day-long meetings maintained focus on project goals, offered a vehicle for problem solving, and allowed mutual support that encouraged learning new ways to teach writing. Having time—away from the daily demands of teaching—to address concerns during the Open Forums was cited as a major reason for individual teachers' growth, as was the sequence of staff development topics that grew out of teacher needs and from project objectives. With the structured activities and available time came one of the project's strongest, unanticipated results: teachers found their colleagues professionally and emotionally supportive, appreciating frustrations and applauding successes as the group wrestled with the challenges of integrating computers into writing instruction.

Lesson 2: Success in Meeting Project Goals

Reflecting on their own learning, our teachers cited valuable lessons in the use of hardware and software, integration of computers and writing process, instructional strategies at every phase of writing process, the significance of varying writing tasks by purpose, managing writing process, and utilizing the computer lab for the best flow of work. Beyond the formal project year, teachers' feelings of ownership and excitement about the connection between computers and language arts have become increasingly evident as they continue to explore prewriting and text-analysis software to increase writing performance and as they express an interest in long-term exploration of using prompts built into word-processing programs.

With the feelings of success they gained from our project, teachers are not only using the computer lab more for writing instruction, but are supporting colleagues uninvolved with the project as they begin to teach with computers. Support typically appears as assistance in the lab, encouragement and explanation of techniques, and affirmation of changes in teacher and student roles. Project teachers themselves have expressed a need for additional support and understanding as they refine techniques learned during the project.

Lesson 3: Altering of Teachers' Managerial and Instructional Practices

Teachers who went through the project felt they needed to be more highly organized if teaching writing with computers was to be effective; lesson plans that involved computers, they noted, became more sequential and clearly laid out than traditional plans had been. In addition, directions for off-machine tasks needed to be highly specific and clearly communicated to students, and teaching in the computer lab had to review or reinforce strategies learned in the regular classroom. Small group teaching on an as-needed basis and conferencing with individual writers dominated teacher time in the lab, mandating a switch to student-centered instruction.

With the demands on teacher time being made more by individuals and small groups, teachers found that classroom management in the computer lab changed because of group dynamics. Greater varieties of activities caused by writers at varied stages of writing at the computer demanded "structuring for freedom"; thus, lab time was typified by clearly stated objectives and activities. Well-defined and consistently reinforced guidelines for the computer lab lessened conflicts and teacher anxiety. Teachers did less redirecting of behavior as students became used to and more relaxed in the computer lab. For example, student participation in supplemental activities, such as learning CAI software, increased as the students' comfort level in the lab increased.

Lesson 4: Effect of Computers and Writing Process on the Curriculum

Because the formal curriculum we wrote during the project is being implemented this year, its structure and resources are a steadfast guide to teachers. We feel that writing instruction itself, as well as students' writing, is improving, and this progress will be evaluated in the year ahead using a process of curriculum evaluation and our adopted writing-competency scales. Project teachers who developed the curriculum find this year's teaching easier to manage in terms of instructional strategies and time.

The issue of time tradeoff was a major concern to teachers during the project year. For those devoting most of their class time to teaching literature, an immediate time conflict arose on two levels—time taken to teach word processing and time given to in-class writing instruction. In retrospect, these teachers did feel that the changes in student writing performance and enthusiasm were worth the time sacrificed. In fact, project teachers found that more concentrated time in the computer lab on writing instruction resulted in great transfer of learning, as seen in writing performance. Students perceived that learning to write was important enough to spend large blocks of time doing it.

Considerations for Teachers and Administrators

From our project we gleaned well-founded and often-heartfelt implications. Echoed time and again during project evaluations was praise for concentrated time and for support given to the teachers who were learning a radically different approach to writing instruction. They collectively felt that continued patience and support would be essential if they were to continue refining their skills as process-oriented, computerized-writing teachers. Stated time and again by project teachers was the need for the entire building staff to understand that innovations can cause disruptions—such as students leaving class late because the teacher is learning the flow of management skills needed in a computer lab.

Colleagues, peers, and department chairs need to be both patient and supportive of the teacher trying new roles, changing techniques, and refining computer skills. Crucial to that process is the value that a teacher places on the computer as a writing tool. Computers must be made available for teacher use in generating class, professional, and personal materials. Training in hardware and software should be offered and run in response to teachers' needs.

Beyond the department level, building and central office administrators wishing to transfer to teachers ownership of the computer/writing-process connection must offer both support and careful management. Providing concentrated time for growth and latitude for trying new techniques is a vital but intangible type of support. More tangibly, providing funds for hardware, software, and teacher workshops will have a direct impact on how much ownership teachers assume in the integration of computers into language arts teaching.

By establishing a computer lab for primary use by language arts classes and by planning for inservice education based on teacher needs, administrators can have a direct impact on the use of computers in language arts. Determining, sequencing, conducting, and evaluating integration tasks are essential for maintaining project focus, continuity, and momentum.

Our project to integrate computers and writing process into curriculum and instructional practices has succeeded because teachers were trained, supported, and given ownership of the project and its goals. Knowing that changes do not come quickly, we have planned our program to progress over several years, giving teachers adequate time to learn about computers and how to teach writing with them. As their levels of comfort and expertise with the computer increase, so does their excitement about new uses of the machine in language arts. At the heart of the excitement and the changes are the sophisticated tools, the computers; not guarantors of change, they are merely catalysts for change.

9 Adapting to a New Environment: Word Processing and the Training of Writing Teachers at the University of Massachusetts at Amherst

Paul LeBlanc, Springfield College

Charles Moran, University of Massachusetts at Amherst

Early research on word processors and writing tried to discover whether word processors helped or hindered writers. More recent research, however, understands that the question is now moot. Word processors are here; they are part of the writer's, and of the writing teacher's, environment. We will not, most of us, most of the time, choose to return to the pen, or to the typewriter.

This fact has special consequences for writing teachers. Our students will be using word processors. We therefore will need to learn how to teach writers who are using word processors. This is, in some degree, a new world. Terms such as *draft* change their meaning, given the fluid text. Revisions become more difficult to track because the writer's alterations no longer appear in margins or between lines. Teachers will read screens, not pages, and their comments will likely be delivered orally, not in written form.

An understanding of the coming change impelled us to establish the Computer Writing Center at the University of Massachusetts at Amherst and to create in it a "computer classroom," one where students have their own word processors and where the teacher "coaches" the writers as they write, working one-to-one sequentially with twenty freshman writers. And thereby hangs our tale.

We are now teaching English 112, "College Writing," for the second year in our Computer Writing Center. Teachers accustomed to teaching the course in conventional classrooms spent the first year teaching in the center and, at the end of the year, requested a training program that would help them function efficiently in the new environment. The training program they wanted had nothing to do with hardware or software. Our teachers, and our students, rapidly learn to operate the computers, and after the first hour or so the technology becomes transparent.

The students' very facility with the word processors, however, creates its own problem for the teachers: with the aid of the computer, students can compose and revise more rapidly than they can with pen and paper. Teachers are therefore faced with the need to react to more writing, and more revising, than standard classroom management techniques can cope with. Our teachers were, they told us, spending more time on their classes than they had before. They were grading more papers, having more individual conferences, and feeling overworked and frustrated. At the end of our first year in the Computer Writing Center, it became clear that either the course and facility design, or the teachers' techniques, would have to change. We believed that the course and the facility were well designed. The best alternative was to help the teachers adapt to the new environment.

To that end we designed a series of workshops that we implemented in the fall of 1986. Most teacher-training programs are inevitably based upon presumed need. Preservice programs are drawn up by program directors who base their program design upon assumptions about what teachers should do and about what teachers are likely to do if left untrained. Inservice teacher-training programs are usually precast, designed by outside consultants without clear reference to the teachers' real needs. Even the programs described in *Training the New Teacher of College Composition* (Bridges 1986) are based upon their authors' assumptions about what new teachers need to know. Charles W. Bridges, for example, assumes that new teachers need to redefine their sense of what is basic (1986, 15); Nancy Comley assumes that graduate student teaching assistants' primary need is the ability to integrate the three components of a graduate curriculum: literary study, creative writing, and composition theory (1986, 45).

As we read through the literature on teacher training, it seems to us that we have had an experience that is rare—indeed, it is almost a luxury. The teachers have come to us; we have not been imposed upon them. Moreover, the us-them distinction is not at all clear: we have simultaneously been workshop leaders and colleagues, teaching English 112 ourselves in the Computer Writing Center. We have been much more in the "helpful colleague" role than in the role of "expert other." In our description of the workshops we will speak of the participants as if they were much more distant than they have in fact been. As we launch into the description of the training program and its context, we need to acknowledge the deeply collaborative nature of this experience and to thank our colleague-participants for their patience and generosity of spirit.

The course that we now teach in the Computer Writing Center, English 112, "College Writing," existed before we developed the center. Our teachers' perceived need for training arose from their attempt to bring this course, with its attendant pedagogy, into the center's classrooms. Before we describe the training program, therefore, we need to establish its context: the course, "College Writing," and the history and design of the center.

English 112, "College Writing"

"College Writing" is an activity-based writing course that derives from the work of James Moffett (1968), Donald Murray (1968), Charles K. Smith (1974), Peter Elbow (1981), Walker Gibson (1950; 1969), and Roger Garrison (1964). It is taken by all but a few of the 4,200 freshmen at the University of Massachusetts at Amherst. All entering freshmen take a placement test, a one-hour essay written on an assigned topic. About 5 percent of the freshmen are placed in English 111, "Basic Writing," a preliminary course to English 112. About 2 percent of the freshmen are exempted from English 112 on the basis of their performance on the placement test. The course is required of the remaining 93 percent of freshmen and is not, therefore, "bonehead English."

In "College Writing," the students' own writing is at the center of the course at all times. Lecture and discussion, normal English teaching modes, are entirely replaced by practice and feedback—that is, in-class writing and peer and teacher response to that writing. Teachers are free to design their own prewriting and peer-editing activities, but writing will always be taught directly: there is no textbook, no anthology, no analysis of prose models, no defined subject matter. There are no lectures on good writing and no whole-class work with such elements as spelling, sentence boundary punctuation, or manuscript format. Much as they might in a course in studio art, students in English 112 complete seven essays or projects, each submitted in rough, midprocess, and final forms. Other writing is assigned as appropriate. Beginning in the third week, students keep a journal, one that functions as a seedbed for essay topics. To enable teachers to bring the students' own writing into the center of the class, all English 112 teachers have unlimited access to the university's copy centers. There they may reproduce student writing for their classes and, four or five times during the semester, publish final drafts of student essays in a booklet (Moran 1986, 111–16).

History and Development of the Computer Writing Center

The University of Massachusetts's Computer Writing Center was developed by the staff of the University Writing Program because we realized that the new technology would complement the "studio" approach to the teaching of writing. If the classroom was to be the scene of writing and editing activity, why not bring word processors directly into the classroom? Our original pilot project involving ten on-loan IBM PCs in a single room has grown substantially. With funding from our dean and provost and a grant from Digital Corporation, we refurbished a language laboratory facility of three connected rooms.

Our center has a control room, a computer classroom with twenty-one DecMate III work stations, and a computer lab with eleven DecMate III work stations. The work stations are stand-alone units, each with its own dot-matrix printer. Twelve sections of English 112C are scheduled directly into the center. To each section we add a one-period lab, using the natural sciences as our precedent. Students are scheduled into the computer classroom during their regular weekly class hours and into the computer lab for a single lab hour each week.

English 112 in the Computer Writing Center

Reminding ourselves that "College Writing" is a course in writing, not in word processing, we simplified the technology and our teaching of the technology. We tried to make word processing transparent: a medium or mechanism, not a subject. We consciously decided not to use integrated writing software, such as *WANDAH* or *Wordsworth,* and not to network the work stations. We tailored the system software, *WPS 2.1,* to simplify functions such as pagination, formatting, and printing, and we reduced Digital's 300-page manual to a concise and straightforward seven-page handout that walks teachers and students through all the steps necessary for writing, revising, formatting, and printing a five-page to ten-page double-spaced essay.

Given the simplified program, teachers and students become comfortable with the system in a matter of hours. When a new teacher joins the staff, we give the teacher our manual and the *WPS* training disk and ask the teacher to write a substantial piece on the word processor before the semester begins. We try to make sure that an expert user is present in the center when the new teacher first takes the plunge, but often this is not possible, and the absence of a coach does not seem to make much difference to the learner. We know that it is important for the teacher to be able to use the program, yet we believe that the teacher's appropriate authority must come from his or her ability to teach writing, not his or her proficiency on the word processor.

Teaching Writing in the Computer Writing Center

When students come to the center for a class period, they begin by taking their writing folder from a file cabinet in the control room. In the folder are two 5¼-inch floppy disks, one a text disk and the other a backup, and whatever "hard copy" the students feel they need. They take their folders to their work stations, insert a text disk, and begin. More often than not, students are busy at work when the instructor arrives. Frequently students work through the ten-minute break between class and lab meetings, and many will stay late if a machine is available. Students' energy and concentration on their writing is the first impression formed by almost all new 112C instructors and visitors to the center. Students quickly come to understand the center is their writing place, and they waste little time doing other things. While they write, the teacher circulates, a roving editor checking on the progress of the twenty writers. On occasion, the instructor will begin the class with some housekeeping or logistics matters, perhaps a new assignment or general instructions. Some instructors take care of the housekeeping details by preparing handouts or by copying an "Instructions" file onto their students' disks. Some days the instructor schedules a peer-editing session, where students exchange papers or monitors and critique each other's work. Because students usually sit in the same spot in class, they often develop an editorial relationship with their neighbors. It is not unusual to see a student ask another to look at a piece of writing. This desirable interaction develops spontaneously over time and needs little official encouragement from the instructor.

As the end of class nears, students run off hard copies to take home with them. We encourage them to do this because current studies suggest the importance of hard-copy review in the work of revising. When the students leave the center, they return their folders to the file cabinet. While they may take hard copies with them to work on at home, the disks stay in the file, partly because they cannot be used on most machines available outside the facility and partly because we want to help the students avoid the disasters that attend taking disks home with them and subjecting them to the hazards of daily life.

Need for a Training Program

The design of English 112, even as it is taught outside the Computer Writing Center, poses some problems for new teachers of writing because this course is unlike any writing course they have ever taken. Teachers look to their own experiences for models. Traditionally, writing has been taught by lecture and discussion or in a workshop that centers upon group critique. Our teachers, chiefly graduate students en route to either an M.F.A. or a Ph.D. in English, have the lecture-and-discussion-based class (Ph.D.) or the workshop (M.F.A.) as their model. The normal classroom environment, with its chalkboard and teacher's desk, makes it possible for these new teachers to draw upon their teachers' techniques and to bring the lecture, the discussion, or the workshop into the writing classroom. As program directors, we do not approve, but we bow to the inevitable.

In our Computer Writing Center, however, lectures are intrusive and unrewarding, and group discussion is difficult to arrange and sustain. In the center, each student has his or her own word processor and is engaged in composing—a powerful, all-consuming activity. The center's environment tells the students to pay attention to their own work, which floats before them at eye level, and to ignore the teacher.

In the center, therefore, teachers are faced with the need to deal with twenty individual writers, each working away at his or her own project at a pace only loosely determined by the writing schedule on the syllabus. The Computer Writing Center becomes something like the writing-editing center envisioned by Ronald Sudol (1985), where student writers write and the teacher-editor circulates—a format described by Garrison (1964) and based on a pedagogy informed by Elbow (1981), Murray (1968), Moffett (1968), Smith (1974), and Gibson (1950; 1969). Given what we now know about the recursive nature of the composing process, and given the dynamics of the word processor, we cannot insist, as Garrison did, upon discrete stages: the list, the structured list, the outline, the draft, the revised drafts. In the center, even the concept of *draft* becomes less clearly defined, given the fluidity of the text on the screen, so the teachers have fewer fixed points of reference. In addition, students in the center write and revise more than they do in conventional classrooms. Their writing may not be better, but there is more of it. The teacher, therefore, has more activity to monitor and more kinds of activity: more prose to read, more *drafts,* if you will, to respond to. The teacher confronts a never-ending stream of prose.

The response of many instructors to this new teaching environment was an attempt to combine the traditional techniques of lecture, discussion, and workshop with the pedagogy that the computer classroom invites—indeed, demands. The amalgamation of old and new resulted in tired and frustrated instructors who found themselves putting in more time and not apparently achieving the gains that we had all hoped for. The teachers found themselves lecturing to inattentive classes and leading discussions that were less lively than those they had led in traditional classrooms in the past; to top it all off, they were not able to keep up with the flow of writing that was emanating from the student writers. When the teachers tried to be editors, they spent ten minutes talking with one student while the other nineteen wrote without guidance. To compensate for what they saw as failure, the teachers kept extra office hours, scheduled more conferences, and brought more drafts home to read and correct. They were doing more work, but achieving results that were not worth the extra effort.

The Training Program

The training program we designed focuses upon the rapid diagnosis of, and oral response to, in-process student writing. Our objective was to improve the teachers' speed and accuracy as in-process editors. At the end of the training sessions, we hoped that the teachers would be able to look at a piece of student writing, read it on the screen rapidly, and, on the basis of that rapid reading, make a diagnosis. On the basis of the diagnosis, they would be able to decide upon a course of action—an editorial intervention. The entire process would take, we hoped, no more than two minutes. With twenty students in a class, a two-minute intervention will make it possible for each teacher to see each student during a fifty-minute class. We knew that this somewhat abrupt style of reading would be resisted by English teachers who, trained in a different critical and pedagogical tradition, would want to read the entire essay closely and comment fully. We knew also that students, themselves accustomed to the full reading and comprehensive commentary, would be unsettled by the new *modus operandi.*

And yet we thought the change worth the effort. If the teachers could learn to function efficiently as in-process, on-screen editors, we assumed that they would become more comfortable in this role and would therefore spend less time in the roles of lecturer and discussion leader. We also assumed that their newfound facility as in-process editors would reduce the amount of writing they took home with them. If this were to happen, our objective would have been achieved: to make it possible for a teacher to teach writing comfortably and efficiently in the Computer Writing Center.

The training program was intended to change the following assumptions, all of which were held, in different degrees, by the participants:

1. Lecture and discussion are essential elements of the writing course, even in the Computer Writing Center.
2. Feedback must be based upon a close reading of the entire essay, despite the new, studio environment.
3. Feedback must be written and comprehensive if it is to be useful.
4. There is a single, "good" reading of a piece of student writing upon which one can base a single, "good" editorial comment.

Each of these assumptions has its roots in the history of our profession, a history that has determined conventional classroom architecture and practice. We hoped that the training program would, through the reading of sample student writing, make it evident that:

1. Practice and feedback are essential elements in a writing course.
2. Useful feedback can be based upon a rapid and/or a partial onscreen reading of a piece of student writing.
3. Feedback can be spoken and can be useful when limited to one aspect of the work.
4. There are multiple readings, or interpretations, of a piece of student writing, many of which are potentially useful and can be the basis for helpful feedback.

The workshops we designed sought to replicate as closely as possible editorial interventions as they would actually take place in the center. We collected samples of student writing and copied them onto workshop disks. Except for the first half of Workshop 1, the instructors read the student writing samples on-screen and under time pressure. They read on-screen because a screenful of writing is different from a set of pages: the screen is smaller than most pages, and scrolling through a long essay is more difficult than turning pages. They worked under time pressure because speed is essential in the computer classroom. The editorial conference may be the only contact between teacher and student. When this is the case, it is important to see everyone in the room at least once each class.

The full program included four hour-long workshops held late in the afternoon at two-week intervals. We began in Workshop 1 with midprocess drafts, pieces that represented substantial composing and revising activity. We began here because our teachers were taking these midprocess drafts home with them and giving them a full read. In Workshop 2 we read writing in an early stage of composition—something approaching a first draft. In Workshop 3 we returned to writing at the midprocess stage, approaching this time from a new perspective as we built on the work of Workshop 1. In Workshop 4 we read late-stage drafts, something that an instructor might read on-screen a day or so before the due date, when time permits the writer little more than the opportunity to polish, proofread, and reflect.

Workshop 1: Diagnosing and Prescribing in the Computer Writing Center

The first workshop focused upon the reading of partial student drafts at a midprocess stage—just the first two hundred words or so, a printed version of a single screenful of writing. We assumed that the drafts were not final so that the teachers' comments could affect the writing, and we assumed that the writers had spent considerable time composing and revising these drafts. The reading was directed by two questions: "What do we have here?" and "What do we say to the writer?" The first question was deliberately broad, permitting such answers as "We have here a writer still finding her way into her subject," or "We have here a voice telling a story." The two questions were treated separately so that we could draw a clear distinction between diagnosis and prescription.

We began reading hard copy—perhaps, in retrospect, an unnecessary step—because we thought our teachers would need to build a bridge between responding to hard copy and responding to the relatively ephemeral text-on-screen that is the currency of the computer classroom. To achieve a certain degree of verisimilitude we used the "print screen" function of our word processors to create a hard-copy facsimile of the screen as teachers would see it in the classroom. We asked the instructors to read the text, keeping in mind the question "What do we have here?" When the reading was finished, we divided the teachers into groups of four and asked each group to agree upon a response to the question—this response was to be written in a single sentence of twenty-five words of less. Here is one of the four student texts we used:

> Throughout my life there has always been a sense of the spirit world involved in my life. As a youngster I was raised in a Jewish home, we were never very religious but I still attended temple, observed the Jewish holidays, and prayed to some unseen, unheard, nontangible being which was revered as being omnipotent, omnipresent, and omniscient. There were times when I'd wonder if this thing we call G—d really existed but would pray to him anyway and there were other times when I was sure that he must be there.
>
> When I am alone is probably when I feel most spiritual. This is when I can be most in touch with myself and when there are no distractions. If I could be in the middle of a vast forest on a fairly warm day with the sun sifting through the branches overhead and maybe just sitting quietly on a blanket on the ground maybe alone or even with one and only one very good friend and thoughts of magic come about, the forest seems powerful and there seems to be some sort of magic around. When I'm in such a place as this then I feel very spiritual, I feel deep within me that all the world isn't as bad as the six o'clock news makes it sound every night, that maybe—

The teachers' answers to the question "What do we have here?" were quite appropriately various: this was a spiritual autobiography, a narrative, a definition. Each of these genres was present in the text, at least potentially. We could see the student's first two hundred words as a description of spiritual growth, or a definition of an abstract concept, or a narrative—the story of change. All of these readings were acceptable.

We then moved the teachers to the second question: given that we have seen what we have seen, "What do we say to the writer?" Because of the range of readings, there was a range of suggested interventions. The minimalist intervention, assuming that the writer had not yet decided and should be allowed to decide, was to encourage the writer to write on. Say, perhaps, "You seem to be well underway. Any problems?" If the answer is negative, pass on down the row to the next screen, the next writer. Another suggested intervention drew the writer's attention, indirectly, to the manifold potential in the writing: "Is this about you, or do you see yourself examining something else—God or religion perhaps?" One instructor would ask the student to "nutshell," or to identify the central idea of the essay in one sentence. Others wanted the student to identify a reader. In each case, prescription followed and was based upon diagnosis. We note in passing: the editing of the manuscript for word-level and sentence-level problems is left for the moment, and perhaps forever, in the hands of the writer.

In the second phase of this workshop we disbanded the groups and asked the teachers to work individually with print-screen facsimile texts. As the workshop progressed, our focus on the first question, "What do we have here?" became more clear and more apparently useful. Finally we left hard copy and turned directly to the computer screens. We had copied student writing onto disks which we distributed. We asked the participants to call up a particular file and to read with the "What do we have here?" question as a focus for the reading. The samples were longer now, perhaps five hundred words or so, and we began reducing the time allowed for the reading and diagnosis. By the end of the workshop, participants were reading, diagnosing, and preparing an intervention in one minute.

Looking back upon this first workshop, we find that the choice of questions was extremely useful. Participants admitted a tendency to bypass the "What do we have here?" question and, under pressure from the situation, to move without appropriate preparation into a search for the right thing to do or say. As the workshop progressed, the participants began to make clearer connections between diagnosis and prescription: "Because this is an X, I would tell the student. . . ." It seemed to us that the answers to the "What do we say to the writer?" question became more consistent as the workshop progressed. Initially the participants had what seemed to be precast, all-purpose responses, such as "Who is this for?" and "What are you saying?" We believe that we began to see a more organic relationship between the writer/text system and the strategies created by the teachers. The workshop was least successful with participants who needed to function at the level of word choice and sentence structure. These teachers focused upon words they thought were wrongly used, and because they were unable to see the larger picture, they were unable to complete their interventions in the allotted time.

Workshop 2: Reading for Potential

Whereas in the first session we read student writing that was at a fairly advanced stage of composition, in the second session we looked at pieces of student writing that were in the early stages—some scarcely drafts, but freewriting that would, at some later time, be reread and considered. Our objective was to help our teachers become more comfortable with nondirective interventions at this stage of the writing process. A full and directive comment on an early draft is not only time-consuming; it may reduce the writer's stake in the writing. Because in the computer classroom we see student writing at an earlier stage than we are likely to in a conventional classroom, the need to learn to refrain from comment is greater here than it is elsewhere.

In this second workshop we worked entirely on the screen. Before we presented the student writing, we told the participants that our focus in this session was on potential: what there might be, what the writing was in the process of becoming. We used an analogy: in the darkroom, the outlines of the image begin to become apparent under the red light. Instead of asking, "What do we have here?" as we had in the first session, we asked, "What potential do we see here?" We wanted the teachers to see a range of possibility so that they could think of the writers as active beings, choosing among alternatives. This question leads the teacher to identify options for the student writer, as opposed to suggesting a single direction and thereby in some degree appropriating the student's essay.

Here is the first student text we selected for this workshop:

> My uncle is dying. I do not understand. I have always been told that death is a part of life, as if this is some bearable excuse for my loved one to leave me. It does not take away my hurt and confusion; nor does it bring me comfort. I ask why, but who am I asking? Death is not concrete; my emotions seem too concrete. I cannot grasp death's meaning, though the anger and loss I feel is a piercing reality. I want my uncle back. How I wish he could wrap his arms around me, give me a big bear hug and say "Hi Kimathy" with the enthusiasm and happiness that he once had. I know this is wishing for the moon, for he is too weak now to be the Uncle Richard I once knew. No one else in the world calls me Kimathy. Who will when Uncle Richard is gone?

The workshop participants, reading this piece, discovered these possibilities: it might become a question-answer piece, or problem-solution essay, or a voyage of discovery. It might become a meditation, an elegy, or a lyric cry of despair. The group determined that directive intervention at this time would be inappropriate, for it was likely that the writer would find her own way. Later in the process, if no clear direction asserted itself, we might voice the several possibilities we thought we saw in the writing.

We read three other early drafts, looking for potential. A piece on water skiing that seemed relatively directionless contained the seeds of narrative, how-to process description, and argument. The suggested interventions were again various: a call for greater sensory detail, a question about desired genre, a question about purpose and audience, and the suggestion that the writer "nutshell" the existing materials. A second piece, this one on the death of a father, contained these possibilities: exploration of consequence, problem-solution, question-answer, elegy. We agreed that the writer should be left to find the appropriate direction at this stage in the composing process. A third piece, on baking bread, was seen to be either process analysis or description. Suggested interventions included questions that would lead to expansion ("Do you have more to say?"), evaluation ("Why do this?"), selection ("Is there a piece of this that is more important than the rest?"), and definition of audience ("What do you imagine your audience to be? And why do you tell the tale?").

With the experience of the first workshop behind them, the teachers in our second workshop adapted quickly to this reading perspective. In the first session the teachers had become comfortable with the fact that different readings of the same text might be equally valuable. In the second session they came to accept the fact that at an early stage in the writing process the teacher-editor is dealing largely with potential. This potential is often multiple, and the multiplicity may be a good thing, for the moment. The text is still open to several readings—and the writer is likely to be too open to suggestion. The teachers were relieved to discover that in the early stages of composition sometimes a rapid and nondirective intervention, such as "Keep going," was more useful, and certainly faster and easier, than a more complicated and directive intervention.

Workshop 3: Discourse-Based Reading

In the third workshop we returned to midprocess drafts and introduced a discourse-based approach to complement the text-based approach of the first two workshops. Although the questions "What do we have here?" and "What potential do we see here?" left open the possibility that one might talk about the rhetorical situation, they drew our focus away from context and toward text.

It may be that a discourse-based approach is even more necessary in a computer-based writing course than it is in a "regular" writing course, where the writing tends to become a "paper," a freestanding artifact composed as a requirement for the course. We do not know yet what effect a computer screen may have on a writer's sense of audience. But from what we have observed, it seems as if student writers can fall into the "writing a paper" mode as easily in our computer classroom as they can when they compose on paper, with pen or with pencil, in an academic setting.

In this session we considered writing primarily as discourse: writing proceeds from someone, to someone, for some reason. Voice, audience, and purpose are hardly separable entities; they are intimately related—a closely knit constellation. To choose one is to suggest that they can be separated. Yet we chose, because one must begin somewhere. And we chose to begin with the audience because we wanted to avoid the pitfalls inherent in drawing our young writers' principal attention either to voice or to purpose. To emphasize purpose is to fall into the communications metaphor, with all writing finally a message to a receiver. This metaphor, while it can be useful, may have a reductive effect upon the teacher's, and therefore the students', sense of what writing can be. To emphasize the adaptability of voice, on the other hand, is to threaten a young writer's sense of self. Using many voices suggests many people. To suggest to a typical nineteen- or twenty-year-old freshman that one can "be" many voices is to run counter to the young adult's search for a coherent self. So it seemed to us that talking about the reader was the least dangerous road to the world of discourse. We did not want, however, to suggest that the reader was a demographically determined audience. Better than that, and more useful to a writer, is the concept of imagined reader, that person whom we imagine as we write. The concept of the imagined reader has its roots in two worlds: those of rhetoric and of reader-response criticism. Its clearest exponent has been Walker Gibson (1950; 1969).

The concept of imagined reader needed explanation. On the board in the classroom we drew this diagram:

```
                          voice                  voice
                            /                       \
WRITER imagines -- reader -- TEXT -- reader -- imagines READER
                            \                       /
                          purpose                purpose
```

Referring to this diagram, we told our instructors that we know that different kinds of writing "compose" different readers—cause them to imagine themselves in particular roles and stances, to become, temporarily, clearly defined characters. When and if we read a "Dear Abby" column we are asked to become voyeurs; when we turn to the editorial page we may be asked to become concerned citizens who want to have the facts interpreted for them; when we read a news article we are asked to become meaning-makers ourselves, readers who want information so that they can form their own opinions. Walker Gibson has said that the function of an editorial board is "to imagine the kind of reader we want to become as we open the covers of that magazine" (1950, 265). The reader reads the text; the text composes the reader.

In this session we read student writing, as before, on the screen. The question we asked our teachers to keep in mind as they read these writing samples was "Who do I become as I read this essay?" Our first writing sample was this excerpt from a student's draft:

> Religion has dominated cultures throughout history. It has served as an explanation of the unknowns. It has stood for society's economical and political organization for many generations. People have used it as the most basic tool to understanding and developing their existence. Religion helped set up the structure of people in a group so that they could function as a unit.
>
> As time has gone on, history has seen the breakdown of religious purposes. People have manipulated religion in different ways to obtain specific goals, giving both positive and negative results. Because religion is so essentially dependent on belief there tends to be a lack of criticism. People are taught that sanction can only be obtained through belief. This allows one person to have a good deal of influence on a larger group.
>
> Throughout time we have seen religions performance in both negative and positive ways. . . .

When asked to respond to the question, "Who do I become as I read this piece?" our teachers responded variously: "I become a reader of an encyclopedia"; "I become an examiner in a history course"; "I become a student listening to a history lecture." We thought these responses perceptive and all firmly grounded in the text. None of the teachers was comfortable in any of the suggested reader roles, and so for the teachers the writer-reader transaction did not take place smoothly or at all. The teachers were not able to become the reader that the text required. An appropriate strategy at this point is to ask the student writer, "Who do you imagine is reading this?" Whatever the answer, the teacher-editor's job becomes one of helping the writer choose and imagine an appropriate audience.

After our work with this piece and our translation of this perspective into specific discourse-based intervention strategies, we practiced on three more pieces of student writing, keeping before us at all times the question, "What kind of reader does this piece ask us to become?" As the practice and discussion continued, we circled about this point: that the academic situation is difficult to see in terms of discourse because the writer is writing, and clearly so, to a teacher. Students most often see themselves writing to the teacher, who is often an unknown; to "the general audience," which is a discourse-free construct; to the neophyte; or, when the course includes peer reading, to peers. We, as writing instructors, do not want to be a generic "teacher" and cannot be the "general audience." We become impatient when asked to become neophytes in most fields, and we would rather not be peers.

The writer's task is to imagine a reader whom the real reader or readers can become. It is as simple, and complicated, as that.

Workshop 4: Reading Final Drafts

In our fourth and final workshop we focused upon editorial intervention at the near-final-draft stage. We wanted to make two rather different points: (1) that intervention at this stage should be a recapitulation of the writer's already accomplished work on the essay, rather than the mapping out of possible new directions; and (2) that this kind of intervention could be short and rapid, given the teachers' prior acquaintance with the essay.

To approximate the reading situation a teacher would face in class, we put together sets of early, midprocess, and late drafts of the same essay. To increase verisimilitude, we brought back two early drafts from Workshop 2, "On My Father" and "Water Skiing." The three drafts of "On My Father" were a record of effective and complex revision; the drafts of "Water Skiing" were a case study of a writer who had done what the teacher-editor had suggested, but who had not written a better essay. We began with "On My Father" and asked the teachers to read the first two drafts, beginning with the draft from Workshop 2, with which they were familiar. Then we asked them to read the near-final draft, keeping these questions in mind: "What has the writer done in the interval between drafts 2 and 3?" and "What pressing word-level or sentence-level problems need consideration?" After we had worked through the drafts, we made the point that certain kinds of intervention were useful at this stage of the process and that other kinds of intervention would be less useful. Because the essay is on the point of submission, asking for major revision is clearly not appropriate. Given that the essay as it stands is the product of almost two weeks' intermittent work, we owe the student writer a summary of what we have seen. In this case the summary was of steady progress and refinement of vision.

With the "Water Skiing" essay the record was not what one would like to see, but what one often finds: the student writer takes an editorial suggestion and runs with it in a direction we might not expect. In a case of this sort, and at this late stage in the writing process, the appropriate intervention, we agreed, takes this form:

> When I saw the first draft, I told you that you had a narrative here, and a narrative without clear point. I sensed your commitment to the subject area—water sking—and so I sent you off to the library to find out something about the history of water skiing—when, where, and why it began. Now you have written the history, and

> simply added it to the end of the pre-existing narrative. You have two essays. You have done what I asked. I enjoy reading the new material you have brought forward. In another world, you would spend two more weeks trying to integrate the two essays. But in this world, you have done what you can in the given time. I am satisfied. Now read the piece aloud and fix sentence boundary errors.

Evaluation of the Training Program

The effect of this series of workshops has been what we had hoped: all of us are teaching writing more efficiently in the Computer Writing Center. At the end of the workshops we asked our colleagues to tell us whether the workshops had helped them adjust to the new environment. Looking back at our objectives, we seem to have achieved our first: to help teachers emphasize writing practice and editorial feedback and to de-emphasize lecture and class discussion. While teachers still do some whole-class instruction, this mode has become less important to most. As one teacher said, "I thought I would miss working with the class as a whole (discussions as a way of brainstorming for topics, etc.) but the workshops helped me to work better on a one-to-one intervention basis and I'm finding I really like that and the focus it requires on the writing."

We may have been less successful in training our teachers to read and respond rapidly to on-screen partial drafts. The teachers generally said that they would need more practice before they could feel comfortable reading as fast as the computer classroom seems to require. One instructor wrote, "I still don't feel entirely adequate at reading quickly on the screen and coming up with good advice." Another wrote, "Although I'm getting better at shorter interventions, I still have a tendency to want to read an entire draft before commenting." Yet another teacher seemed to have made a clean break with the past:

> I had never before given feedback on a partial reading of student writing—that which is visible on the screen when I move through the lab. Providing feedback on the drafts we examined in the minute given was helpful not only in letting me see that I could do it, but also in learning that it is not necessary to see the entire draft in order to say something of value to the student.

We seem to have been successful in suggesting to the teachers that limited feedback—that is, a response that addresses one aspect of the essay—may be better, and certainly is faster, than comprehensive feedback. And we seem to have helped the teachers see that there is not just one good editorial response, but a range of possible responses to a given piece of student writing. Teachers need not spend time, therefore, searching for this "good" response, but they can assemble alternatives and make a choice.

The training program we have designed has clearly helped our teachers work more efficiently in the center. Most report that they are taking fewer student essays home with them and that they are doing most of their editorial coaching on-screen, in the center's classrooms. Most teachers state that they are more able to cope with the volume of writing generated by their classes. With these gains, however, comes the feeling that something has been lost. One teacher writes,

> I feel more relaxed, but at a cost. I'm not doing nearly as many in-class writing assignments; we work on [the major] essays usually twice a week now. I miss the sense of fun other kinds of assignments generate.

Another teacher was even more explicit: "It [the rapid intervention model] works too well. My workload is a lot better, but I miss the discussions. I'm getting bored." Here we encounter the necessary human limit: teaching styles differ; human beings have sharp edges. There are differences among people that no training program can, or should attempt to, eliminate.

If we had the workshop to do again, we would make two major changes in procedure. First, we would be more careful in our selection of student texts for the reading sessions. We would attempt to assemble coherent sets of student drafts by selecting and tracking a small number of students from our classes. We would therefore have to schedule the workshops weekly rather than biweekly so that the reading could keep pace with the students' writing. And second, we would give the teachers more practice at rapid reading and diagnosing. This practice seemed a bit repetitious to us during the workshops, but some of the teachers felt that this was the most valuable aspect of the program. Aside from these changes, we would proceed again much as we have proceeded. What we have done has clearly been shaped by particular circumstances: our freshman writing course, our Computer Writing Center, and our instructors' needs. Nevertheless, we believe that the basic elements of our teacher-training process can be usefully translated and adapted to other computer-based writing programs.

Works Cited

Bridges, Charles W., ed. 1986. *Training the New Teacher of College Composition.* Urbana, Ill.: National Council of Teachers of English.

Comley, Nancy. 1986. "The Teaching Seminar: Writing Isn't Just Rhetoric." In *Training the New Teacher of College Composition*, edited by Charles W. Bridges, 47–57. Urbana, Ill.: National Council of Teachers of English.

Elbow, Peter. 1981. *Writing with Power*. New York: Oxford University Press.

Garrison, Roger. 1964. "One to One: Tutorial Instruction in Freshman Composition." *New Directions for Community Colleges* 2: 55–84.

Gibson, Walker. 1950. "Authors, Speakers, Readers, and Mock Readers." *College English* 2: 265–69.

———. 1969. *Persona: A Style Study for Readers and Writers*. New York: Random House.

Moffett, James. 1968. *Teaching the Universe of Discourse*. Boston: Houghton Mifflin.

Moran, Charles. 1986. "The University of Massachusetts Writing Program." In *New Methods in College Writing Programs*, edited by Paul Connolly and Teresa Vilardi, 111–16. New York: Modern Language Association.

Murray, Donald. 1968. *A Writer Teaches Writing: A Practical Method of Teaching Composition*. Boston: Houghton Mifflin.

Smith, Charles K. 1974. *Styles and Structures: Alternative Approaches to College Writing*. New York: W. W. Norton.

Sudol, Ronald. 1985. "Word Processing in a Workshop Model." *College Composition and Communication* 36: 331–35.

10 Preparing Teachers for Computers and Writing: Plans and Issues at Governors State University

Deborah H. Holdstein, Governors State University

Introduction

When I became Director of Writing Programs at Governors State University (GSU) in University Park, Illinois, I reasoned that the trial and error of my previous six years of work with computers and writing at Illinois Institute of Technology could be channeled into an effective teacher-training effort for our uninitiated colleagues (full-time and adjunct) and teaching assistants. Interestingly, there would be even more trial and error at GSU. In the few pages that follow, I will sketch what was right—and what my colleagues and I decided was less right—about notions of training models that had developed over the years, and the salient issues that keep teacher training a flexible, ongoing, always-fresh process.

Identifying Philosophical Assumptions

When we began the program at Governors State University, we decided to start with wide-ranging questions that illustrated all too well the complexities (often unforeseen) of initiating any effort in teacher training for computers and writing. (For a discussion of the politics of computers and writing, see Holdstein 1987 and Holdstein 1988.) We knew that the following guidelines were not as prevalent in practice as good sense and theory would have us believe:

1. Writing specialists have to be trained—to proficiency—in the software and hardware their students would use.
2. The writing specialist's responsibilities as an instructor are increased and enhanced when computers are used as writing tools—and not relinquished, as was often erroneously assumed.
3. Teacher preparation for using computers in writing classes de-

mands that discussion leaders include components on the ethics and responsibilities (for both teacher and student) of "computer writing."

4. Good training efforts acknowledge the problems as well as the joys of writing and the computer; acknowledge that some colleagues might not wish to use the computer to enhance their interpretations of the curriculum; and recognize that tenable, successful training supports—not supplants—instructors' various ways of teaching writing.
5. The trainer-leader has to be a writing specialist with more than just a casual interest in computers and writing. Training cannot be left in its entirety to a lab assistant from the computer center, although these colleagues offer the leader valuable assistance.

The Departmental Context and University Facilities

We learned another important lesson from one we already knew: that any successful English department effort in teacher training for composition stems from the context of that department—its students, its size, and the interests and skills of the faculty—and that efforts in training for computers and writing could be treated no differently. In fact, we do not suggest that any "models" we present in this chapter be taken quite as such, since efforts will vary widely among different types of colleges and universities, with different students, budgets, and facilities, and will vary within the department, with excellent writing instructors who approach their craft in completely different, unique ways.

Given these variations, however, there were some methods that seemed better than others. First, for example, any faculty member who considered accepting the role of "leader" in a teacher-training process (or who considered accepting the "nomination" or "election" to do so) faced the following practical, if rudimentary, concerns well before training could begin (keeping as context the demands of the first list of philosophical assumptions). We generated our list of concerns, at least in part, through hindsight:

1. What facilities will be available for the training effort? How flexible is the availability of the facilities? If the English or humanities department has its own laboratory, the effort is off to a wonderful, less controversial start than if the department must first negotiate for computer time in the university's central laboratory.

2. How cooperative are those who run the lab or work as the lab assistants? And how helpful does the leader want them to be? Will someone be "on call" for troubleshooting?
3. Does the laboratory (or department, or other host facility) have enough copies of the software the leader will want to use in workshops? Can the facilities meet the demand in terms of space, scheduling, software, and assistance? Out of whose budget will these resources come?
4. What, if anything, does the department or university hierarchy have in mind for training? Are such ideas compatible with those of the leader, who is presumably a writing specialist?
5. Most importantly, training must be optional, not mandatory; a small group of potentially enthusiastic colleagues is better than a large group of hostile or potentially frustrated, vindictive ones.

We found that if leaders' resource needs could not be immediately satisfied, we at least had them in sight and in mind, and we adapted our program for immediate realities and demands with an eye toward the future.

As serendipity would have it, my arrival at GSU coincided with (and helped to foster) expansion plans for the computer center. During the first trimester, we scheduled five sections of English 381 ("Advanced Writing") and one section of English 382 ("Technical and Professional Communications") for the one IBM PC room on campus. (We also have an Apple IIe room.) These gestures alone put new, significant demands on existing resources that others, in other fields, had also discovered. New computer equipment was purchased. By 1985, IBM and IBM-compatible equipment and a few Apples lined the common corridors of the center, available for use at any time, and by fall of 1986, GSU could boast of a room of twenty Zenith IBM-compatible PCs and two demonstration classrooms with projection screens.

But while some resources expanded, budgetary considerations restricted our word-processing choices to the usefulness of a particular software package for other, university-wide applications; however, in 1986, we decided to support our dean's suggestion to add *Microsoft Word* to our available software, *PC-Write* and *WordStar*. Our training effort demanded that we learn each type of software thoroughly—whether it was our "favorite" or not, and particularly if it was not—so that we could best help our colleagues (and students) approach it from the writing specialist's point of view.

Our work in learning the software was deliberately integrated with issues in writing, the curriculum of our particular writing program, and the needs of our students. The practice "assignments" through which participants learned the word-processing software became actual documents our colleagues would use in their teaching or research (or for administrative purposes within the department). And despite our individual methods and goals for teaching writing (even with a core syllabus for English 381), we all raised concerns relevant to the learning and teaching of composition and to composition as a discipline.

Framing an Effective Workshop Approach

After considering the interaction among participants in early workshops, their needs, their feedback, and our own sense of what seemed to work best given the context of our particular university, we developed the overall "scheme" and theoretical backdrop for a two-day, intensive workshop that seemed most easily scheduled (given discrepancies in scheduling and vacations) during registration week.

The following description also includes a plan for a follow-up series of colloquiums in computers and writing to keep participants (and trainers) fresh and familiar with new approaches and developments in the field. We also determined that, ideally, it seemed best to begin training the semester or quarter before participants wished to start using the computer with their classes.

Between the time we had planned and completed the first two-day event, we devised another list of considerations, a list that we revised both during and after the workshop. During that time, we learned that there were several tasks that participating teachers would not even consider doing:

1. Teachers would not learn anything else until they had mastered the software package that served as the focus for the workshop. Without a firm grasp of the software, any discussion of classroom applications was far too theoretical (and anxiety producing for the novice). This was no different than the collective fate of the students these colleagues would teach—students could not always be expected to learn to write and learn the computer at the same time. Donald Ross (1985) discusses this "double-bind" effect.
2. Teachers initially had no interest in the computer's innards (motherboards, buffer commands) or in programming. We learned to leave these topics until much later in the training

process, preferably during the follow-up colloquiums, when participants were proficient in using the computer.

3. Teachers would not learn or share anything productive if the workshop, even in its most preliminary stages, did not integrate participants' technical knowledge of the computer with issues contextually based in the syllabus amd writing curriculum of our particular department. For instance, writing activities to help participants learn word-processing software had to involve "real" documents they would want to or have to write anyway—letters, memos, articles, class handouts, syllabuses.
4. Teachers at first would not feel relaxed before the computer. For many of our colleagues, the computer was tantamount to stress. However, the ones complaining the most loudly—or who seemed to lose the most material—eventually became the most enthusiastic.

This advice stems from our own mistakes in some of our earlier efforts and from our responses to those who would decree that preliminary computer instruction be handled exclusively through university computer facilities, thereby hindering a discussion of computers integrated with composition issues and pedagogy. When, in fact, we had naturally integrated the curriculum and its related issues within the process, the learning was cooperative, producing much brainstorming and many ideas, suggestions, and disagreements, which was as it should be. As trite as it may sound, teaching ideas grew "organically" from the practical, sometimes-technical training in word processing.

Planning the Training

The overall scheme for preparing teachers to use computers to teach writing is outlined below. We developed and continue to revise this workable pattern in keeping with the issues noted above. The following components are in various stages of implementation:

1. Two-day, intensive workshop (held during registration week, or at another time convenient to colleagues). The workshop should be lengthened to even more hours, if possible. We assumed that participants would also put in additional time on their own.
2. Computers and writing colloquiums (held monthly).
3. Integration of the computer within "regular" writing and professionally oriented classes: "Advanced Composition" (English 381), "Technical and Professional Communications" (English

382), and a seminar, "Advanced Composition and Rhetorical Theory" (English 830).

4. Development of related courses: a 500-level course, "Computers and Writing," and a 600-level course, "Workshop for Teachers of Writing," with a computers-and-writing component (taken by those who teach elsewhere or who are graduate students).
5. Eventual "mainstreaming" of computers and writing issues in colloquiums with other research and theoretical issues in composition.

While the two-day, "baptism by fire" immersion approach worked well given the inevitable schedule conflicts (the computer center versus us, one person's teaching schedule versus another's), we had most success when we followed up the workshop with regular meetings throughout the semester. These were not necessarily additional workshops, but rather gave us an excuse to create the departmental "writing colloquium" and, later, to create a new colloquium with a new focus. We planned, in the next trimester or so, to make computer-related discussions part of a "regular" colloquium that dealt at different meetings with different issues of research and theory in composition. To us, this eventual "mainstreaming" heightened technology's credibility as a legitimate part of any ongoing discussions in the field of composition.

The Two-Day Workshop: An Overview

During the morning hours of the intensive workshop, participants learned to create at the terminal documents related to their scholarship or teaching. In the afternoons, we followed up with discussions and brainstorming about applications for our students—some that we devised alone and some that we devised together with participants in the workshop. Most importantly, instructors performed these applications themselves as they designed invention ideas or practiced, allowing them to anticipate at least some student reaction to the exercises or ideas and gaining some sense of how the activity might need to be adapted or redesigned. Most good instructors found that they could quickly devise ways of incorporating various types of software into their own ways of teaching writing after they had become familiar with word-processing and/or CAI packages.

During the second day of the workshop, we showed teachers how to have students bring to class the hard copy of drafts written at the computer so that they could discuss the drafts with their peer-revising groups. After more revision with pencil or ink, writers then returned to the computer center (on their own time or as part of classroom activity) and entered their revisions at the terminal, including whatever changes occurred to them at the computer.

During the second afternoon session, we also discussed teaching methods for GSU instructors eager to use our projection and demonstration computer classrooms, emphasizing that a student's text could be displayed on a large screen in front of the entire class for discussion and reworking—a technological variation on the traditional technique of reproducing a student's paper for classroom distribution. With the computer, most participants felt that this type of revision process became much more active and interactive as participants role-played the method themselves.

During these workshops, the possibilities seemed endless and, as advertisers say, "limited by our own imaginations" and capabilities. But what about computer-aided instruction? While we stressed word processing in our workshops, we did include work with CAI as part of the afternoon sessions. (For a further discussion of CAI in the classroom, see Holdstein 1988.) For example, in our discussions, one instructor wanted to work on microstructural aspects of the writing process using CAI packages for grammar or sentencing. In this instance, we discussed a plan whereby students who needed the work might use CAI for subject-verb agreement, for example, while other students used the same time to begin drafts of the latest assignment (particularly if there were not enough computers or CAI disks to go around). During these sessions we made use of my own *Write Well* programs on the comma, other forms of punctuation, parallelism, subject-verb agreement, and other aspects of writing.

As students finished their CAI work, we explained that they could then pair up with other students who had used the programs and together make certain that the latest "lesson" was incorporated within the writing process itself. Participants later reported that they had particular success with our approach of pairing students before a CAI lesson that required them to discuss or reason the appropriate response. Then the same two students assisted one another in reworking the papers they had been writing and revising, in part by hand and in part at the computer, with particular attention paid to the CAI lessons. Training workshop participants used this same approach to devise their own methods for using CAI and for becoming familiar with various types of software.

Most importantly, colleagues in the workshop realized that innovative classroom ideas with the computer could be compatible with their own traditional, tried-and-true methods, reinforcing an important theoretical underpinning of our workshop process: that technology adapts to the instructor, as he or she wishes, and not necessarily the other way around—unless that is a deliberate choice or part of an innovative teaching plan. Familiarity with the computer did not mean eliminating tradition for the sake of joining the "computer bandwagon."

The Follow-up

We determined that too many important issues surfaced during the workshops to let the two-day effort stand alone. To provide ongoing dialogue among workshop participants, to troubleshoot and provide the forum for questions that might arise, and, simply, to provide another form of continuous training, a series of fairly informal follow-up gatherings seemed appropriate. Participants welcomed the idea of what we began to call "The Writing Colloquium." These monthly meetings meant that we did not have to rush through the important theoretical, political, and practical issues that had come up during workshops. While these issues were related to the hands-on task and would influence the efficacy with which computers and writing plans would work, just knowing that we would have follow-up sessions meant that many concerns could be addressed more fully later on.

Ideally, writing colloquiums should be held as often as schedules will allow during the regular school year. At first, once a month (or more frequently) seemed ideal; as time passed, different faculty schedules demanded a reduction to several times a trimester. However, less formal meetings and special-interest group meetings were another possibility as long as colleagues would gather en masse often enough to know what everyone was up to. In the future, our gatherings might well occur through electric conferencing, particularly if we begin an effort that might implement computers for writing across the disciplines.

Once an initial acquaintance period had passed, we found that teachers used the computer as uniquely and innovatively (and as distinctly from one another) as they had used any other enhancement tool—or as they had taught composition in the past. But most important during the training period was the flexibility of the workshop, its contents, and its leader.

Nothing, we knew, could be chiseled in rock, so to speak, which was why the leaders' thorough familiarity with issues in computers and writing and with the field as a whole were so essential for appropriate responses to and guidance of workshop participants, particularly when discussions became constructively spontaneous and freewheeling.

Evaluation and Some Conclusions

Our first attempt at designing a workshop has undergone much change. Initially, day one was called "An Introduction to Computers" and day two, "Using Word-Processing Software." Gradually we changed the plan, realizing that the writing curriculum had to be integrated from the start and, like good Monday morning quarterbacks, devising most of the other questions and suggestions in this chapter.

One evaluation from a graduate student participant commended the redesigned effort: "It makes so much more sense to talk about word processing as it really relates to writing (and our students) from the first! Everything was so much more accessible to us." Another participant agreed with our restructuring of the sequence of material: "We really didn't need to know a lot of that stuff in the first session—it was too intimidating, and kept us from plunging in."

We continue to evaluate and rethink all aspects of our training program, part of a long-term process that includes informal discussions as well as written evaluations (often anonymous) of training sessions.

Above all, we learned that whatever the institution, an important goal of any good training model using technology is to prepare teachers for effective, student-centered work in computers and writing while acknowledging and respecting the individual differences of the colleagues involved in the training process—and those who do not want to be involved. While time, logistics, and the wide scope of issues to be discussed as part of computer-related training efforts demand that these projects exist apart from other teacher-preparation work in composition, their gradual integration within "regular" programs (already begun at some institutions) will lend legitimacy not only to the colleague committed to the computer as an enhancement tool for writing, but also to the computers and composition discipline itself as an appropriate forum for research and scholarship in the English department.

Works Cited

Holdstein, Deborah H. 1987. "The Politics of Computers and Writing: Issues for Faculty and Administrators." In *Writing at Century's End: Papers from the UCLA Conference*, edited by Lisa Gerrard, 81–90. New York: Random House.

———. 1988. *On Composition and Computers.* New York: Modern Language Association.

Ross, Donald. 1985. "Realities of Computer Analysis of Composition." In *Writing On-Line: Using Computers in the Teaching of Writing*, edited by James L. Collins and Elizabeth A. Sommers, 105–13. Upper Montclair, N.J.: Boynton/Cook.

11 Integrating Computers and Composition at Southern Illinois University–Carbondale

Stephen A. Bernhardt, New Mexico State University

Bruce C. Appleby, Southern Illinois University–Carbondale

Introduction

As our profession has moved to integrate computers into the teaching of composition, we have increasingly been confronted with the need to train English faculty to be comfortable and productive in a microlab environment. While college departments have always recognized a responsibility to train graduate assistants to teach composition, the computer has created a new responsibility: training faculty across the ranks. Few precedents exist. Unlike the public schools, which recognize the need for inservice programs, universities have traditionally assumed their faculty know how to teach.

As we write, we are in our second year of integrating computers into the composition program at Southern Illinois University–Carbondale (SIU–C). We have trained approximately fifty of our faculty to use computers in their teaching, and approximately twenty-five have now taught classes in a microlab setting. Our lab is large, so controlling the attention of a group of students is difficult. We know that teachers need to change their instructional approaches in order to be productive in this setting, particularly by learning to manage individualized, process-oriented instruction. They have discovered a need to plan carefully and to use time efficiently, in the lab and out. We feel we have been successful in training faculty to adjust to the demands of teaching in a new situation and that recounting our experiences might help other English departments develop their own strategies for integrating computers into their writing programs.

After reviewing the background to our project and describing our microcomputer labs, we will describe in turn the several components of our program:

1. Faculty development workshops—sixteen two-hour sessions involving approximately twenty-five faculty
2. Follow-up activities, including opportunities for released time to attend composition and rhetoric seminars, a series of one-night sessions to introduce university faculty and staff to *PC-Write,* and biweekly discussions with those teaching in the microlab
3. Research activities to assess the effectiveness of computers in teaching composition

Background

Our composition program is a traditional one, with students taking a first-semester 101 course, best described as process-oriented with an emphasis on purpose and audience throughout. The three-part course moves from personal and experiential writing, through objective and informational writing, to persuasive and argumentative writing. Most of our use of the computer has been in this course, which enrolls a total of approximately 3,500 students per year. Of these, five hundred or more are typically in computerized classes. Our students come from various backgrounds. Many come from the greater Chicago area (since our school is as far from home as they can get without paying out-of-state tuition). We have large numbers of minority, international, and disabled students. Our incoming freshmen rank above the national average on their ACT scores, but only slightly. We have a large number of students who do not meet our minimal admission requirements but who come in under a "special admissions" rubric.

Early in 1985, we submitted a proposal to the state of Illinois to enhance our undergraduate composition program. We prepared a proposed budget of $330,700. After much negotiation, we received a $128,000 permanent addition to our department budget for "Enhancement" purposes. We proposed money be used to train faculty and graduate assistants in the use of the computer as a tool to teach writing. Because our computer laboratory was being built and because we had priority on its use, we needed to be sure we had the teachers trained to use the facility. We also proposed buying computers for teaching and administrative functions in the department and funding for a graduate assistant to work alongside the teachers in the computer classes. Other aspects of our proposal were reduction of class size in all introductory composition classes to a maximum of twenty and addition of tenure-track lines, term positions, and graduate assistants to cover the increased number of sections. Like other Illinois public universities, we found that state "new program" money was the best source for funding. In addition to the training of full-time faculty and graduate assistants, we also planned research to evaluate our success. The first year of our work with computers allowed us to plan and pilot our research procedures. We had the opportunity to go beyond the prevalent anecdotal research through a combination of experimental and observational research which would give insights into the effectiveness of the computer as a tool to teach writing.

Our PC Lab

The microlab at SIU–C was planned by an interdisciplinary committee to provide access for students taking courses in departments which traditionally do not have their own labs. Some of us in English were anxious to use computers in composition classes; the vice president wanted to meet demands for computer literacy (which he saw as a bogus issue) by incorporating computer work into existing requirements. Introductory composition seemed a natural fit, and so English had a heavy involvement in the lab from the start, with assurances from the vice president that English would be entitled to a major portion of lab time. This support proved extremely helpful as we worked with faculty from other disciplines who were not apt to appreciate the power of the PC as a tool for teaching writing. Over time, several of these same faculty (engineers and computer scientists, in particular) became our greatest champions as they realized our work would help prepare students for advanced computer applications.

Our lab has two large adjoining rooms with thirty-two IBM PCs in each room and a control room in the center. One side is a classroom, with the machines in rows of four or five oriented toward the front, where there is a teaching station, a teacher's PC, and a large-screen Sony. Each row has an Epson printer, controlled by a T-Switch box. We have no networking, though we often talk about what we would like and where the money would come from. The second room, designed as an individual, drop-in lab, also has thirty-two PCs, arranged in star clusters, with a printer shared within each star. The individual lab provides for special uses of PCs. Some machines have beefed-up memory; some are linked to letter-quality printers or graphics plotters; two stations are built for wheelchair access. Both rooms are attractive, with window walls looking out over the campus woods. The facility was expensive to build, largely because of physical renovation. Schools planning to build new labs should look hard for existing space which can be readily adapted to computer labs without major renovation. For our $600,000 lab, we spent only about $225,000 on computer equipment per se.

The committee decided to provide only general applications software for the lab: *PC-Write*, a word processor; *Random House Proofreader*, a spelling checker; *Grammatik* and *Punctuation and Style*, grammar and style parsers; *Lotus 1-2-3; P-C Calc; P-C File; IBM Filing Assistant;* several programming languages and compilers; *CRISP*, a statistics package; several graphics packages; and a CAD/CAM package. The choice of software reflects both philosophical and pragmatic positions. We wanted the lab to focus on the computer as a tool for applications, not as a self-instruction center. We wanted students skilled in general applications on the most general business machine, the IBM PC. Pragmatically, we realized the lab could not provide multiple copies of the very expensive software our faculty wanted for individual classes. Choosing *PC-Write* was also a pragmatic decision, since it meant we would not have to buy multiple copies of expensive word-processing software. We haven't regretted choosing *PC-Write* and have seen its use expand across campus. After the initial purchase of the applications software, the policy has been that individual departments need to buy their own software if they have special needs.

Working cooperatively with the SIU–C office for Computing Affairs has proven advantageous in several ways. They staff the lab with work-study students who maintain the machines, check software in and out, refill paper and reink ribbons on the printers, and solve endless problems, whether with word processing or other applications. The lab and classroom are open from 8:00 a.m. until 2:00 a.m., five days per week, with shorter hours on the weekends. When we hold class in the lab, the machines are unlocked before we arrive, with requested software at each station. When no classes are scheduled in the evening, the lab is open for drop-in use. Computing Affairs has also trained staff to repair the PCs, so when a machine malfunctions, the technical staff simply pulls the machine and replaces it with another while the first is being fixed. Thus far, Computing Affairs has paid for the paper and ribbons, an expense the English department is glad not to cover.

There have been a few drawbacks to the university-wide lab. The biggest drawback was that it took us nearly two years and countless hours of committee work to plan and build the lab. In the negotiating process, we frequently compromised. For example, we would not have put thirty-two machines in a classroom, since we like to keep our writing classes at twenty to twenty-two students. The classroom is very large, and the forward-facing arrangement makes it difficult to know what is on the screens. There is a fair amount of distracting noise, with students coming and going. We feel, though, that the benefits of strong support from Computing Affairs, especially our not having to worry about technical difficulties, make a cooperative approach worthwhile. For faculty apprehensive about moving instruction into a new technological setting, having the technical and managerial services of Computing Affairs has been wonderful.

The Faculty Development Workshop

We realized—fortunately at an early stage—that if our goals were to be met, we had to convince our faculty of the potential value of the computer as a tool for writing. We thought it important to involve as many faculty as possible through incentives. Our dean made a point of supporting our work and had offered released time to any liberal arts faculty member who wished to develop instructional uses of the computer. Within the department, the chair offered to all tenure-track faculty the opportunity to be released from one class if they would attend a once-a-week workshop on computers and the teaching of writing. With the state Enhancement money described above, we hired lecturers to cover released classes for the leader and the participants.

One of the first tests of our program and goals was how many faculty would take advantage of the offer. We did not fool ourselves into believing that everyone who asked to take part in the Enhancement activities was doing so out of a driving desire to be a better composition teacher. We did feel that we could convince the faculty of the usefulness of computers if we had the opportunity to work with them every week in the lab. Three full, one associate, and four assistant professors signed up for the weekly two-hour course. Once the chair (until then a dedicated Macintosh user) decided to attend the course, others picked up on the idea. The assistant to the chair and three secretaries joined us, as did several lecturers (non–tenure-track, full-time teachers) and a number of graduate assistants. We cut off enrollment at thirty participants.

At the time we started our course, we were concerned about having too many people in the group. At several computer and composition conferences, we heard speakers say that a teacher would find working one-on-one ideal, working with several people comfortable, and working with seven or eight a practical limit. In addition to the size of the group, we were concerned that the mix of ranks, ranging from civil service through graduate assistants to full professors, might make the going difficult. The official participants might demand full attention and resent those who joined informally. We ended up with a faithful contingency of twenty-five, with several more who attended occasionally. We quickly learned that it is possible to work with a large group through individualizing instruction, encouraging collaboration, and acquiescing to the natural forces of learning that develop in a computerized composition classroom.

We spent most of the first two sessions working in concert: we taught the participants how to format a disk, prepare a working copy of *PC-Write,* and begin word processing and printing. We taught control keys, cursor movement and function keys, the "delete" and "insert" routines, on-line help files (fascinating to the uninitiated), and the simplest print routines. Getting people quickly into actual production of text and printing has become a hallmark of the training system we advocate: immediate success with word processing—often within two hours—is the best way to convince word people like English teachers that the computer offers possibilities for their writing and their teaching.

After the first two weeks, people were on their own, many working with a self-paced tutorial which led them through the word-processing package. Scattered throughout the room were advanced learners, mostly lecturers and graduate students who had been working on their own prior to the faculty workshop. Many of the questions people had were answered by turning to the person at the next machine. Anyone who has taught in a computerized writing classroom knows that this pattern quickly develops and that it is one of the most heartening aspects of teaching in such an atmosphere. It is exciting to see theories of learning in action when students view each other as teachers. We roamed—answering questions, getting people unstuck, retrieving lost files, commiserating over files that were really lost, and only occasionally making comments to the group as a whole. All of this was a wonderful process to observe and be a part of: a busy, serious atmosphere, punctuated by occasional outbursts, hands waving, and cries of success. The atmosphere surrounding this group of adults was much the same as we found in our introductory composition classes with freshmen, where a teacher and a lab assistant trained in composition worked one-on-one with busily composing students.

Our general pattern was that people started immediately on their own projects. A fast-two-fingered-typist graduate student put the first draft of his novel on disk, making his capturing of it in a new medium the second draft. Many people worked on articles and chapters of books. Many of the graduate assistants worked on materials for their own classes or on seminar papers. Our secretary put our memos on disk. The chair wrote letters to his son, away at college for the first time.

We generally let people work for a half hour without interruption. Then we would often break in and introduce new features of the system. Sometimes we rehearsed routines previously taught, and always we answered questions. Most paid attention to this instruction, with others continuing on their individual paths.

One lesson of our workshop, a lesson we all know but need to be taught time and time again, is that people have different learning styles. Some of our participants never needed our help, yet turned up each week to be part of the group. Others clung to the tutorial as though it were a life raft. Still others discarded the tutorial and learned new routines, such as underlining or pagination, as needed. We encouraged learners to take on real tasks—a letter or a memo—if they were not working on a seminar paper or their next article.

We wanted everyone to experience quickly the success of printing, as we have found with all age groups and ability levels that watching your own text as it is being printed is a boost to further success and learning. With some participants, we could not force even this small success. They would not quit the tutorial, feeling they needed to learn everything before trying anything on their own. Some participants finished the tutorial and then turned back to page one and started over on the same lessons, believing they needed the reinforcement of repetition. We encouraged them to open a file containing a composition assignment so they could swap files and gain some ideas on teaching writing. Only a few did so. They were determined to use the machine in their individual ways and to make the lab and software fit their own learning styles.

The process of learning we saw in this faculty workshop contains lessons for composition instruction in general. The computerized writing classroom forces individualization, a goal we have long recognized but not realized in composition instruction. Instead of standing at the board and lecturing about good writing or leading recitations over textbook elements, teachers in a computer classroom work one-on-one, helping students as they write. Teachers can roam, answer pertinent questions, and encourage substantial revision. We were worried initially over not doing enough and about how to prepare the class. Having a group of university teachers as students is disconcerting, particularly if you know that many of them believe that "teaching is telling" and that learning takes place only when the teacher decides what the learning will be. Yet, over the weeks we saw that it was working. At widely varying paces, the participants were gaining skills. It took time, but the teachers in our class started to see the value of individualization where entry skills are divergent, where learning styles and motivation vary. Since this describes nearly all composition classes, we were realizing part of our goals through the serendipitous discoveries that take place when teachers are learners.

Faculty who work with computers need to become problem solvers, and the problems are often technical. As soon as serious printing starts, to take the most common example, a host of technical problems inevitably arises. Those accustomed to working only with words on the printed page are acutely uncomfortable when faced with technical difficulties, letting their cyberphobia rule. A lab assistant with technical and pedagogical skills can help, but the teacher must become a problem solver.

As in the learning of any new content area or skill, one learns the jargon and vocabulary of the field. Teachers become technical communicators who work to disambiguate language, demonstrate through explanation and example, clarify procedures, and solve problems with documentation. *Page breaks, ruler defaults, font changes, headers* and *footers, hard-returns,* and *soft-hyphens* are just a few of the new words that surface. The healthy respect for language which most English teachers share makes it possible for them to laugh at themselves as they learn to talk and behave like technical problem solvers.

Happily, the computerized classroom brings about an approach to teaching and learning that changes the relationship between teachers and students. Teachers and students are often on a par with each other, confronting problems together, working out solutions, sharing frustration and success. Repeatedly, participants had the opportunity to teach what they had just learned, demonstrating and leading another through a newly acquired process. Our role was that of matchmaker, forcing the behavior of teacher teaching teacher, in the same way we hoped the faculty would become accustomed to matching student to student in collaborative learning and teaching. All had ample opportunities to see us fail, work through problems, and seek assistance from others who had an answer when we did not.

Typically, teachers think immediately about instructional applications. In our workshop, questions of how to get students on the machines, how to devise assignments, how to use the machines to increase student willingness to revise, and how to *teach* with the machines could easily have become the prime questions.

However, we felt a better first step was for the faculty to begin using the machine as writers—preparing courses or organizing research or working on a publication. As teachers used the machines to save materials, keep records, develop syllabuses, and print handouts, they learned how the machine works and what it is good for. They gained a conceptual familiarity with its operations, coming to understand how information is stored, retrieved, and manipulated. Seeing the machine in their own lives as writers and teachers, they gained a realistic perspective on its classroom applications. We generally feel that in schools with a limited number of machines, it is better to devote them to the teachers' use rather than trying to give as many students as possible some small measure of experience. Classroom applications can follow as more hardware is acquired, and when that time comes, the teachers will know what to do.

After ten weeks in the lab, we found it helpful to get away from the machines and to discuss their effects on writing, including the implications for composition instruction. During four two-hour sessions, we read and discussed several articles (Bridwell, Nancarrow, and Ross 1984; Cleveland 1985; and Daiute 1983), organized a roundtable of those teachers who were teaching in the lab, and had an open discussion of the future of the computer in our department. These meetings were announced to the full faculty, and a number of people who were not in the workshop joined in. It was important that these discussions followed the hands-on, skill-development portion of the workshop. It is a mistake to try to do too much talking when people are just learning how to use the machines. Developing a feel for the machines, comfort with computer talk, and ease with word processing puts people in a better frame of mind to discuss the implications for teaching composition.

These discussions proved valuable for the department. Though the focus was on computers, at the same time we discussed teaching writing as process, making assignments, individualizing learning, and encouraging student collaboration. Stories such as the one about the football player who brought the whole team over to learn word processing were heartening (the coach did buy an IBM PC for the football study room). The descriptions of the students who arrived early for an 8:00 a.m. class, of those who did not want to leave class, and of those who attended both sections taught by their teacher stimulated positive talk among seasoned faculty that is rare and welcome.

On returning to the lab after our discussions, we introduced software other than word processing. Most teachers have unrealistic expectations, expecting the machine to do the teaching and the software to use language in human ways. There is a paradoxical clash of expectations as teachers run a grammar check or work through an invention program. They see the immediate value of the program's abilty to check spelling, but other software is often disappointing. Having heard from zealous colleagues about the wonders of the computer, teachers feel an inevitable letdown and wonder what all the fuss is about. We know that software which teaches students to write better has not met our expectations. What we fail to realize is that this means that teachers are free to concentrate on creative uses of word-processing packages and other standard applications software. The shift away from expecting the computer to be the teacher and toward the use of the computer as a tool is important, a shift well documented by Tucker (1985).

Giving teachers ideas for building instructional files within the word-processing package was an important final part of our training workshop. The teachers wrote files containing models of student and professional writing, heuristic prompts, sentence-combining exercises, revision checklists, and other activities for individual and class-wide use. A training workshop can encourage teachers to write and swap assignments on disk. Such files are tremendous resources for teachers and a vast improvement over copies of handouts fading in steel files. As Rodrigues and Rodrigues (1986) suggest, we urged the participants to discover the teaching possibilities in the creative use of text files.

Follow-up Activities

In addition to the semester-long development workshop, we have continued to provide opportunities for interested faculty to develop their backgrounds in composition and computers. In the semester following the computer lab workshop, we used state Enhancement funds to offer faculty released time to attend one of two graduate seminars: one on research in composition and another on rhetorical theory. We were unsure how responsive the faculty would be to the idea, given that both seminars were taught by untenured assistant professors in areas often held in suspicion by literary scholars. But a tactful presentation by the chair encouraged two associate professors (one a Renaissance scholar and the other a Victorian scholar) to attend the research seminar. Several other colleagues decided not to audit the class during the full term, but followed along with the readings of one of the courses and attended selectively. In both classes, the participating professors contributed respectfully to a lively interchange, with the result that the regularly enrolled students and the instructors both felt positive about the mix of participants.

To encourage wider use of *PC-Write* across campus, we held a series of five two-hour workshops during which we gave faculty and students a copy of the program and a brief introduction to using it. Each session enrolled between thirty and fifty participants. We started them on the tutorial and showed them how to get help. Our intention here was to create a community of knowledgeable users as a support group.

Each term, on a purely voluntary basis, the group of computer teachers has met biweekly to discuss their classes. Time has been given to whatever most concerns the teachers. At the beginning of the term, procedural matters dominate—how to do things in the lab, how to make copies, how to find the various tutorials and help sheets, and so on. One teacher, for example, told us she had identified those students with computer skills and, with their permission, seated them on the ends of rows so they could be resource people. Several of the others picked up on the idea and arranged their classes similarly. Teachers who developed short tutorials on key aspects of computer use brought their handouts and shared copies. Teachers copied various activity files to their own disks for future use, and in our duplicating office we kept a master file of handouts for the computer sections. It was easy enough to organize resources in such small ways to pay large dividends to busy teachers who needed quality instructional materials.

The teacher meetings were also a good opportunity to discuss general teaching strategies, to share assignments that work well, to compare student reactions to classes, and to make notes about what to try the next time around. Our teachers have had to learn they cannot move a class into a lab and teach as in a traditional class setting. Because our arrangement has classes meeting in two seventy-five-minute periods, one in and one out of the computer lab, there is a strong feeling of not having enough time. Most of our teachers feel they have to cut back on the number of formal assignments and to look for ways to stage assignments.

This move toward linked, staged assignments, rather than discrete, nonrelated assignments, takes advantage of the machine's power to do major text revisions. Texts are refined, combined, and edited repeatedly. Fewer major assignments mean that students write several drafts as audiences or purposes change or as more sources of information are added. One teacher has pairs of students brainstorm and then outline collaboratively in class, write up the text independently, and then collaborate once more in an effort to combine their two independent drafts into a single text. Other teachers lead students to revise supposedly "finished" texts. For example, during the lab the teacher might instruct students to examine the first sentence of each paragraph to determine its effectiveness as an introductory sentence. After a series of such revisions, students print out copies to be turned in. For students, the benefits of a lesson on revision are immediate, recognizable in their own texts.

We made it clear from the beginning that the teacher meetings were purely voluntary and asked each term whether the teachers wanted to meet. They did. They have been willing to meet continually, over several semesters, to engage in discussions of teaching practices with their colleagues. The chance to get together and to talk about teaching with computers has sparked a continuing interest.

Research Activities

From the beginning of our computers and composition project, we have insisted on the importance of linking a basic research program with teacher training. In general, we feel that an active research program stimulates interest throughout the department, among both graduate students and faculty. In our research, we have been concerned with three primary objectives:

1. To measure the effects of teaching composition with computers on student and teacher attitudes, writing quality, attendance, assignment completion, and other quantifiable variables
2. To document the effects of teaching composition with computers on patterns of classroom interaction, with attention to how instructional strategies and classroom discourse change in a lab setting
3. To document the effects of computers on patterns of student composing, specifically in revising habits

We began our research with the fall 1985 term and have continued collecting data, refining our instruments, and analyzing our results over each consecutive term. During fall of 1986, we collected masses of data from the classes of twelve teachers, each of whom taught one lab section and one regular section.

To get at student attitudes, we used the short form of the Witte/Faigley instrument for assessing the effectiveness of composition instruction. To their twenty-one items, we added several more questions which gave us specific data about how computer sections compared with regular sections. In addition, students in the computer sections also completed an additional list of yes/no questions targeted specifically at their feelings about using computers and answered a list of open-ended questions about their course. Course evaluations from both semesters during the first year consistently favored the computer classes. The only exceptions were the items related to the perceived usefulness of the texts: a rhetoric and a handbook. On all other measures, students gave their teachers and their courses in the lab higher marks, finding the teachers more intellectually stimulating, more fair about grading, and better at helping students while they composed; computer students even found their teachers' remarks on their papers easier to understand than did those in the regular classes. We do not suppose that the perceptions of students in the lab classes necessarily indicate differences that might be objectively documented. We suspect a halo effect from using computers. Because students liked the computers as a part of their writing class, they rated all aspects of the class more highly than did students in regular classes.

However we might explain the consistently more favorable attitudes toward the computer sections, it remains a fact that teachers appreciate the improved student attitudes. In their course evaluations, the students say that they like revising on the computer, that they believe the class will be useful to them in the future, that they would recommend this course and this teacher to their friends. Knowing that students feel good about the course helps teacher attitudes. Before our computer and composition research began, it was the practice in our department to use only open-ended evaluations. Our research efforts, with their detailed questionnaires, have provided teachers with new kinds of data which can be compared across sections and against department norms. By getting detailed feedback, teachers gain in confidence and begin to identify specific areas of strength and weakness in their teaching.

All through our project, we have been careful to collect data on teacher as well as student attitudes. We have encouraged the teachers to keep logs on their experiences, as a resource for research data and as a record to which they can return to trace their development as teachers. We have not been successful in getting all our teachers to keep logs. Those who have chosen to keep records apply the lesson we try to teach our students: writing can be a means of discovering what we think and why we behave as we do. Keeping teaching logs is good practice for any teacher concerned with developing successful classroom strategies, and we see the encouragement of logs as another strategy in our overall effort to train teachers.

In addition to collecting attitudinal and evaluative data, we have devoted a major portion of our research energies to observational studies of computer versus regular classes. During spring of 1986, the research team visited a number of the computer classes, keeping detailed observational records of what went on in the classes, what the patterns of interaction were, and how teacher and student behavior contrasted between regular and lab settings. We identified two teachers, both of whom were experienced with computers and both of whom seemed to have a good sense of how to teach productively in both computer and regular settings. These two teachers became our subjects for observational case studies during fall of 1986.

That semester, we observed every minute of instruction in the two sections of these teachers, in the lab and out. We kept detailed time lines, as well as observational logs which recorded our impressions, the language of the classrooms, the reactions of the students, and whatever other kinds of data we could gather in an unobtrusive fashion. The research team met weekly to boil down the observations, which we then shared with the teachers for their comments. This aspect of the research involved the researchers intimately with individual classroom communities. Researchers and teachers together began to see emerging patterns which characterized what it is like to teach in a lab environment.

We also tried to get closer to the students' experiences with computer sections by isolating a major writing assignment and following selected students through the experience of writing a paper, again contrasting computer students with regular students. Additionally, researchers spent time in the drop-in lab to watch students and to interview them about their writing habits.

By systematically collecting data, the research project makes the experience of teaching composition a more public, more shared experience. The research helps us overcome the isolation of teacher and class, which is characteristic of the profession. The research context provides a setting for comparing experiences, attitudes, and practices. For many of our teachers, the research represents the first time they have thought seriously about how to evaluate successful teaching. Though the research claimed both class and personal time, the teachers have been highly cooperative. Research creates a sense of community which stimulates a continuing dialogue about being effective teachers.

Conclusion

In our experience, effective workshops for training teachers to use microcomputers to enhance composition instruction should have the following characteristics:

1. Teachers quickly begin to use the machines, encouraging immediate small successes on practical tasks and giving minimal whole-group instruction.
2. A true workshop atmosphere dominates, with people working together and helping each other, facilitated by emphasis on individual progress and constructive collaboration.
3. Teachers become accustomed to solving technical problems, consulting with other learners, and using manuals.
4. Teachers use the machines for their own purposes before considering how students might use the machines.
5. After the teachers are familiar with the machines, time is reserved for discussion of the implications for teaching writing.
6. Activity files are developed through discussion of the creative possibilities of the machine and through file swapping.
7. Follow-up activities continue to support teachers who are changing their methods of teaching composition.
8. A research program provides teachers with data to evaluate the success of their new methods.

Postscript

The work we have described does not stop with the workshop. Shifts in faculty, particularly as graduate assistants leave, mean there must be continuous training efforts. We were lucky to have funding for our initial year of activities, but in our second year of the program the money became part of our general operating budget, and we were unable to keep money earmarked specifically for faculty development, lab assistants, or adding computer resources. Large institutions such as ours typically do not acknowledge the extensive training necessary to teach writing, especially when that training involves new and sometimes-unfamiliar technologies. In times of budget difficulties and (for us) increasing enrollments, such efforts are often seen as dispensable luxuries.

We have found personal and professional satisfaction and growth in this work and feel we are a part of a national network of educators who share our goals. We know we have seen changes in the attitudes of our faculty, with greater collegiality and greater respect for composition as a discipline. The revolution in the teaching of composition that the computer has brought about is only beginning. Those who choose to integrate computers into their composition programs should realize the tremendous commitment of time and energy involved. Getting a lab is a first step, followed by continual efforts to keep the program working and expanding. Now, if we could just figure out where to get the money to put a couple of PCs in the Writing Center. . . .

Works Cited

Bridwell, Lillian, Paula Reed Nancarrow, and Donald Ross. 1984. "The Writing Process and the Writing Machine: Current Research on Word Processors Relevant to the Teaching of Composition." In *New Directions in Composition Research,* edited by Richard Beach and Lillian Bridwell, 381–95. New York: Guilford Press.

Cleveland, Harlan. 1985. "Educating for the Information Society." *Change* (July/August): 13–21.

Daiute, Collette A. 1983. "The Computer as Stylus and Audience." *College Composition and Communication* 34: 134–45.

Rodrigues, Dawn, and Raymond J. Rodrigues. 1986. *Teaching Writing with a Word Processor, Grades 7–13.* Urbana, Ill.: National Council of Teachers of English.

Tucker, Marc S. 1985. "Computers in the Schools: Has the 'Revolution' Passed or Is It Yet to Come?" Paper presented to the Association of American Publishers, Ryetown, N.Y. (Available from Carnegie Forum on Education and the Economy, Suite 301, 1001 Connecticut Ave., NW, Washington, DC 20036.)

12 Faculty Development for Computer Literacy at the University of Wisconsin–Milwaukee

Eleanor Berry, Cedar Grove, Wisconsin

William Van Pelt, University of Wisconsin–Milwaukee

Neil A. Trilling, University of Wisconsin–Milwaukee

Introduction: The Need for Faculty Computer Literacy

With the advent of powerful, relatively inexpensive microcomputers, many English departments are beginning to teach writing in well-equipped microcomputer labs. *The English Microlab Registry* for spring 1986 reported over one hundred colleges and universities equipped with microcomputers for teaching writing and composition (Barker 1986, 2). According to Thomas T. Barker, who compiled the registry, most schools are moving away from "drop-in" writing labs to formal classroom instruction with microcomputers, yet few English departments have formal training programs for developing faculty computer literacy. "Training" in computers frequently takes place in a non-programmatic, ad hoc, one-on-one situation. Valuable administrative support, budgetary resources, and existing faculty expertise remain underdeveloped and untapped.

This chapter describes the three courses developed at the University of Wisconsin–Milwaukee (UWM) to avoid such waste:

1. An English department noncredit instructor-training course, for those instructors—mostly lecturers and teaching assistants—teaching writing courses in the English microcomputer classroom
2. An English department graduate-credit course on computers and writing, open to all graduate students in English
3. A Computing Services Division campuswide faculty computer-literacy program, available only to tenured faculty (including deans and other high-level administrators)

This chapter recounts how the English department and Computing Services Division programs arose, evolved, and interacted. Finally, it evaluates the success of our efforts and provides advice to English departments and administrators developing their own computer-literacy programs.

Background: How Our Program Took Shape

In early 1984, a small group of new faculty, lecturers, and teaching assistants in the English department pressed for an experimental computer classroom to support the teaching of writing, and the department presented a five-year plan for incorporating computers into the English curriculum to the College of Letters and Science administration. At about the same time, the campus approved an academic computing plan calling for an annual investment in instructional microcomputer labs. As a result, the UWM vice-chancellor's office allocated approximately $80,000 to establish a twenty-one-station microcomputer classroom operated by the Computing Services Division for the English department. The department could hardly have attracted such a sum through the normal budget process. Equipment for the lab currently consists of twenty-one IBM-compatible microcomputers, six printers, five speech synthesizers, and word-processing, text-analysis, and programming software. The English department teaches fifteen to twenty courses a semester in the lab, including remedial through advanced composition, business and technical writing, and creative writing.

Faced with the immediate need of training instructors to be effective teachers in a microcomputer environment, the English department developed an initial training course in the summer of 1984. The English department training, which has evolved considerably over the last three years, attempts to help instructors develop the confidence, technical know-how, and teaching strategies for incorporating computers into the existing writing curriculum by presenting the computer as a writing instrument, a pedagogical tool, and a research tool.

An instructor was paid for teaching the initial training course as if it were a regular four-week summer course. For the next two years, the College of Letters and Science funded released time (presently two courses per semester) for a lecturer to coordinate microcomputer classroom use for the English department, including instructor training. In addition, in 1986–87 the English department offered a graduate course on computers and writing.

The English department's computer-literacy effort has also relied heavily on technical support and advice from the Computing Services Division (CSD). CSD advised the department on initial lab purchases; CSD personnel continue to install new equipment and help with daily administration of the lab.

In June 1985, CSD implemented a campuswide faculty computer-literacy program. This general program supports the English department training effort. Every six months, CSD loans twenty selected faculty a complete microcomputing environment—microcomputer, printer, modem, software, documentation, and talented consultants—in their own offices. Out of the twenty faculty selected from the campus at large, two English department faculty have been included in the CSD program every semester.

The Faculty Development Program

Initial English Department Training Course and Modifications

The training course for instructors in the English department has been directed primarily at the lecturers and teaching assistants who do most of the teaching in our large composition program. In their writing courses, our English instructors teach their own students how to use the computer and word processor; the rationale here is that a writing instructor is the appropriate person to have control over the presentation of a writing technology. First, however, the writing instructors must themselves be trained in our instructor-training course. This training course does not purport to teach the nature of the computer nor to present anything like the full range of its possible applications in the humanities, even in English. Its goal is simply to present the computer to writing instructors as a writing instrument and a pedagogical tool, and to encourage participants to develop strategies for, and facility in, using it in these two capacities. In its original version, the instructor-training course emphasized the possibilities of the word processor as a composing—not just an editing—tool.

Our first training course for instructors took place in the time between the arrival of the equipment for the English department microcomputer classroom/laboratory in July 1984 and the beginning of the fall semester that August. In that course, twenty instructors were trained to write and teach writing with computers. Participants (mostly lecturers or teaching assistants) signed up on a first-come, first-served basis for a training course combining hands-on experience with discussions of articles and research on writing and teaching writing with computers. For this initial training course, most of the computers were temporarily installed in the offices of participating instructors. A few of the computers, with printers, were temporarily installed in a large, unoccupied office, where the hands-on sessions were held.

For each of the four weeks of the course, participants met once for a hands-on session and once for a session devoted to discussing readings. Between meetings, they were expected to practice using the computers for their own writing (with the training-course instructor available for consultation) and to read the assigned articles (see the selected, updated reading list at the end of the chapter).

Conducting hands-on sessions in cramped quarters with four or five people per machine was less than ideal. It was impossible, for example, for everyone to try freewriting with a word processor. And while it was ostensibly easy for participants with machines in their own offices to practice, a computer in every trainee's office did not guarantee that every individual worked and played with the machine enough to get comfortable and creative with it. The trainees varied widely in how fully they exploited the opportunity of using a computer in the privacy of their own offices.

The sessions devoted to discussion of readings stimulated instructors to consider not only how to incorporate the computer in their teaching of writing, but also how they might improve all aspects of their writing courses. With computers, these instructors came to realize, students could do more in-class writing than they had ever been able to do with pen and paper; thus, the microcomputer classroom would become a new kind of writing environment. The discussion sessions helped prepare instructors for the new opportunities and new risks they would face in the computer classroom: students would develop collegial relationships with each other and with their instructors more easily than in a traditional classroom; instructors would learn more about their students' writing processes than they had ever been able to do when most assignments were written out of class; and teachers would be able to intervene in those processes at more points than ever before.

At the end of this initial training course, a number of the participants collaborated in preparing a manual for students on how to write with *WordPerfect* on a Zenith Z-150 microcomputer; the manual was designed to help teach writing, not just computer operation. It presented word-processor operations in such an order that student writers would quickly learn how to compose, edit, and print text and then more gradually acquire the tools of sophisticated revising and formatting.

And rather than simply giving the sequences of keystrokes for particular word-processor operations, the manual discussed when and why a writer might want to use each operation.

Growing Pains: Developing a Modified Training Course

The 1984–85 academic year was no sooner under way than the English department program for using computers in writing instruction had entered a new phase, and the problem of training instructors had also changed. Because some instructors had attended our summer course and others had not, instructors now had varying degrees of experience writing with computers and varying degrees of readiness to adapt their instructional roles to teaching in the computer classroom. Hence, the second training course had to be designed with a modular structure: a structure that allowed instructors to participate in both, one, or neither of the two hands-on sessions and in all, none, or only the more advanced of the discussion sessions.

By 1985–86 a further problem had arisen: instructors had to be introduced to newly acquired software and hardware. In this second year of its operation, the UWM English department computer classroom/laboratory was enhanced with the addition of an alternative word processor *(Volkswriter)* for use in lower-level courses, an outline processor *(ThinkTank)*, and speech synthesizers. In response to this, we had participants in the two training courses work with *Volkswriter* instead of *WordPerfect;* some of the other instructors experienced in using *WordPerfect* decided to join the new trainees for the hands-on sessions with *Volkswriter*. The final hands-on session, devoted to going "Beyond Word Processing," was intended to introduce trainees to the speech synthesizers, *ThinkTank,* and our text feedback software, *Punctuation and Style.*

The modified training course, offered during each semester of the 1985–86 academic year, met once a week for seven weeks, first for three three-hour hands-on sessions, then for four two-hour discussion sessions.

The hands-on sessions, now much more structured than in the original summer training course, required the trainees to write—with computers—about their attitudes toward computers, about practical matters they were learning (such as how to care for disks), and about strategies for using computers in writing. Their writings reflected a wide range of expectations and apprehensions about computer use for writing. One participant with considerable previous computer experience in programming as well as in writing with a word processor wrote:

> I wanted to take this course primarily to learn how to teach others how to write using computers, but I also . . . wanted to see how you made use of everyday language to simplify computer instructions. . . . I'm so excited about what computer writing offers any writer, that I want to get on with it. . . .

At the other end of the spectrum was a poet who had never touched a computer:

> I am terrified of computers. First, I do not have a scientific mind. Second, I panic when I come within a few feet of a machine. One reason computers frighten me is they're so much more clever than I am. . . . For example, I've heard that computers have whimsical properties, magically shutting themselves down just when the operator is onto something impressive.

Nonetheless, they all proved able to articulate these attitudes through writing with the computers; this accomplishment in itself was a valuable learning experience for many of them, and what they wrote was a valuable aid to their teacher in shaping the training to the participants' needs. During the hands-on sessions, participants gave and received peer feedback as they worked with printouts and with text on the screen—just the kinds of things they would be asking their students to do.

From the first full year of computer use in undergraduate writing instruction at UWM, it had become evident that helping individual writers discover how they could best incorporate the computer into their own writing process would be more fruitful than insisting on the value of the computer for all phases of any writing project. So in the 1985–86 training courses, the emphasis on the word processor as a composing tool was replaced by an approach stressing how widely writers could vary in the computer uses they found congenial and productive. In the initial training course, instructors had been strongly advised to require their students to do all their writing—raw writing, notes, and rough drafts as well as revisions—on the computer. Now, in the modified training course, they were advised to develop assignments that forced their students to learn, first, how to use the computer for a variety of writing tasks and, later, how to choose between the computer and traditional tools to suit their individual inclinations and the needs of specific writing projects.

From the first year of courses in the English computer classroom, it had also become apparent that users, both teachers and students, needed a basic conceptual and practical understanding of the disk operating system (in our case, MS DOS) to be successful in using applications software independently. So in the 1985–86 training courses, instruction in the use of the word processor and other applications programs was supplemented by instruction in the function of the operating system and the use of its most frequently useful commands. Course participants got practice moving in and out of applications programs and using resident and transient DOS utilities. The instructor explained the DOS conventions (for file names, "wild card" characters, etc.) that must be followed both to give commands to DOS directly and also within a word-processing or other program running under DOS. To help trainees see that DOS was "always already" there when they were using the word processor, the instructor showed them the batch file set up to load the word processor automatically.

For the 1985–86 training courses, the readings were slightly modified and expanded. They now covered the following areas:

1. Instructional uses of computers in writing classes at other institutions
2. Research on word processors and the writing process
3. Other writing-related software and its uses
4. Humanists' uses of computers beyond the writing classroom
5. UWM student papers, written with computers, about writing with computers

Thus, when it came to adapting course syllabuses to include students' using (and learning to use) computers for writing, instructors who had taken our training course could benefit from other writing teachers' reports of their experiences in computer classrooms. Further, through analyzing existing research on computers and writing, participants in our training course for instructors not only gained a sense of whether, when, and how students' writing could change when they used computers (and hence, what sort of instructional intervention might be most appropriate and when), but also developed a sense of what kinds of questions needed to be asked in this field and what kinds of research strategies and designs might answer them.

Formalizing the Training Effort

By the third year of our program, we recognized the need to formalize the computer-training effort as part of the English department's regular academic plan for staffing, new instructor orientation, and curriculum development. We wanted to encourage pedagogical innovation and to appeal to a broad spectrum of individual needs within the department. To achieve these ends, we made the following changes:

1. We standardized our training materials.
2. We increased the frequency of our staff meetings for English department instructors teaching in the computer classroom.
3. We encouraged new trainees to exchange information with experienced instructors.
4. We developed model syllabuses and exercises for courses using the computer classroom.
5. We integrated graduate student and faculty research into the modified training program.

To help standardize our training materials, we streamlined the instructional manual for the microcomputer classroom by reducing its bulk and giving it a more accessible modular format. Instead of a longer, comprehensive document on the computer as a writing tool, we combined a brief tutorial, reference guide, and quick reference summary into a multipurpose training manual focused on only the most basic computer tasks needed for the writing process. The modular format made the manual easier to use as a tutorial guide during the three hands-on sessions of the instructor-training course and easier for instructors to incorporate into their course syllabuses as a three-step lesson plan for students. The shorter manual also worked well as a self-paced introduction for individual faculty members who preferred to learn on their own.

Deleting sections in the manual that dealt specifically with writing instruction, however, required compensation. Although the streamlined manual helped reduce training time, we realized that microcomputer syllabuses had to be more carefully planned around teaching in the lab. During the first year of writing instruction in the lab, we had compared the progress of experimental sections (microcomputer sections) with control sections (sections of the same course not using the microcomputer). We had learned that computer sections usually fell about two weeks behind control sections in covering the same course material simply because more class time was required for learning the computer and for conducting writing exercises on the computer. So we are now collecting and refining our instructors' computer exercises to build a library of usable exercises and to develop model syllabuses for each course taught in the lab.

We have also begun inviting new trainees to the staff meetings of English computer-classroom instructors. This approach allows trainees to discuss their classroom expectations and strategies with more experienced computer instructors. The exchange between new trainees and experienced instructors works well, and we have increased the frequency of staff meetings to accommodate the amount of ad hoc training and retraining that now takes place in these meetings.

One of the most valuable training experiences, however, now occurs outside of our instructor-training course when instructors discover how to incorporate the computer into their own writing process and then transfer that discovery into effective teaching strategies in the microcomputer classroom. This transfer reveals a crucial link between pedagogical uses of the computer and the computer's value as a tool for scholarly writing. Not surprisingly, many of our graduate students who teach in the microcomputer classroom are also writing their dissertations in the lab. All of our full-time faculty who teach in the lab used microcomputers in their scholarly writing first. Thus, the next logical step in formalizing our training program was to reinforce the link between using computers in academic scholarship (including writing, research, and experimental studies) and classroom teaching by offering a graduate course on computers and writing. The graduate course does not replace the noncredit instructor-training course: teachers using the computer classroom for the first time still need the practical experience of hands-on training offered in the noncredit training course. The graduate course, however, builds on and augments the noncredit training course by examining the impact of computer technology on current theories of writing, pedagogy, and composition research.

This graduate course on computers and writing has a twofold goal: to introduce students to methods of scholarly research and to provide a theoretical framework for evaluating the impact of computers on traditional research and pedagogical practices. The course begins with a reading list similar to that for our noncredit training course (see the selected reading list at the end of the chapter), but it broadens the scope of that list by adding selections on rhetorical theory, the history of composition research, and the methodologies of academic research in general. The course asks graduate scholars to examine assumptions about writing, pedagogy, and computer technology and to consider how these assumptions have shaped current research. Given this critical and theoretical framework, graduate students design their own research projects. They begin with a literature review on a topic of interest to them; then they write their own formal proposal for a larger research project based on their findings. The final proposal may involve an experimental, ethnographic, or holistic study of how computers influence student writing; a design for instructional software; or even a more polemical, theoretical response to published results in the field of computers and writing instruction. If graduate students later decide to carry out their proposed research, either as an independent study or as a dissertation project, the department's microcomputer lab may provide valuable primary research material. Although this graduate research seminar can never replace the noncredit instructor-training course, it can help teaching assistants evaluate and improve their pedagogical uses of computer technology.

Over the past three years, computer literacy among our teaching assistants and lecturers has grown rapidly. Out of ninety graduate students and lecturers currently teaching in the English department, about thirty have completed the noncredit training course and are qualified to teach in the lab. Fifteen graduate students are currently enrolled in the credit course on computers and writing. Computer literacy among regular faculty (tenured and tenure-track) has taken a different route: out of a department of forty faculty, only four have taught in the lab, three of whom request courses in the lab on a regular basis. These figures are not surprising if we consider that the lab is used largely for writing courses, which are taught by relatively few of our tenured and tenure-track faculty. Consequently, our regular faculty's main interest in computer literacy emerges from scholarly and administrative needs first; their interest in pedagogical applications may come later.

Twelve out of forty regular faculty have purchased their own microcomputers and trained themselves for the purpose of writing articles and books. Ten more have received training through the department's noncredit training course, one-on-one instruction, or the Computing Services Division computer-literacy program (described in the next section). Of the remaining eighteen regular faculty, most seem interested in computer literacy, but cannot commit time to the noncredit training course, are shy of the technology, or simply need to be prompted by a more concrete sense of the computer's usefulness to them as professors of English. If we could focus our training more directly on research applications (mainly writing scholarly papers, but also generating bibliographies, indexing, and database searches), we might draw more faculty into our training effort. What hinders our effort most here is the lack of equipment specifically dedicated to faculty research: the current instructional lab is too crowded with classes and students to serve faculty needs well, and the department cannot afford to buy microcomputers for individual faculty. Fortunately, our university's campuswide CSD computer-literacy program helps bridge this gap in the English department's resources.

The Computing Services Division Faculty Computer-Literacy Program

The CSD Faculty Computer-Literacy Program, implemented in June 1985, is directed toward senior faculty in all departments, whether they would use computers for instruction, for research, or for improving personal productivity. It focuses on the needs of the computer-phobic, or at least computer-anxious, faculty member, as opposed to those faculty who have already come to grips with computers and want to enhance their computing knowledge. The objectives of the program are to provide faculty with sufficient computing experience to enable them to evaluate the use of computers in their instructional and research activities and to expose faculty to computing tools that could enhance their personal productivity.

After introductory training (presently four three-hour sessions), the program loans twenty selected faculty a complete microcomputing environment in their own offices for a six-month period. So far, eight English faculty have participated in the program. Participants take part in an initial orientation, devote five hours per week to using computer tools, and respond to questionnaires, surveys, interviews, and follow-up studies designed to evaluate the success of the program. CSD established the following guidelines to ensure the program's success:

1. Providing participants with sufficient microcomputing resources
2. Providing a nonthreatening learning environment
3. Minimizing the use of technical terminology
4. Promoting a hands-on instructional environment
5. Having participants work on "real" projects, not "toy" exercises, during the learning process
6. Establishing the computer as the participants' personal tool, always available, and not something shared with colleagues
7. Using electronic mail for individualized consulting

By following these guidelines, we hoped to make it easy for faculty to learn to use the computer for their work, rather than taking time away from their work to learn computer operation.

Conclusion

Evaluation of the English Department's Instructor-Training Program

The most obvious strength of our noncredit training course for instructors in the UWM English department is its hands-on, practical focus on the microcomputer as a writing tool and on teaching strategies that maximize the advantages of the computer classroom as a new kind of learning environment. Instructors have discovered new ways of approaching their students' writing processes, including intervening constructively in student work-in-progress, holding conferences at the microcomputer with the student's text immediately visible and revisable on the computer screen, and using the lab as a healthy workshop environment for peer consulting and collaborative exchange.

A survey of instructors teaching in the English computer classroom in spring 1985, asking how they and their students used the facility, elicited responses that showed the value of the instructor-training course and the ongoing staff meetings. Typical of the responses to the question, "What use of the computer equipment for teaching has been most successful for you?" were the following:

> Individual conferences, showing the fluidity of writing by moving, editing, and re-thinking writing on the student's machine.
>
> Being able to show students possible revisions on the computer AS they are writing . . . [moving] to blank lines and working on alternative sentences with them, for example.
>
> One to one personal contact at the student's terminal.

Instructors also described innovative adaptations of assignments to the computer-writing environment. One instructor, who was teaching a basic writing course, described the following experience:

> . . . one night the class learned the prewriting strategy of cubing when I passed out a stick of gum to each of the students and then had them (1) describe it, (2) compare it, (3) associate it, (4) analyze it, (5) apply it, and (6) argue for or against it. Many students seemed amazed at the amount of text they generated [on the computer] about such a simple item.

This exercise helped the students learn to use the computer to generate ideas and compose text; here the computer induced fluency, a primary goal in our basic writing course.

Another instructor described how her intermediate composition class used the computer in a series of assignments. For example, her "In-Class Worksheet for Science Articles" assignment asked students to extract two or three poorly written paragraphs "from a particularly obtuse science article" they found on their own in a journal and to enter them on the computer. Then students used our manual's instructions for running the paragraphs through the text feedback program, *Punctuation and Style.* Finally, they rewrote the paragraphs, using the help of the computer and their own judgment. This assignment forced students to learn how to use the computer as an aid for revision; other assignments forced them to use it as an aid in other aspects of the writing process, such as planning, prewriting, or composing. For the final assignment in this intermediate composition class, students had to decide for themselves how and when to use the computer for the various writing tasks involved in producing their papers. This assignment forced them to learn how to adapt the computer to their individual writing needs and how to combine it with such traditional tools as paper and pen.

The problems instructors have encountered with computers reflect the variation among students in how they are inclined to use the computer in their writing and the need for ongoing exchange between experienced computer instructors and new trainees. One instructor in freshman composition complained:

> I was amazed at how many students were simply using the machine as a typewriter. Some were extremely cautious because of their inability to type; others were very set in their ways as writers, having very set composition patterns. I had to force them to brainstorm by requiring a printout of each day's work. However, those more set in their ways seemed to like to use the computer for creating an outline and filling it in.

In general, we have learned that integrating instruction in computer operation with instruction in writing requires both experience and experimentation to help students discover what word-processor functions are truly suitable for them in what writing tasks. Our training for writing instructors continues to evolve, informed by the successes of experienced microcomputer instructors and the innovations of new graduate students, lecturers, and faculty.

Evaluation of the CSD Faculty Computer-Literacy Program

Just as the English department's training effort for instructors has enjoyed success, the separate campuswide faculty-development program of the UWM Computing Services Division has also achieved positive results. CSD's evaluation of the Computer-Literacy Program's success stems from empirical data and observation. We see several areas of achievement, some intended, some not.

Primary areas of success include the following:

1. A high proportion of the participants purchased microcomputers. Some even purchased two: one for the office and one for home.
2. Several faculty began using electronic mail to communicate with colleagues, students, and our consulting staff.
3. We now see a growing interest in information services and national networks. The free flow of information is attractive to university faculty.

Secondary areas of success include the program's influence on academic administrators. In the first group of twenty faculty, we deliberately included seven deans or associate deans. For the most part, these participants became enthusiastic proponents of academic computing, resulting in the following benefits:

1. Deans set the tone in many campus divisions by matching their new enthusiasm for computers with funding for divisional computing programs. As their personal knowledge of computer applications grows, the deans empathize more with campus computer initiatives and respond more readily to faculty requests for increased computer support.
2. The deans' experience in the program enabled them to identify faculty who would derive the most benefit from it.
3. Some deans strongly encouraged faculty on their administrative teams to participate in the loan program, building a base for divisional communication and the effective use of electronic mail.

We see a critical mass developing that should constitute a strong political base on our campus in the near future. At some point, this base may change instructional computing by making software development a potential criterion for tenure evaluation. Furthermore, because the program has catered to computer-anxious faculty, there has been a significant computing growth in disciplines, like English, not traditionally associated with computing.

We are hard-pressed to find negative results from the program. Five to ten percent of the participants did report that the technology was not useful to them in their work or that they could not devote the time necessary to make their participation more positive. Although this may indicate a failure in the teaching process, it may also reflect the fact that for certain faculty, the computer is of limited value.

Advice to Other Instructors and Administrators

A recent survey of Modern Language Association members completed in the spring of 1985 indicates that more than half were writing with word processors (Doland 1985). Does this mean that English departments do not need to provide some kind of computer training for their instructors? We think not: on the contrary, instructors need guidance on how to use the computer effectively as an instructional tool. Both experienced and inexperienced instructors will benefit from a program that shows them how to incorporate the computer into their courses, profiting from the experience and research of those who have already implemented and tested successful classroom applications.

In the UWM English department instructor-training course, discussion of a wide range of theoretical and practical readings has proven at least as important as required writing with the computer, but participants need adequate time to do the reading and writing, and neither graduate students nor lecturers in composition typically have such time to devote to a noncredit course during the regular academic year. One solution to this difficulty is to conduct training during the summer, as we did initially. For teaching assistants, theory and research on computers and writing might better be introduced in a regular graduate course than in a special training course. In any case, to put the trainees under pressure to do sufficient writing with computers and sufficient associated reading, an instructor-training course should be quite formal.

Furthermore, as microcomputer facilities expand with new hardware, software, and pedagogical techniques, English departments cannot go on indefinitely expanding their training efforts; new instructors need time to absorb one software application before being overwhelmed by several new ones. Single-purpose workshops may provide the best means of training instructors to use new equipment and new techniques in computer-assisted instruction.

Besides solutions to the problems of adapting training to the instructors' varied degrees of preparation, of finding a way for teaching assistants and lecturers to fit adequate reading into their heavy schedules, and of teaching instructors to use upgrades and enhancements to computer facilities, ways must be found to involve the English department's regular faculty in computer-assisted instruction. Without tenured faculty involved in the development and administration of the program, computer instruction may not receive the resources and attention required for growth in a rapidly changing field.

To this end, we cannot overemphasize the need for and value of high-level administrative support for a faculty-development program. In addition to providing funding (a computer loan program is expensive), high-level administrators (the college deans, the English department chair) have various ways—released time, space allocations, schedule assignments, political influence—to create enthusiasm for a program. In leading by example, these administrators can make the difference between the success or failure of a faculty-development program.

But even with all the good will and individual effort imaginable, a program for developing computer literacy in a faculty will not succeed without a commitment of considerable resources. Hardware, software, and supplies are the beginning, but staff support is a continuing necessity. English departments have to "grow" their own technical expertise or look for it elsewhere. Wherever they find it, it will have a cost. Because faculty are both a critical and defensive audience, the choice of instructional staff can make or break a faculty development program. In addition to being technically knowledgeable, the training staff must be tactful, nonthreatening, patient, and enthusiastic. And they must plan the training carefully. Instructional staff, for instance, must be able to recognize when enough becomes too much. The rich functionality of word-processing software and the complexity of a disk operating system like MS DOS may tempt trainers to offer far too much detail before providing closure. It is a mistake to assume that because the participants are university faculty, they can absorb information and instructions on computer use more rapidly than other learners. Yet because faculty are typically very busy, they need to acquire learning quickly. The secret is to teach as *little* as possible. Everything taught must be of immediate use. Faculty should be in a hands-on situation where they can produce a tangible product as quickly as possible. With word processing, training staff should teach a minimum number of commands at first, so that some success is assured early, and then teach more advanced features individually, when the need arises and when there are questions.

However, even with high-level administrative support, adequate resources, and carefully chosen training staff, tenured faculty are not likely to develop an interest in computer-assisted English studies unless the concept of computer literacy for English departments extends beyond developing an individual's proficiency in using hardware and software. Computer literacy should also help individual faculty identify what the computer can or cannot do for their specific professional goals and how to adapt the computer to those goals. English departments should keep their notions of computer literacy broad enough to exploit the links between instructional, research, and administrative uses of the computer. And they should consider joining their efforts at developing computer literacy with those of other departments and services on campus. Even though most English faculty may never teach in a computer lab, as the researchers in a department develop their own uses of computers, they will take a new interest in the progress of instructional applications. Similarly, as department administrators learn to use the computer for administrative tasks, their newfound enthusiasm will lend political support and encouragement to their teaching staff's efforts in computer-assisted instruction.

Because the gains associated with computer literacy appear as instructional or research improvements, not as real dollars that can be banked or tapped, the cost-effectiveness of programs for training instructors and faculty cannot be gauged directly. We are convinced, however, that increases in instructional quality and faculty productivity will quickly amortize the costs of any such carefully planned programs.

Selected Readings

The following is a list of readings from the University of Wisconsin–Milwaukee English department's instructor-training course and graduate course in computers and writing:

Bean, John C. 1983. "Computerized Word-Processing as an Aid to Revision." *College Composition and Communication* 34: 146–48.

Berry, Eleanor. In press. "Writing in the Age of Electronic Text Production." In *Literacy in the Computer Age*, edited by Barton Thurber. Osprey, Fla.: Paradigm Press.

Brannon, Lil. 1985. "Toward a Theory of Composition." In *Perspectives on Research and Scholarship in Composition*, edited by Ben W. McClelland and Timothy R. Donovan, 6–25. New York: Modern Language Association.

Bridges, Charles W., ed. 1986. *Training the New Teacher of College Composition*. Urbana, Ill.: National Council of Teachers of English.

Bridwell, Lillian, Parker Johnson, and Stephen Brehe. In press. "Computers Composing: Case Studies of Experienced Writers." In *Writing in Real Time: Modelling Production Processes*, edited by Ann Matsuhashi. Norwood, N.J.: Ablex.

Bridwell, Lillian, Paula Reed Nancarrow, and Donald Ross. 1984. "The Writing Process and the Writing Machine: Current Research on Word Processors Relevant to the Teaching of Composition." In *New Directions in Composition Research*, edited by Richard Beach and Lillian Bridwell, 381–95. New York: Guilford Press.

Carlson, Patricia Ann. 1983. "Computers and the Composing Process: Some Observations and Speculations." In *Sixth International Conference on Computers and the Humanities*, edited by Sarah K. Burton and Douglas D. Short. Rockville, Md.: Computer Science Press.

Case, Donald. 1985. "Processing Professorial Words: Personal Computers and the Writing Habits of University Professors." *College Composition and Communication* 36: 317–22.

Catano, James V. 1985. "Computer-Based Writing: Navigating the Fluid Text." *College Composition and Communication* 36: 309–16.

Collier, Richard M. 1983. "The Word Processor and Revision Strategies." *College Composition and Communication* 34: 149–55.

Collins, James L., and Elizabeth A. Sommers, eds. 1985. *Writing On-Line: Using Computers in the Teaching of Writing*. Upper Montclair, N.J.: Boynton/Cook.

Daiute, Colette A. 1983. "The Computer as Stylus and Audience." *College Composition and Communication* 34: 134–45.

———. 1985. *Writing and Computers*. Reading, Mass.: Addison-Wesley.

Feldman, Paula R., and Buford Norman. 1987. *The Word-Worthy Computer*. New York: Random House.

Gere, Anne Ruggles. 1985. "Empirical Research in Composition." In *Perspectives on Research and Scholarship in Composition*, edited by Ben W. McClelland and Timothy R. Donovan, 110–24. New York: Modern Language Association.

Gerrard, Lisa, ed. 1987. *Writing at Century's End: Papers from the UCLA Conference*. New York: Random House.

Halpern, Jeanne W., and Sarah Liggett. 1984. "The New Systems Require New Composing Strategies." In *Computers and Composing*, 13–46. Carbondale, Ill.: Southern Illinois University Press.

Harris, Jeanette. 1985. "Student Writers and Word Processing: A Preliminary Evaluation." *College Composition and Communication* 36: 323–30.

Hawisher, Gail E. 1986. "Studies in Word Processing." *Computers and Composition: A Journal for Teachers of Writing* 4: 6–31.

Hilligoss, Susan. 1983. "The History of Composing Tools and the Future of Word Processing." In *Sixth International Conference on Computers and the Humanities*, edited by Sarah K. Burton and Douglas D. Short, 273–80. Rockville, Md.: Computer Science Press.

Marcus, Stephen. 1983. "Real-Time Gadgets with Feedback: Special Effects in Computer Assisted Instruction." *The Writing Instructor* (Summer) 156–64.

Marling, William. 1984. "Grading Essays with a Microcomputer." *College English* 46: 797–810.

Pufahl, John. 1984. "Response to Richard Collier." *College Composition and Communication* 35: 91–95.

Rodrigues, Dawn. 1985. "Computers and Basic Writers." *College Composition and Communication* 36: 336–39.

Rodrigues, Raymond J., and Dawn Wilson Rodrigues. 1984. "Computer-Based Invention: Its Place and Potential." *College Composition and Communication* 35: 78–87.

Schwartz, Helen J. 1984. "Teaching Writing with Computer Aids." *College English* 46: 239–47.

Schwartz, Mimi. 1982. "Computers and the Teaching of Writing." *Educational Technology* (November): 27–29.

Smith, Charles R., Kathleen E. Kiefer, and Patricia S. Gingerich. 1984. "Computers Come of Age in Writing Instruction." *Computers and the Humanities* 18: 215–24.

Southwell, Michael G. 1983. "Computer-Assisted Instruction in Composition at York College/CUNY: Grammar for Basic Writing Students." *The Writing Instructor* (Summer): 165–73.

Sudol, Ronald A. 1985. "Applied Word Processing: Notes on Authority, Responsibility, and Revision in a Workshop Model." *College Composition and Communication* 36: 331–35.

Thurber, Barton D. 1985. "Computers, Language, Narrative." Paper presented at the Seventh International Conference on Computers and the Humanities, Provo, Utah, June.

Van Pelt, William. In press. "Microcomputers and Writing Instruction: Research, Results, and Implications." In *Computers and the Humanities, 7,* edited by Randall L. Jones. Osprey, Fla.: Paradigm Press.

Wresch, William, ed. 1984. *The Computer in Composition Instruction: A Writer's Tool.* Urbana, Ill.: National Council of Teachers of English.

Young, Richard E. 1982. "Concepts of Art and the Teaching of Writing." In *The Rhetorical Tradition and Modern Writing,* edited by James J. Murphy, 130–41. New York: Modern Language Association.

Works Cited

Barker, Thomas T., comp. 1986. *The English Microlab Registry.* Vol. 2, no. 2 (Spring). Lubbock, Texas: Texas Tech University.

Doland, Virginia M. 1985. "Computer Utilization in the Profession of Literature: A Systems Theory Analysis of a Revolution." Paper presented at the Seventh International Conference on Computers and the Humanities, Provo, Utah, June.

Part II: Toward Model Programs—General Features and Specific Strands

13 Developing and Implementing Computer-Training Programs for English Teachers: A Game Plan

Dawn Rodrigues, Colorado State University

Background

When it comes to computers, many public schools and universities have put the cart before the horse. They have purchased computers before they have figured out how teachers and students will use them. And in many cases, they have purchased computers without developing training programs to help teachers prepare to teach with computers. Simply making computers available to teachers and students will not guarantee improvement of any kind. Without some kind of inservice training program, teachers and administrators may have no sense of what to do with the computers they purchase for their schools.

But what kind of training is appropriate? Gene Hall and Shirley Hord (1987) recommend a "game plan" approach to teacher training. According to this approach, leaders of training programs develop plans similar to the kinds of game plans often used in sports and in business. Game plans from the business world are known by such terms as "zero-based budgeting" and "management by objectives" and are developed after extensive research into a company's previously successful ways of operating. Game plans for the sports world are just as carefully developed. In order to lay out game plans in sports, researchers catalog "tendencies of coaches and players to do particular things under certain conditions" (Hall and Hord 1987, 185).

As teachers and teacher trainers struggling to find appropriate ways to introduce teachers of English and language arts to computers, we may want to consider a game plan of our own, developed by examining the successful experiences of previous computer training projects. Obviously each school and university needs to develop a computer project suited to its individual context, but some overall guidance based on the experiences of others may be useful. As Hall and Hord note, "With a plan in mind at the outset, however, it is much easier to adjust and adapt as the unexpected occurs and still maintain an overall perspective."

The Game-Plan Concept Applied to Computer-Training Projects for English Teachers

The contributors to the first part of this collection of essays have, indirectly, worked out a game plan for us. When they began their courses and training programs, they were not sure how to proceed. Yet as they proceeded, they came to many similar conclusions. From their collective experience, we can see some patterns: similar ways of integrating computers and language arts instruction, similar ways of responding to problems, and similar attitudes towards change. There is no need to reinvent the wheel. By heeding some of the lessons of the early program developers, a district or a department can begin developing a computer-training program even before the computers arrive.

After examining the training projects and courses described in Part I, seeking commonalities and key ingredients, I discovered that before most project leaders or teachers began their training programs or courses, they took time to assess the needs of the teachers. Specifically, whether a training program or course was designed for an individual school or college, or whether the training program or course was run by a central agency to serve teachers from diverse situations, the leaders first customized the training to the participants' needs by helping them:

1. examine the existing curriculum, preparing to revise it if feasible so that computers can be used to support a pedagogically and theoretically sound language arts or English program.
2. consider the contexts in which computers will be used (lab, classroom, classroom-lab combination, etc.).
3. consider the special needs of students in their schools, colleges, or universities.
4. consider their own backgrounds and needs (and the needs of other teachers in their schools, colleges, or departments).
5. determine the role of the computer by identifying how it will be most effective in their settings (considering the needs of the curriculum, the context in which computers will be used, the needs of students and teachers).

To implement the computer-training projects, leaders in many of the projects followed a similar process:

1. They established plans carefully and considerately (sometimes by writing grant proposals).
2. Even though they had few models to turn to, they assessed their individual training plans and computer projects by considering the experiences of others (often meeting with experienced teachers and project administrators).
3. They considered their plans to be tentative and thus implemented them confidently, expecting to make changes.
4. They planned from the outset to conduct ongoing research and evaluation of their efforts.

In this chapter, I would like to detail what a model game plan might look like, a game plan intended to help teachers and administrators develop computer-training programs that integrate writing-process theory with computer technology. These guidelines, based on the experiences of the training projects described in Part I and on my own experiences as a teacher trainer, should be useful to instructors planning computer courses and to teachers and administrators designing inservice sessions or workshops. With the confidence that what they are doing has worked for others, leaders of new training programs may be able to move forward with their own versions of general guidelines, adjusting them and revising them to meet their own needs.

Developing the Game Plan

1. Begin with the Curriculum

A computer-supported curriculum will only be sound if the curriculum is sound to begin with. Thus, before computers are incorporated into the classroom and before any training program is developed, it would be wise to examine the curriculum thoroughly.

The following list of questions should be considered by prospective participants in a training program:

> Do the participants' departments or districts have a curriculum or a syllabus that teachers are required to follow?
>
> Is the existing curriculum appropriate for the students and the teachers at their schools?

Do the teachers follow the curriculum?

Should the curriculum be revised?

What are teachers' goals for their students?

How is writing taught?

Do teachers have sufficient training in writing-process theories?

How is literature taught?

Do teachers know how to integrate composition and literature?

How is student achievement evaluated?

Do teachers need to be trained to evaluate writing?

If the curriculum needs to be revised, project leaders can follow W. Edward Bureau's lead and use the computer as a catalyst for change, revising the curriculum with computers in mind (see Chapter 8). Even if the curriculum does not need to be revised substantially, teachers may need some inservice training in writing-process methods before a full-scale computer project begins. But as several projects described in Part I reveal (see, for instance, Chapter 5 by Jane Zeni Flinn and Chris Madigan) it is possible—and even valuable—to introduce teachers to computers at the same time that they are learning writing-process theory and pedagogy.

With the curriculum established (or with a plan to revise it underway), training-program participants should be encouraged to answer such questions as these:

How can computers help me achieve my goals for each course I teach?

How can computers help the students in these courses?

What parts of the curriculum or the course syllabus lend themselves to computer support?

What parts of the curriculum or the course syllabus do not seem applicable to computer support?

Teachers will not be able to answer these questions too early in their training, but thinking about how they might want to use computers in their own teaching will help them answer more challenging questions later.

2. *Consider the Contexts*

Leaders of training programs should consider the contexts in which computers will be used: a classroom with ten computers in the back of the room, a computer lab which students visit in their free time, a computer classroom in which class sessions are conducted, or many other variations of these setups. Each context will demand a different pedagogy. Currently no one model seems inherently better than others. And even if research should show that computer labs are more effective than computer classrooms, schools and universities have to live within many constraints, such as the budget, space availability, numbers of students taking English courses, and teachers' preferences for one configuration instead of others.

What seems to matter is not that we prepare teachers to face the demands of any situation, but that we help them confidently face their individual situations. Of course, no training program will meet the needs of any one particular teacher in all of these teaching contexts; teaching and learning strategies will vary considerably from one kind of computer classroom to the next and from one kind of teaching style to the next. Teachers themselves will inevitably need to discover how to incorporate much of what they learn into their own classrooms. Still, training programs should attempt to provide teachers with some context-specific guidance. As Deborah H. Holdstein notes, "any successful English department effort in teacher training . . . stems from the context of that department" (Chapter 10).

At Southern Illinois University–Carbondale, Stephen A. Bernhardt and Bruce C. Appleby adapted their training program to the conditions imposed by their lab: "Our lab is large, so controlling the attention of a group of students is difficult" (Chapter 11). Their classes meet once in the lab and once in a regular classroom. Their teachers learned "they cannot move a class into a lab and teach as in a traditional class setting." At the University of Massachusetts at Amherst, the Computer Writing Center was developed because Paul LeBlanc and Charles Moran "realized that the new technology would complement the 'studio' approach to the teaching of writing" that they used in their writing program (Chapter 9). As a result, the teachers needed specialized training.

Decisions about hardware and software are likewise tied to the contexts of a given school or department. As Amy L. Heebner notes, consistency of equipment may be a factor in public schools, but in colleges, it may even be useful to expose students to a variety of computers (Chapter 4). Whereas elementary teachers, for example, may want to use Apple computers because more software is available for them, college teachers may not mind if their students use a variety of word-processing equipment and a variety of computers for their writing.

Another hardware consideration with implications for training is whether the computers that participants will be using can be "networked" (see Chapter 19). If students and teachers can send files or notes to one another, then more collaborative teaching and learning is possible than with stand-alone microcomputers. Because networking changes the dynamics of the classroom, special training sessions will probably be needed by teachers who are preparing to teach in networked labs.

3. Consider the Students

In order to plan a student-centered training program that meets the needs of a particular department or school, program leaders should consider the students' writing backgrounds. Ask prospective participants to answer such questions as:

> What writing experiences are the students likely to have had?
>
> Will the students already have developed fluency as writers?
>
> Will they be anxious about writing?
>
> What are students' individual needs as writers?
>
> Will all students be willing to write with a word processor?
>
> Will all students have equal access to computers at different times of the day?
>
> What kinds of supplementary software might be useful?

Before implementing a training program, project leaders should find out about students' varying experiences using computers. (Similarly, before teaching an inservice course, instructors should learn about the background and range of interests of the group.) Some students may have been using a word processor at home for many years. Students who have moved from other districts may be unfamiliar with the computer software and hardware available in their new districts. Some students may have taken "keyboarding" classes. Other students may never have touched a typewriter. Still others may have had negative experiences with computers in other courses and be reluctant to try again. A teacher-training program needs to address these variables so that teachers will have the opportunity to think about how to handle potential problems before they occur.

4. Consider the Teachers

Since teaching with computers is challenging yet potentially frustrating, teacher trainers need to pay considerable attention to the teachers and their teaching situations. Not all teachers are sufficiently experienced to handle the kinds of challenges computers bring to their teaching. Similarly, depending on how teaching is evaluated in their schools, not all teachers will be able to use the same techniques. Computer classrooms are noisy. Computer labs—and traditional classrooms—are more controlled. If a principal or teacher evaluator expects a tightly controlled classroom, only an experienced, secure teacher may be ready to handle the challenges involved in teaching in a computer classroom. Teachers in computer-intensive sections run the risk of getting lower evaluations than their colleagues. Program leaders can keep the following questions in mind as they reflect on teachers' situations:

Who evaluates the teachers?

How are they evaluated?

What is the evaluation instrument: a generic set of questions or a set of questions designed for English teachers?

What are the expectations of the evaluators?

How much teaching experience do the teachers have?

How much computer experience do the teachers have?

How much writing experience do the teachers have?

If teachers are new to writing-process theory and new to computers, they will need different training than if they have been teaching for many years and using a computer themselves. In order to be effective as they teach English with computers, teachers need to be computer writers themselves. They should not try to learn a word-processing program one day and begin teaching with computers the next.

5. *Determine the Role for the Computer*

With a particular department or school in mind—its curriculum, its computer context, its students, its teachers—project leaders should think about the role computers might have in English classes. Some uses of the computer are more time-intensive than others. For instance, if teachers in a department or district want students in English classes to have the opportunity to do all of their writing at the word processor, they may need to limit the use of the computer lab to students in writing classes (instead of making it available to students for writing assignments across the curriculum).

An alternative to having students use the computer for composing might be to require that some prewriting be done on paper to save time at the computer itself. A consideration to keep in mind with some software (such as style-analysis programs) is whether the results can be printed so that students can make revisions at their desks or at home rather than at the terminal (see Chapter 16).

Some computer programs may be more appropriate for some schools than others. Software that includes what is sometimes called a "management" feature—a capability of keeping records (for instance, the number of students who have completed a computer exercise along with the score they received) may be useful to large school districts in which students use computer labs when teachers are not present. The same program may be of no value whatsoever to a teacher in a small district or department.

Implementing the Game Plan

1. Establish the Training Program or Course Plans

After project leaders have thought through the above considerations, they need to flesh out plans for their workshops or courses. It is not possible to recommend one model syllabus or one model workshop that will suit everyone's needs. Training programs and courses must be designed by individual project leaders to meet the needs of local participants.

But once a program leader has become familiar with the needs and the constraints of the participants, the syllabus for the training program should start to fall into place. In most cases, it will include (but not be limited to) the following components, topics that are covered in detail in the remaining chapters of this book:

- Word processing
- Software selection and evaluation
  - prewriting programs
  - literature programs
  - style-analysis programs
  - other (e.g., database programs)
- Computer contexts
  - networking
  - computer classrooms
- Evaluation concerns
  - programmatic evaluation
  - teacher evaluation

If the workshop or training project includes teachers from diverse backgrounds, leaders can easily customize their syllabuses or their workshop designs to accommodate teachers' different situations. For instance, teachers who need to learn how to use a powerful word processor for their business writing classes can learn how to use *AppleWorks* while the elementary teachers learn how to use *Bank Street Writer*. Similarly, high school teachers in the class can work with different prewriting programs than the ones elementary teachers work with.

Another possible way of individualizing a training program would be to provide a common strand in the training for all participants and to include separate strands for participants who need to develop special skills for specific contexts. For instance, if the entire group is focusing on software selection, teachers who will be teaching in a computer classroom might be asked to visit several schools where computer classrooms are already in place; teachers who will need to learn how to teach in a networked classroom, similarly, could be asked to make some site visits and to read articles about networking.

If literature teachers are especially interested in using computers, a significant amount of the training might consist of evaluating literature software. If a school or a department has chosen to use only the word processor and no supplementary software, then several sessions might be devoted to training teachers to create their own teaching materials with the word processor. If some teachers express an interest in learning how to use database software in their classes, a special workshop on that topic would need to be included.

In all situations, teacher trainers should use hands-on experiences in the training sessions. They should use training strategies that will give the participants a sense of what it will be like to use computers in their own classes. Training programs can simulate or be based on actual conditions. Elizabeth A. Sommers and James L. Collins write: "While addressing theory, practices, and computer uses, we take the opportunity to model an integrative writing course" (Chapter 3). The small group learning that takes place in Heebner's computer-training classes simulates the small group work that leaders want teachers to use as they teach writing in their own classes (Chapter 4). By taking computers with them, teachers in David Humphreys's project learn word processing at their own pace as they use it for real writing tasks. According to Humphreys, "The teachers learn the fundamentals of word processing in much the same way that we recommend teaching these skills to the students: within the context of the writing process as they work on real writing tasks" (Chapter 1). Holdstein agrees: "Writing activities to help participants learn word-processing software [have] to involve 'real' documents they would want to or have to write anyway" (Chapter 10).

Finally, project leaders need to understand that training takes time and that follow-up workshops are necessary. As Heebner says: "Staff development programs need to be conceived in terms of years, rather than weeks or months" (Chapter 4). Flinn and Madigan speak of a "longer-term need for assistance in applying that training in actual school situations" (Chapter 5). Bureau writes, "Knowing that changes do not come quickly, we have planned our program to progress over several years, giving teachers adequate time to learn about computers and how to teach writing with them" (Chapter 8). Flinn and Madigan report that when school administrators contact them to do teacher training, they usually "are thinking of a brief introduction to word-processing software with a few techniques for teaching writing. Our first task is . . . to convince this audience that teachers really need a more thorough, more integrated experience" (Chapter 5). Bernhardt and Appleby report: "Those who choose to integrate computers into their composition programs should realize the tremendous commitment of time and energy involved. Getting a lab is a first step, followed by continual efforts to keep the program working and expanding" (Chapter 11).

2. *Assess the Training Program or Course*

Leaders of training programs and courses described in Part I had to develop their projects independently, without the benefit of others' experience. But future project leaders can use the experience of these innovators. They can see if their projects or courses meet the following criteria for successful computer-writing training efforts, based on the successful training programs listed in Part I of this text. They can reconsider any major discrepancies between these suggestions and their own emerging projects.

Teachers are at the center of the programs, helping conceptualize them, implement them, and shape their direction. Teachers thus develop ownership of the project and its goals. Eleanor Berry, William Van Pelt, and Neil A. Trilling explain what has happened at the University of Wisconsin–Milwaukee: "Our training for writing instructors continues to evolve, informed by the successes of experienced microcomputer instructors and the innovations of new graduate students, lecturers, and faculty" (Chapter 12). Teachers must remain at the center of computer-writing projects, for computers themselves will not improve writing, but good pedagogy can.

Successful projects are rooted in writing-process theory. In some projects, the teachers are presumed to know already writing-process pedagogy; in other projects, teachers study writing-process theory and pedagogy before they consider computer integration. In still other projects, teachers learn about the writing process as they learn about computer applications. LeBlanc and Moran explain why: "We know that it is important for the teacher to be able to use the program, yet we believe that the teacher's appropriate authority must come from the teacher's ability to teach writing, not his or her proficiency on the word processor (Chapter 9).

Successful projects focus on the integration of computers with effective writing theory and pedagogy. Sommers and Collins make the point most emphatically: "Computer skills . . . are not an appropriate focus of instruction for English and language arts teachers." Teachers need to keep "the focus on language skills and on using the computer as an instrument to enhance the learning of language, writing, and literature" (Chapter 3). After some experimenting, Flinn and Madigan report that they have "pulled together the computer strand and the writing-process strand of [their] training" (Chapter 5).

Leaders of successful projects recognize that instructional change requires support from administrators and others in charge. Referring to their attempts to integrate computers at the university level, Berry, Van Pelt, and Trilling write: "We cannot overemphasize the need for and value of high-level administrative support for a faculty-development program" (Chapter 12). Bernhardt and Appleby also value higher-level administrative support. They note that "assurances from the vice president that English would be entitled to a major portion of lab time" proved invaluable (Chapter 11). And Bureau suggests the kinds of support administrators can provide: "Providing concentrated time for growth and latitude for trying new techniques is a vital but intangible type of support. More tangibly, providing funds for hardware, software, and teacher workshops will have a direct impact on how much ownership teachers assume in the integration of computers into language arts teaching" (Chapter 8).

Successful training programs emphasize sharing and collaborating. Teachers can learn much from one another when different kinds of sharing and collaborating take place. In some training courses, collaboration takes place between high schools and colleges and between teachers and researchers. At Columbia University's Teachers College, sharing goes on amongst teacher trainers, school computer specialists, and

English teachers. Similarly, at Indiana University–Purdue University at Indianapolis, Barbara L. Cambridge and Ulla Connor report that "cooperation among public school teachers and university instructors brought mutual admiration [and] also increased productivity" (Chapter 6). LeBlanc and Moran have "simultaneously been workshop leaders and colleagues, teaching English 112 ourselves in the Computer Writing Center" (Chapter 9). Bureau, too, feels that sharing is essential: "To help each other succeed in teaching writing with computers and to guarantee project success, we also set aside time to maintain project continuity." Participants had an "Open Forum" segment in each of their regular meetings, a time when "teachers could address each other's concerns, questions, and needs" (Chapter 8).

Successful programs begin with word processing and emphasize word processing. Holdstein explains how she came to the conclusion that word processing should be presented first: "Day one was called 'An Introduction to Computers' and day two, 'Using Word-Processing Software.' Gradually we changed the plan, realizing that the writing curriculum had to be integrated from the start" (Chapter 10). Sommers and Collins write: "We concentrate on word-processing software because we believe this is the most useful software to date for writers" (Chapter 3). Humphreys says: "The most effective training program does not begin with bits and bytes . . . but with applications" (Chapter 1).

Successful programs help teachers learn how to integrate supplemental software into the curriculum. Most programs stress word processing, but recognize that teachers need to understand how supplemental writing software can be incorporated into their curricula. Bernhardt and Appleby explain their reservations about software: "We wanted the lab to focus on the computer as a tool for applications, not as a self-instruction center" (Chapter 11). Further, they feel that "most teachers have unrealistic expectations, expecting the machine to do the teaching and the software to use language in human ways." Humphreys agrees: "While the emphasis of the class is clearly on word processing and its application to the writing process, we feel it is important for teachers to spend some time evaluating the various kinds of software that have been produced commercially for use in the composition classroom" (Chapter 1).

Leaders of successful projects recognize the demands of the technology and the need for some technical support. Some knowledge of how computers work is essential—it helps teachers understand limitations and helps them set realistic expectations. But language arts teachers should not have to do it all themselves. Bernhardt and Appleby explain: "For faculty apprehensive about moving instruction into a new technological setting, having the technical and managerial services of Computing Affairs has been wonderful" (Chapter 11). If teachers need to do a lot themselves, then technical aspects of computers need to be built into the training. That is why Humphreys teaches how to set up and connect the Apple IIc machines that his students will take home with them. Cambridge and Connor report additional technical needs: "Although we had included in our original plan computer experts from both the school system and the university, we needed an instructional media specialist and a programmer" (Chapter 6).

Computer-training programs should include a research component. Different kinds of research complement one another. As Sommers and Collins note, "research on computer-assisted language instruction is so new that we really cannot claim unequivocally at this point that we know the best ways to integrate computers into the English language arts classroom" (Chapter 3). Some quantitative studies are needed. But in order to discover what strategies work best, qualitative research is vital: case studies of teachers teaching, ethnographies of classrooms, and protocols of student writers will reveal patterns of behavior and are part of many current projects (Bernhardt and Appleby, Flinn and Madigan, Heebner). Bernhardt and Appleby feel that "research creates a sense of community which stimulates a continuing dialogue about being effective teachers" (Chapter 11). Flinn and Madigan have action research as one of the components in their program. They observe what happens in the classrooms of experienced computer teachers and feel that what they learn each year "from this practical, ethnographic research becomes part of what we teach the next summer's teachers" (Chapter 5). Heebner uses videotapes to gather data, and she notes that "in viewing these videotapes, teachers learn how to structure classroom environments in which students write independently, both on and off the computer, and in which equipment resources are utilized fully" (Chapter 4). And research informs teaching. Teachers in Bureau's project learned how to do holistic evaluation at the same time that they were evaluating the students' preproject and postproject papers. As a result, they gained insights into their students' writing processes.

3. Maintain Flexibility

With a carefully conceived plan to guide them, program leaders are ready to begin their training programs. But they should not feel bound by their plans. They should adjust their training as necessary to fit the participants' backgrounds and needs.

They need to pace the training program or course appropriately, allowing time for teachers to learn and to reflect on their experiences. As Berry, Van Pelt, and Trilling remind us: "New instructors need time to absorb one software application before being overwhelmed by several new ones" (Chapter 12). Sandra Hooven feels that it may be good that teachers at her school have not yet used computers in the labs extensively, for those teachers in particular feel a need to learn more before they will know how to use computers effectively. As she says, "What can be best and most appropriately done by each teacher at each grade level is still being hotly debated in our department. We need . . . to decide . . . whether the broadest computer education might not go forth with two or three computers placed in each English classroom rather than a single lab" (Chapter 7).

It is essential that teachers do not see a course or a workshop as the only training they will need. Leaders should make it clear from the outset that training never stops. Teachers need to develop perspectives; they need to understand that they have to continue learning. To that end, Flinn and Madigan try to "encourage experimentation, help novices develop problem-solving strategies, and debug aloud" (Chapter 5). As Bernhardt and Appleby put it, "The teacher must become a problem solver" (Chapter 11).

Leaders should not get upset when problems arise. Problems are natural parts of the training process. For example, most teachers will have some difficulties adjusting to the special demands of a computer classroom. One teacher at the University of Massachusetts felt that her workload was "a lot better," but she missed the time for class discussion (Chapter 9). Some problems are unexpected. Bernhardt and Appleby report: "The biggest drawback was that it took us nearly two years and countless hours of committee work to plan and build the lab" (Chapter 11). Other problems are potentially longer range. Humphreys cautions teachers, observing that "the introduction of any new element into the curriculum . . . will inevitably raise a furor, especially among humanities scholars." He adds, "Power structures within the department must change to accommodate the new experts," threatening "the image that teachers have of themselves as competent, experienced teachers of others" (Chapter 1).

4. *Conduct an Ongoing Evaluation of the Training Program or Course*

On the basis of an evaluation, project leaders need to make whatever changes seem necessary (see Chapter 21 for specifics on evaluating teaching in computer-assisted writing classes). Honest evaluation is essential. If certain aspects of the project or the course are not working well, leaders should reconsider their training methods.

Training programs have to be modified and evaluated continually. Holdstein writes about changing her program as a result of what she learned in early workshops. So do Berry, Van Pelt, and Trilling. They note that by evaluating their first efforts, they began to do such things as increase the frequency of their staff meetings, encourage new trainees to exchange information with experienced instructors, develop model syllabuses, and begin integrating research. Flinn and Madigan write about how project evaluation caused them to reorient their training strategies. Initially, they were convinced that their "focus would be on writing, not on technology." Participants in their project met in the morning for writing-process instruction; in the afternoon, teachers took turns using the computer lab. In effect, Flinn and Madigan at first "divorced the writing workshop from the computers." After evaluating the results, they decided to integrate computers throughout their writing process training (Chapter 5). Similarly, Sommers and Collins plan to change their course when they next teach it. Originally, they selected the software they wanted teachers to examine. Now they feel that teachers should choose their own software, for "teachers need to learn to fend for themselves" (Chapter 3).

5. Share the Results of the Training

Even if a district or a department has no plan to do large-scale research, teachers should, nonetheless, develop a researcher's mindset. Along with program leaders, they can try to determine what changes have occurred as a result of implementing computers into their classes, and they can share the results with colleagues—on the national as well as on the local level.

Teachers should answer the following kinds of questions and share their findings with others:

Has technology changed the way they teach?

What general changes have they observed?

What specific teaching strategies have they discovered?

Have teachers' attitudes toward teaching changed?

What in their experiences is similar to the experiences of others? What is different?

Many teachers in the projects reported on in Part I have developed new and exciting strategies as a result of computers. Humphreys feels that "computers . . . change not only what we teach in the English classroom, but how we teach as well" (Chapter 1). Bureau considers computers to be "catalysts for change" (Chapter 8). According to Joan Dunfey, instructors at Lesley College hope that computers "can help transform ineffectual teaching methods by offering teachers a new and creative way to teach language skills" (Chapter 2). Berry, Van Pelt, and Trilling feel that computers bring with them new opportunities and new risks: "Students . . . develop collegial relationships with each other and with their instructors more easily . . . instructors . . . learn more about their students' writing processes, and teachers . . . intervene in those processes at more points" (Chapter 12).

Many authors in Part I also report that teachers' careers were transformed as a result of their involvement in a computer project. Bernhardt and Appleby state: "We know we have seen changes in the attitudes of our faculty, with greater collegiality and greater respect for composition as a discipline" (Chapter 11). Similarly, Humphreys writes: "Most important . . . is the teachers' observation that writing was again 'exciting to teach'" (Chapter 1).

Cambridge and Connor report that one of the benefits of their program was "teachers' perception of themselves as teachers" (Chapter 6). Bureau also observed positive effects on teachers' attitudes towards their career: "With the feelings of success they gained from our project, teachers are not only using the computer lab more for writing instruction, but are supporting colleagues uninvolved with the project as they begin to teach with computers" (Chapter 8). Dunfey has had similar success with the teacher-training program at Lesley College: "Many teachers find that the work they do using a computer is the most creative and energizing of their careers" (Chapter 2).

Conclusion

When computer-assisted instruction was first developed, educators everywhere predicted that computers would soon replace English teachers. Patrick Suppes, one of the leaders in programmed learning, argues that "with computer-based teaching devices . . . the student will study a sequence that is tailored to his individual needs" (Suppes 1966). Fortunately, between those days and today, researchers have learned much about how students produce writing. They have learned that, above all, writers need to develop fluency. Thus it is not surprising that today's teachers prefer word processing to canned programs.

Some teachers may, indeed, choose to supplement their computer-writing programs with programmed materials, but as the successful computer projects described in this book suggest, a computer-training project for English teachers should emphasize teaching writing, not using fancy software. Contrary to predictions of futurists in the sixties, English teachers will not be replaced by teaching machines. With careful training, teachers—not computers—will continue to guide their students' development as writers.

Works Cited

Hall, Gene E., and Shirley M. Hord. 1987. *Change in Schools: Facilitating the Process.* Albany, N.Y.: State University of New York Press.

Suppes, Patrick. 1966. "Plug-In Instruction," *Saturday Review,* July 23. Cited in Edmund J. Farrell, *English, Education, and the Electronic Revolution.* Champaign, Ill.: National Council of Teachers of English, 1967.

14 Creating Writing Activities with the Word Processor

Helen J. Schwartz, Indiana University at Indianapolis

Teachers can realize a number of advantages by creating writing activities involving word processing. As with computer-assisted instruction (CAI), word processing can support student learning by building on student strengths and responding to individual needs. And depending on the level of computer use available to teachers, both CAI and word processing can change the architecture and dynamics of the classroom. However, unlike most CAI, word processing can enable teachers to prepare easily modified materials that reflect each teacher's preferred methods of instruction and the students' actual classroom experiences (as opposed to textbook materials or CAI written by others, which might use terminology unfamiliar to the students). Most important, word processing supports writing instruction that helps students orchestrate the various skills involved in writing and do so with their own texts rather than with textbook examples.

Before illustrating these advantages, let us first distinguish between CAI and word processing. CAI is preprogrammed to provide structured learning, whether with a great deal of feedback (as in many drill programs) or with relatively little feedback (as with some prewriting programs). Although teachers can be creative in the ways they integrate CAI programs into their classes, such software can only be used for the tasks it has been designed to perform. However, a word-processing program is a utility that can be used for many different purposes: for writing the great American novel, for pornography, for letters to the editor, or for writing letters to Aunt Millie. Most word-processing programs allow such standard functions as adding, deleting, moving or copying text, searching for particular phrases or letters, and, possibly, replacing them. Work done with word processors creates "text files" that can be printed or revised or saved on disk (or some other storage medium). Because work can be created, modified, printed, and saved, the teacher can create writing activities with text files within the content-free context of word processing.

Writing activities for the word processor may lack some of the features and convenience of CAI, but the low cost and flexibility of word processing makes it an important source of teacher-created writing activities. Besides, many CAI programs now produce text files that can be loaded into the word processor, so the teacher's choice should not be *either/or* but *both/and*.

Writing Activities throughout the Writing Process

Whether dealing with generation of ideas, organization, or work on logic, structure, or mechanics, word-processing activities allow teachers to write exercises tailored to their teaching situation and enable students to concentrate on different writing skills using their own texts as content for the exercises.

Coming Up with Ideas

The electronic medium of word processing encourages playful risk taking. Teachers can design activities that let students explicate the "minimax" strategy of simulation: a minimum of risk in case of failure and a maximum of benefit in the case of success. Timed exercises limit the student's investment, with no messy or crumpled papers around to bear witness to failure. The capacity to save satisfactory work maximizes beneficial results. For example, the teacher can ask students to do some of the following activities:

1. *Jottings* produce a wealth of ideas. Saved jottings then form the basis for narrowing the topic, selecting relevant items, and organizing them in later activities.
2. *Freewriting* involves having students write nonstop for a timed interval to get ideas flowing and to build the students' investment in the topic.
3. *Invisible writing* helps students overcome writer's block. Students turn down the contrast on the monitor until text can be entered "invisibly"—that is, with no contrast between the blank screen and text. Because students cannot see what they have written, they must write quickly, without revision. After a short period (perhaps three to five minutes), they can bring back the contrast to see and edit their work.
4. *Heuristic questions* guide students in covering the topic systematically, whether the teacher uses a generic set of questions such as Aristotle's topics (including comparison and contrast, cause and

effect, or definition); Young, Becker, and Pike's tagmemic matrix (looking at an object in itself, as it changes through time, or as one thing in a field); Burke's dramatistic pentad (combining act, actor, agent, agency, and purpose); or visual synectics encouraging creative analogies. Questions can be typed in a special file that can be accessed by students. Student work can then be saved with a new name. This leaves the original heuristic blank, as it was when the student started, so that the heuristic can be used again, without retyping or revising. The filled-in version can form the basis of the student's work on an assignment, with useful ideas and phrasing moved to the draft created later in the file.

In all of these exercises, student work can be saved and printed or revised for inclusion in a draft or finished product.

Forming Ideas

Students can gain experience testing ideas by working collaboratively to critique ideas. Teachers can provide a number of appropriate activities using word processing:

1. *Models for critiques* can be provided when the teacher puts criteria and a sample essay and critique in a text file. All students can use the same text file, but they save their responses to the same essay separately under their own names.
2. *Peer review* can be added to student drafts when the reviewers type their comments in bold type or all caps or in a glossary item (depending on the capabilities of the word processor being used).
3. *Debate on disk* can be achieved by having timed "rounds" of argument (with students assigned to a pro or con position on an issue), followed by switching of computers for a timed period of rebuttal. If, for example, students are debating academic qualifications for extracurricular activities, Susan might be assigned to argue in favor of them, and Lee to argue against. After five minutes, with each at a different word processor, Susan and Lee could change places, with Susan now writing with the "caps lock" key down to insert rebuttals to Lee's arguments (and vice versa).
4. *Anti-papers* get students to test and discover ideas by adopting a "secret voice" (Schwartz 1985, 215–16). Knowing that the text can be scrapped or printed allows students to vent their true feelings

on a topic, with the possibility of integrating any new ideas uncovered.

Because the text on the computer screen seems so malleable, point and counterpoint seem gamelike. Besides, as Sudol (1985) has noted, the person whose hands are on the keyboard "owns" the text in the revision process. Teachers would do well to make sure the writer's hands are on the keyboard during conferences concerning drafts.

Organizing Ideas

Word processing can help students see the structure of their essays or the shape of their ideas either before or after the fact:

1. *Template outlines* provide a structure for ideas, with main ideas numbered with capital Roman numerals, subordinate points with capital letters, and so on. The student can work first with main ideas (replacing all the Roman numerals) or can develop one idea fully (working through I, A, 1, 2, 3, B, 1, 2, and so on). For example, the first entry read: "I. (Type a main point you might want to make here.)" The student who calls up such a template would then replace the parenthetical phrase with the first main idea for his or her paper, such as "I. Language doesn't change social behavior."
2. *De facto abstracts* show students the actual shape of their first drafts and encourage paragraph cohesion. The student scrolls through the essay, putting an asterisk in front of the controlling sentence in each paragraph (or providing a controlling sentence if necessary). Afterwards, the student saves the text under a new file name (for example, *emilyrev*) and then deletes all text except the starred sentences, leaving only a paragraph-by-paragraph description of the actual contents.
3. *Paragraph marking* of a sample text shows students the reality of the paragraph. Students can compare where they inserted paragraph markers to see what cohesion accomplishes and to discover the signs of paragraph boundaries.

Editing

Word processing seems to help students with some kinds of editing even though it may interfere with surface revisions. The word processor always allows students to see neat and legible text. Some students feel an increased detachment, an ability to read their work like a reader. However, as Linda Flower and her colleagues at Carnegie-Mellon University (Flower et al. 1986) discuss, students need ways to detect and diagnose writing problems before revision seems useful or becomes effective. Teachers can help students develop diagnostic skills with exercises like the de facto abstract described above, or by providing a self-assessment form for students to complete. For example, my students use a four-question self-evaluation form created by Lyn Hamilton (Schwartz 1985, 40). The file, named *self-eval,* is on each student's disk (or is available on a hard disk or on a master disk). Each time a draft is due, students fill out the form, save it under another name (for example, *self-eval3*), and print it out with their papers for use in peer-group work and submission to the instructor.

Polishing

Students can also use their own papers or those of peers for drill on grammar and correctness. Teachers can give directions, making them specific to the word-processing program being used. Here are several possibilities:

1. *Homonym checking* is possible through the "search-and-replace" command once the student's typical pattern of error is diagnosed. If the student typically misuses *there* for *their,* then the student should search for every use of *there,* check it in light of the rule, and replace it with *their* if necessary.
2. *Sentence diagnosis* involves inserting a break (either a carriage return or a page break) after every period. By reviewing the essay from back to front, the student can often identify sentence fragments when out of the contextual flow of an essay.
3. *Sentence variation* can be shown visually by setting the word processor for hanging indentation (as in the references or bibliography section of a paper) and by inserting a carriage return at the end of each sentence. This makes the length of sentences visible and highlights the way each sentence begins.

Throughout the writing process, therefore, teachers can help students use their own texts to work on separate skills needed to orchestrate a writing assignment. A text file with freewriting can be revised or cannibalized to create a draft, which can be checked for organization with a de facto abstract or critiqued with peer review. Errors in spelling or problems with sentence structure can be checked with the student's text as exercise sheet, instead of using a handbook (or these techniques can be used to supplement a handbook).

Teachers can also prepare materials more easily and individually with the computer and can use the medium of the computer to change the design and dynamics of the classroom. Student text files can easily be printed as classroom exercises, using either a whole paper or sections from several different papers as the basis for the activity. Student conferences around the computer allow instant revision, without jeopardizing the original (safely stored on the disk or in another file). My favorite bit of advice to people planning computer labs is to get plenty of one certain peripheral—extra chairs.

Training Teachers to Create Word-Processing Activities

Many teachers work comfortably writing lesson plans that utilize sections of textbooks, integrate different media into lessons, and create additional materials in the form of handouts, quizzes, and overhead transparencies. In a sense, computer use is only another medium to incorporate into lesson plans. However, only someone comfortable with word processing will feel at ease using computers and will see how to modify even some of the good ideas that can come from source books.

Therefore, the first important point in training teachers is for them to use word processing to write journals, letters, outlines, lesson plans—whatever they would normally write. They should feel comfortable with the standard features of a word processor and should know the special features of the program with which they will be working. As much as possible, this introduction and some practice should be achieved several months before a workshop, with at least a summer between the learning of word processing and its first use in a class.

In training sessions, I recommend introducing materials to teachers gradually, in the following order:

1. Discussion of the goals of writing instruction.
2. Listing of the problems teachers face in writing instruction.
3. Demonstration of activities that deal with typical writing problems (such as those described above).
4. Discussion of different situations for computer use (for example, a roomful of microcomputers to be used for one hour a week, or one microcomputer always in the classroom).
5. Creation of a template to set up a checklist that teachers can use for adapting demonstrated activities.

6. Creation of projects by participating teachers to create a lesson plan using word processing in support of a writing activity. Essentially, teachers fill in the checklist they created in step 5, starting with planning and peer critiquing; create the lesson plan, including any text files; and end by demonstrating their project to the group.

Conclusions: Changing the Classroom Dynamics

Textbooks provide material that is carefully prepared and edited, but unchanging and prepared from afar. Diversity comes from having too much material to use with any one class. In addition, teachers supplement textbooks with hastily prepared but relevant material, often responding to the individual needs in the class. The ease of creating and revising word-processed text files means that teachers can prepare and refine materials over time, but can also revise them to keep them responsive to current events and issues or modify them to fit the needs of individual students.

Furthermore, work prepared on disk can be printed out at the student's need or can be made available for all students to use, as in a collaborative assignment. In addition, assignments made in text files can provide virtually unlimited room for student response, unlike the fixed room for response on a handout. Finally, a teacher can prepare writing activities in text files that stage-manage a work unit, providing direction and guidance for individual and group work while the teacher provides short mini-lessons or, more typically, circulates among the students for short conferences.

Works Cited

Flower, Linda, John R. Hayes, Linda Carey, Karen Schriver, and James Stratman. 1986. "Detection, Diagnosis and the Strategies of Revision." *College Composition and Communication* 37(2): 165–55.

Schwartz, Helen J. 1985. *Interactive Writing*. New York: Holt, Rinehart and Winston.

Sudol, Ronald A. 1985. "Applied Word Processing: Notes on Authority, Responsibility, and Revision in a Workshop Model." *College Composition and Communication* 36: 331–35.

15 Incorporating Prewriting Software into the Writing Program

Michael Spitzer, New York Institute of Technology

Composition theorists and classroom teachers alike proclaim the virtues of prewriting, yet prewriting strategies are not frequently emphasized in the classroom (Rodrigues and Rodrigues 1984). For whatever reason, many teachers seem to leave students to their own devices when it comes to prewriting. This is true even though the prewriting stage is "the really hard part of the writing process" (Corbett 1977), and despite the fact that "to apply invention strategies independently, students need abundant practice and guidance—more than class time permits and more than many instructors choose to include" (Rodrigues and Rodrigues 1984). Perhaps invention software can provide the necessary practice without infringing on class time.

Often students can be as fearful of the blank screen as they are of the blank page. Computerized prewriting software can help students overcome this fear. It can help all students who need or want assistance as they develop ideas at the prewriting stage of the composing process. The computer's special characteristics make it a natural vehicle for presenting invention heuristics (question patterns that encourage students to investigate their subjects), and in retrospect the marriage between the computer and invention appears to have been inevitable. Of course, neither invention strategies nor computer software can teach creativity, but they can, as Richard E. Young (1978) indicates, "coax imagination and memory; the intuitive act is not absolutely beyond the writer's control; it can be nourished and encouraged." This chapter will focus on prewriting programs that help students generate ideas and that can therefore function as important tools in support of the word processor in a writing program.

Prewriting Software

Invention programs differ in purpose and approach from drill-and-practice grammar programs. Invention software presents students with a series of open-ended questions, questions for which there are no right or wrong answers. The software does not understand the student responses, although some programs, as Fred Kemp (1987) points out, do try to convey the illusion that they understand. For example, Hugh Burns (1982) cites the following exchange between his program, *Topoi*, and a student:

> *Program:* Now I need to find out what you are writing about. So would you please type in your subject. I am looking for one to three words.
> *Student:* Entropy in Maxwell's Demon
> *Program:* Holy electronics! That's weird. I used to date a computer interested in entropy in Maxwell's Demon.

Nor can invention programs evaluate the responses students make to the questions they are asked. Instead, the programs try to build on what students already know, and they try to stimulate students to see the relationships among those thoughts. They can also prompt students to think about how to organize their thoughts coherently and persuasively.

Carefully designed prewriting programs should be easy to use, and while they need not be entertaining, they should maintain the interest of students using them. The programs should also capitalize on the strengths of the computer: its patience, its ability to individualize, its capacity to manipulate data. More importantly, carefully designed programs should be improvements over paper-based invention strategies and should also be based on effective invention heuristics. These are demanding criteria, because our profession has produced no persuasive evidence that says that a given heuristic is valid or not.

Judging invention software will remain problematic until we can firmly say that specific heuristics are valid, or that some heuristics work better than others for some writers at certain times. In assessing and selecting computer aids to invention, then, we need to evaluate not only the software but also the heuristic on which the software is based. Some studies, such as the dissertations of Hugh Burns (1979) and James Strickland (1984), compare structured heuristics to unstructured invention strategies like freewriting. These studies do not conclusively establish the superiority of one or the other approach. Probably this is because no single heuristic can work for every writer; nor can one heuristic serve any individual writer for every writing task.

We will probably not have the best possible invention software until we know a lot more about invention. Nevertheless, some recent invention programs bring invention software beyond the capacity of paper-based heuristics: Helen J. Schwartz's *SEEN* and *ORGANIZE*, *Writer's Helper* by William Wresch, *HBJ Writer* (formerly *WANDAH*) by Ruth Von Blum, Michael Cohen, and Lisa Gerrard of the University of California at Los Angeles, *Access*, developed at the University of Minnesota, *Idealog* by Fred Kemp of the University of Texas, and *Invent*, a program I am developing. Each of these programs does things that cannot be readily duplicated on paper, and each begins to take advantage of the flexibility and individualization made possible by the computer. For example, *SEEN* provides a disk-based bulletin-board facility that allows students to comment upon one another's ideas, making invention a collaborative enterprise impossible to duplicate on paper. *Writer's Helper* offers a variety of invention strategies, from brainstorming to listing to "crazy contrasts," and a section that allows teachers to write their own questions. *ORGANIZE* offers students choices from among several different rhetorical perspectives. *Access* and *Invent* allow teachers to change sets of questions or to create entire sets of questions. Student responses to all these programs can be saved on disk and incorporated into word-processor files to serve as the basis for writing a first draft.

A description of *Invent* will illustrate the variety of invention strategies that can be accommodated by current prewriting software. *Invent* is not one program, but two. The first program allows the teacher to create or modify a script, the set of questions the program will present. For example, the following are several questions from a script intended to help students write an essay on national defense:

> How does the issue of national defense affect peoples' lives? Try to be specific here.
>
> Can you recall a personal experience—your own or that of someone you know—which you can relate to the issue of national defense?
>
> When they argue about national defense, some people say that our military is strong enough. Others say we need to increase our military strength. Which view do you share?
>
> 1. We need to increase our military strength.
> 2. Our military defense is strong enough.

By moving the cursor to the space before any of the questions, the teacher can select that question and then choose to revise, replace, or remove it. No programming knowledge of any kind is needed. By following the prompts and typing in the questions, the teacher can create scripts with up to a hundred questions. There is no limit to the number of scripts that can be created. Thus, it is possible to have scripts that are based on freewriting, listing, the *topoi,* the tagmemic matrix, creative problem solving, or any other heuristic.

The scripts could be specific to a particular writing assignment, as in the example given above, with questions geared to a particular topic, or the scripts could be rhetorically based, with sets of questions on audience analysis, for example, or definition or persuasion. Optional explanatory information and suggestions to students could be included at several points in the program.

The program also has a branching capacity, so that students using the same script might be asked different questions based on their responses to previous questions. For example, the last question from the script on national defense asks students to choose a position. Students who say that our military defense is strong enough will next be presented with a series of questions intended to help them support that view. Students who think we need to strengthen our military defense will be asked a different set of questions.

Numerous scripts can be on the same disk. When students sit down to use the program, they can specify which of the many scripts they want to use. They can experiment with a variety of different heuristics or can attempt the one they think would prove most relevant to their needs, given their knowledge of the subject and their relative readiness to begin composing. After completing the program, students can print out their sessions or save their output on disk. The disk files they create can then be loaded as text files into their word processors. In other words, students can use the output from the program as the basis for the first draft of their essays. Students can then revise their drafts and can later run them through a spelling checker.

Incorporating Prewriting Programs into the Curriculum

Once we learn more about invention and develop prewriting software that permits a range of valid invention heuristics, we must then begin to think about how to incorporate this kind of software into the curriculum. In an ideal learning environment, each student would have the opportunity to meet with an informed teacher to discuss the subject of the student's next paper. In conference, the two would review the student's knowledge of the subject, the intended audience for the paper, and the student's purpose in writing the paper. Many teachers find the time to have one or two of these individual discussions with each student. But how many teachers can meet with every student for a conference preceding every writing assignment?

An invention program can provide a meaningful and effective substitute for the student-teacher conference. In some ways, the software is an improvement. In a conference, the teacher is both a source of knowledge and an authority figure. In a study in which they analyzed students' recorded reactions to conferences with their teachers, John Daly and others (Daly et al. 1987) report that students perceive such conferences as evaluative. As a result, they become defensive, especially about comments on their ideas. They often leave such conferences with misinformation, at least partly because their defensiveness prevented them from hearing what the teacher actually said. Unlike the teacher, the computer program has no answers and is not judgmental. Helen Schwartz (1984) points out that students "soon realize they cannot get answers from the computer. They soon revel in the fact that they are doing the thinking, not the machine." If the software is effective, it may also help students internalize the question-asking process, so that over time students could learn to ask themselves the same kinds of questions without the help of the software.

Once we accept the fact that prewriting programs can be helpful, we must address their place in the writing curriculum. The most appropriate use of prewriting software will necessarily vary depending upon the configuration of the computer resources available. Do students meet in a computer-writing classroom, or do they go to a computer lab to do their work? Is there a computer for every student, or are only a few machines available for the class? Is the teacher present when the students compose?

Ideally, during whole-class writing activities, students would work individually at their own computers. They also would have access to computers at other times. Unfortunately, this ideal situation is not always possible. The creative teacher can compensate in many ways. Students can work together collaboratively, either on texts or on prewriting software. If there are only a few computers, the class can be divided into groups, and while some students engage in one activity, such as peer editing, others can work on a prewriting program in preparation for their next writing assignment.

Training Teachers to Use Prewriting Software

Just as prospective teachers must learn that prewriting activities are part of the writing process, so, too, they must learn that prewriting software is but one way of providing students with prewriting activities. Teachers who desire to use such software should familiarize themselves with a variety of programs. They should examine the heuristic on which the program is based, and the extent to which the software successfully adapts the heuristic to the computer. The best way to evaluate the software is to use it the way a student would, that is, by seeing how well it helps generate ideas for an essay. If the program provides a variety of heuristics or the capacity for teachers to create their own sets of questions, teachers need to think about the writing assignments their students will be given and then determine which heuristic, or group of heuristics, might work best with these assignments.

Before students use any prewriting software, the teacher should spend time explaining prewriting and its place in the writing process. Several prewriting activities, such as brainstorming, should be undertaken by students collaboratively, with the teacher's guidance. Depending upon the level of experience of the students, it might be a good idea to continue collaborative work, forming the material generated during the brainstorming session into a rough draft. Only after students have had some experience with prewriting activities should the teacher demonstrate prewriting software to them. Again, it is best to conduct such a demonstration with a group of students, perhaps an entire class, especially if all the students can observe the software in operation, either through the use of a large-screen monitor or one of the devices currently on the market that connect to a computer and can then be projected through an overhead projector. (Eastman Kodak is one of several companies marketing these devices.)

While demonstrating the software, the teacher should explain its features and point out how it can help students. If the program has any limitations (and they all do), these should be mentioned. In almost all programs, for example, if the student responds thoughtlessly, the program will be of little benefit. ("Garbage in, garbage out" is an especially appropriate bromide when it comes to using prewriting software.) If the program incorporates a variety of heuristics, the teacher should explain what each is intended to accomplish and how it can be helpful. Because it is difficult to predict which heuristic will be successful for a given student, the teacher should encourage students to experiment with several of them.

Conclusion

In a cautionary essay, Irvin Hashimoto (1985) suggests that exposure to one or two heuristic procedures will not automatically help students "discover interesting [and] abundant things to say about all subjects."

Heuristics, he warns, will neither help students change their perceptions, nor necessarily enable them to discover meaning or clarify thought. It is well to keep this caution in mind and to remember that not every invention strategy will work for every student, nor for any one student at all times.

The ideal invention software would provide students with an array of invention strategies on a single disk and would permit students to choose the appropriate heuristic for a particular writing situation. Students who used such software over a period of time would in effect be training themselves to select and use a variety of heuristics appropriate for particular writing tasks. Such students will be able to adopt meaningful prewriting strategies that should enable them to discover meaning and clarify thought.

If used properly, invention software can be a dynamic tool that encourages students to discover, arrange, and manipulate ideas and language in new ways and at all phases of the writing process. Because the computer reinforces the recursiveness of the writing process by permitting writers to move forward and backward through a text, to move easily from one stage to any other of the process, it makes the malleable nature of text a reality rather than a metaphor, and from invention to final product, it encourages writers to play until their texts are properly sculpted.

Works Cited

Burns, Hugh. 1979. "Stimulating Invention in English Composition through Computer-Assisted Instruction." Ph.D. diss., University of Texas.

———. 1982. "Computer-Assisted Prewriting Activities: Harmonics for Invention." In *Computers in Composition Instruction,* edited by Joseph Lawlor, Los Alamitos, Calif.: SWRL Educational Research and Development.

Corbett, Edward P. J. 1977. *The Little Rhetoric.* New York: Wiley.

Daly, John A., Anita L. Vangelisti, Heather Neel, and David Webber. 1987. "Protocol Analysis of Computer-Mediated Conversations." Paper presented at the annual meeting of the Conference on College Composition and Communication, Atlanta, Georgia, March.

Hashimoto, Irvin. 1985. "Structured Heuristic Procedures: Their Limitations." *College Composition and Communication* 36: 73–81.

Kemp, Fred. 1987. "The User-Friendly Fallacy." *College Composition and Communication* 38: 32–39.

Rodrigues, Raymond J., and Dawn Wilson Rodrigues. 1984. "Computer-Based Invention: Its Place and Potential." *College Composition and Communication* 35: 78–87.

Schwartz, Helen. 1984. "Teaching Writing with Computer Aids." *College English* 46: 239–47.

Strickland, James. 1984. "A Comparative Study of Systemic and Unsystemic Heuristic Strategies in Computer-Assisted Instruction and Traditional Instruction." Ph.D. diss., Indiana University of Pennsylvania. *DAI* 45, 2749A.

Young, Richard E. 1978. "Paradigms and Problems: Needed Research in Rhetorical Invention." In *Research on Composing: Points of Departure*, edited by Charles R. Cooper and Lee Odell, 29–47. Urbana, Ill.: National Council of Teachers of English.

16 Style-Analysis Programs: Teachers Using the Tools

Kate Kiefer, Colorado State University

Stephen Reid, Colorado State University

Charles R. Smith, Colorado State University

Nearly every year since the early 1980s, new, often expensive programs for style analysis have appeared in teachers' software catalogs. Although they are impressive at first glance, style analyzers must be used with good judgment if they are to be effective in teaching writing. Teachers must know the strengths and weaknesses of style analyzers, understand their proper and improper roles in the writing process, and provide for their integration and proper sequencing in the writing classroom.

Programs for Style Analysis

The oldest of the style analyzers is *Writer's Workbench* (WWB), developed by Bell Laboratories in the late 1970s. This program is now available in three different versions: a collegiate edition adapted specifically for student writers, an interactive version, and a noninteractive version; each requires a UNIX operating system. Included among its subprograms are some seven or eight for analyzing style. Based on word-class counts and other information derived from a part-of-speech analysis, WWB identifies passive constructions, forms of "to be," sentence types, sentence openers, and other elements descriptive of syntactic style. Teachers select model or target essays that represent attainable standards for their students. These essays are entered and run through a subprogram called *makestandard.* WWB then compares each student's essay with the standards according to several stylistic criteria, such as variety in sentence length, structure, and opening, or percentage of passives and nominalizations. Other WWB subprograms rely on special lists of words to identify and comment on wordy and inflated diction, sexist language, abstract words, vague words, and the like. Because WWB includes a part-of-speech analyzer, it requires more computer memory and speed than most microcomputers can provide, and so its use has been limited mainly to facilities with access to minicomputers or, more recently, micros with hard disks (such as the AT&T 3B2 series or IBM ATs with a UNIX operating system).

Many of the style analyzers are also available as microcomputer programs. The better known include *Grammatik, Homer* (later revised for *HBJ Writer), MacProof* (perhaps the most thorough of the style analyzers for micros), *Wordy, Right Writer,* and *Writer's Workshop* for younger children. Each of these programs offers information about such features as sentence length, passive constructions, nominalizations, and forms of "to be." Like WWB, these programs also rely on special word lists to identify vague and wordy diction. (See Figure 16.1 for comparisons of common style-analysis programs.)

Students' Assumptions about Style Analyzers

Students can misuse the best-designed, best-tested analyzers when they have mistaken assumptions about writing and revising. Nancy Sommers's research on revising (1980) shows dramatically that students do not think of revising in the same ways that experienced adult writers do. Most students simply edit superficial features of text: they change spelling, punctuation, diction. But by and large, students do not revise for global features—purpose, audience, structure, level of detail, and so on. All style-analysis programs—to the extent that they point to superficial features only—can reinforce this tendency among student writers. Diction checkers, frequently cited for this weakness (Dobrin 1986), and programs merely flagging vague words and "to be" verbs, for example, can create the false impression that improving one's writing consists only of improving its surface features. Moreover, some students use style analyzers to relieve them of all responsibility for editing papers for grammar or style. Thus, students who use style analyzers too soon in the writing and revising process can mistakenly assume that once they polish the surface of the text, nothing remains to be done. To be sure, this assumption creates difficulties for any writer with or without style analyzers, but teachers must note that these computer tools can contribute to this tendency. If teachers are aware of students' misconceptions, however, they can use style-

	Hardware	Cost	Sentence length	Sentence openers	Simple/ complex	"To Be"	Passive voice	Wordiness/ diction	Vague diction	Nominalizations	Readability
Writer's Workbench	UNIX operating system	$2000	X	X	X	X	X	X	X	X	X
Homer	Apple II and IIe	$100	X			X	X	X	X	X	
HBJ Writer	IBM-PC		X			X	X	X	X	X	
Right Writer	IBM-PC		X	X	X	X	X	X			X
MacProof	Macintosh		X	X	X	X	X	X	X	X	X
Wordy	Apple	$100				X		X	X		
Grammatik	TRS-80 IBM-PC	$79	X	X		X	X	X		X	X
Thelma Thistleblossom	IBM-PC	$90	X	X				X	X		X

Figure 16.1. Comparisons of features of style-analysis programs.

analysis programs effectively to help students with revising and editing.

Before Using Style Analyzers: Some Caveats for Teachers

As teachers integrate style analyzers into their writing classes, they may begin with unrealistic expectations. Teachers need to know what a style program can and cannot do, and how they should or should not use style analyzers in their classes.

1. Style analyzers cannot "grade" papers; nor should they replace teachers' evaluative comments on papers. The percentages of sentences in the passive voice, "to be" verbs, vague words, or nominalizations are not equal to grades, nor should they be assigned evaluative levels. Some teachers may be tempted to prescribe a percentage of vague words (say, below 5 percent) or sentences in the passive voice (below 10 percent) which is "passing" work. But determining value based on "acceptable" percentages of style elements ignores rhetorical considerations of purpose and audience and tends to reinforce students' narrow conceptions of editing.
2. Revising an essay based on advice from style analyzers may, if students fail to consider the rhetorical context, hurt an essay more than help it. While changing a vague word to a more precise word usually improves a text, changing the percentage of passive-voice or complex sentences may destroy coherence or style in the process.
3. Style analyzers often create the illusion for students that an "intelligence" is responding to their writing. While the artificial intelligence usefully mimics audience-response for students, the intelligence behind the computer is a teacher or programmer who has set the computer to count, match, and label certain configurations.
4. Style analyzers sometimes catch items that do not require change, and they do not identify constructions with 100 percent accuracy. Diction programs often flag words and phrases that, in context, should not be changed. Programs assessing variety in sentence openers are not more than 85 percent accurate. All passive-voice programs fail to distinguish between past participles and certain predicate adjectives. Style analyzers' inherent

inaccuracies require that teachers continually remind students that the programs merely "flag" items for possible revision.

5. Style analyzers do not necessarily shorten teachers' grading time. In studies at Colorado State University using WWB, only 30 percent of forty-three teachers surveyed in 1984 reported that WWB shortened their grading time, while 16 percent reported that the programs increased their grading time. Nearly half (47 percent) reported, however, that using style analyzers gave them more time for substantive comments on content, clarity, and development.

Used with care and good judgment, however, style analyzers can be most helpful.

1. Style analyzers provide immediate response for the writer, in that a student can get a screenful of suggestions within seconds of asking for analysis. Or the student can get a printout of suggestions within minutes of completing a revision and asking for style analysis.
2. Style analyzers respond objectively and predictably, in that they note the same misspelling or wordy phrases each time they appear in any piece of writing. Moreover, the advice does not change, and students can determine just what standards teachers are using in setting targets or models for editing.
3. Style analyzers give writers practice in responding to flagged items as possible areas for editing or revision. Students are repeatedly asked to attend to possible stylistic flaws in papers to judge which constructions are most appropriate in a given rhetorical context.

Moreover, as writers learn how to generate alternatives to highlighted items and how to revise according to their purpose and intended audience, they also learn how to respond to peer readers' suggestions.

Using Style Analyzers: Teachers' Decisions

Once aware that style analyzers are only aids to revision and evaluation, teachers then need to determine which parts of an analysis program to use. The temptation with any new technology is to use all of it—just because it is there—but only certain analyses are appropriate to specific courses or writing programs. Students in basic writing, for example, rarely use nominalizations (words ending in *-ion, -ance, -ment, -ence),* but students in advanced courses often do. Students writing primarily narrative prose, moreover, need different programs from those writing argumentive prose.

After teachers select features of a style analyzer to use, they must remember that style analyzers, like any other revision tool, should be used in a rhetorical context. The writer's purpose and the intended audience should provide the guidelines during the revision process. Just as teachers remind students to consider peers' advice carefully rather than making immediate or automatic changes in a text, so they need to teach students that style-analysis programs are merely advisory. Certain passive constructions—for instance, "Young children are manipulated by television advertising for sugary cereals and expensive toys"—may be preferable to equivalent active sentences in context. A vagueness program may "advise" a particular student that "2.9 percent of the words are vague, an appropriate score," but there may still be vague words in the text which should be revised. A "to be" program may caution: "Your percentage of 'to be' verbs (29 percent) suggests that your text might benefit from more sentence combining and from more careful selection of verbs denoting action." However reasonable the advice sounds, it is based on statistical probability, not on an item-by-item judgment. Writers cannot deal directly with statistics or percentages; they must consider each item by itself, in the context of the essay. Perhaps when teachers point out that readers are more likely to judge quality based on nonstylistic features, students will remember to trust their own judgment as readers and to put the style analyzer in its place as a mechanical aid to revision. Initial studies correlating features of style checkers with holistic evaluation suggest that essay length, spelling, word length, and sentence length correlate with holistic scorers' judgments of essay quality (Reid and Findlay 1986). Other features, however, such as number of "to be" verbs, percentage of passive voice, nominalizations, vague words, or complex sentences, do not correlate with holistic rankings. Holistic scorers, whether professional teachers or student peers, are apparently affected more by content and organization than these style features.

Finally, teachers need to recall that each style-analysis program bases its advice on different authorities. WWB, for instance, bases some standards on data from research, as, for instance, in the abstract program that relies on a dictionary of 314 words identified as abstract by subjects in psychological testing. Other WWB standards can be set by individual users, such as the percentage of vague words that triggers a list of all vague words in the text. Finally, WWB uses caveats from writing texts for still other standards—for example, start no more than 75 percent of sentences with the subject. Before using a style-analysis program, teachers must also determine if the standards are ones they feel comfortable setting forth to students. If not, the program must allow teachers to modify the standards.

In short, those programs that permit selection and change, those that offer options and flexibility, have important advantages over those that do not, especially when they will be used in large and varied programs with instructors having diverse interests and abilities.

Using Style Analyzers to Teach Writing

Teaching in the Classroom

After teachers have decided which style-analysis tools to use in their particular program or course, they should design a suitable sequence of computer analyses for their writing assignments. Even though students are curious about all the style aids, teachers should not use them all at the beginning of the course—just as they would not start off by assigning four chapters of a handbook. Ideally, style-analysis programs should be itemized or menu-driven, so the teacher or the student can ask for certain programs for certain kinds of writing, for papers of certain lengths, or at specific points in the course. If teachers can modify the printout to have only certain analyses appear, students can attend to analyses as teachers sequence them. If teachers cannot modify the printout, they should instruct students to ignore certain analyses.

Because teachers should establish peer-revision groups and strategies first and then gradually integrate the computer's feedback into the revising process, the following sample progression of style analyses is appropriate. As students move to the next writing assignment, more complex analysis is called for:

1. Word-processing functions only—work on composing process without any style analysis
2. Vague words
3. Vague words, diction and usage
4. Vague words, diction and usage, "to be," passive voice
5. Vague words, diction and usage, "to be," passive voice, nominalizations, sentence style

Since WWB has separate analyses for vague words and diction, we introduce the vagueness program first. More students have greater difficulty with overusing vague words than they do with errors in diction highlighted by WWB. Of course, depending on individual classes and style analyzers, teachers would select and sequence analyses differently.

A sample peer worksheet for writing assignment 5, which uses all the main style analyses offered by WWB, follows:

Read through the paper completely, noting the writer's purpose and intended audience.

1. As you reread the essay, comment first on content and organization. Considering the intended audience, where might the writer add more evidence or examples? Are the main points clear and in some logical order? How might the lead-in, the thesis statement, and the transitions between paragraphs be more effective for that audience? Ask if the writer has any lingering questions about sections of the paper that you found clear or well developed.
2. Now turn to the style analysis. Look at the vagueness index. If it exceeds 3 percent, go through one body paragraph that has a high number of vague words and suggest specific details or precise words or phrases for each vague word. Where possible, suggest several different versions.
3. Check (or calculate roughly) forms of "to be" and passive voice. If the passive voice exceeds 15 percent, suggest alternative revisions. If forms of "to be" exceed 25 percent, try sentence combining to reduce "to be" forms in a body paragraph containing a high number of "to be" verbs.
4. Check the number of nominalizations. If it exceeds 2 percent, choose one body paragraph and suggest alternative revisions.
5. On the style analysis, note the average sentence length. In one paragraph, try combining sentences to produce at least one sentence that is ten words longer than the average.
6. Consult with the writer about which of your suggested alternatives he or she finds appropriate for the purpose and audience of the paper.

Writer's name ______________________________

Editor's name and phone number ______________________

It is important that the computer's suggestions for revision be integrated with the other advice the student receives from teachers or peers working in collaborative groups. The collaborative groups compensate for the computer's inability to adjust for purpose and to react to intended audience, and they also help the writer generate alternatives to the original version. In a group context, the writer can consider what items the computer has flagged, what changes might be needed, and whether the changes would be effective. In addition, the computer's mode of merely flagging potential items provides a convenient form for peer response. The peer reader can flag items that do not "sound" right, and the group can then collaboratively offer the writer advice. Student writers thus receive flagged items both from peer readers and from computers, and they learn to treat them as alternatives. Such a system benefits peer readers as well—computer flagging provides an accepted, objective format for their responses, reducing the feeling that they are being unnecessarily picky, bossy, or subjective. Their explanations, however, unlike the computer responses, can address issues only human readers can attend to.

Selected Collaborative Revision Exercises

1. An effective way to integrate style analyses into the revision process is to run "before" and "after" versions of a single passage. Teachers can take a sample paragraph from a student essay or a sample exercise paragraph from the text, run it through a style-analysis program, and then have students work collaboratively to revise the paragraph based on the analyses and their own judgment. Then the students run an analysis on the revised version and compare, in groups, the resulting differences in the computer's analyses. Such comparative exercises allow students to discover, for example, that the vagueness percentage is changed both by adding details to an example as well as by merely changing a flagged vague word.
2. Students with high percentages of vague words choose one paragraph from the essay, circle vague words, and discuss adding specific detail. (Clearly, this exercise often turns into a good brainstorming session for writers working on detail.)
3. Students (in small groups or pairs) pick out five highlighted diction "errors" they do not understand and then discuss whether the computer flag is appropriate for the context. Students might also role-play as the intended audience when discussing clarity of diction and suggested changes.
4. Students having difficulty with passive voice choose one paragraph, identify the passive sentences, and then try multiple revisions with sentence combining, rewriting specific sentences, and so on.
5. Students in small groups or pairs run a "to be" program on a sample paragraph. After revising the paragraph, groups compare the different ways they combined sentences, changed nouns and adjectives to verbs, and varied sentence structure.

Conferencing

Conferences allow student writers to ask additional questions about the computer's responses, to experiment with alternative versions of words, phrases, or sentences, and to weigh their effect on the paper as a whole. If students request conferences on papers or if teachers are able to build conference time into the writing schedule, style-analysis printouts can help focus students' attention on specific revisions.

For example, the following paragraph is taken from the original draft of a paper written by a student in an advanced composition course at Colorado State University:

> The plasma membrane keeps the cytoplasm inside the cell. The cytoplasm consists mostly of water, seventy-five to ninety percent. Proteins, carbohydrates and lipids compose the other part of the cytoplasm. The cytoplasm has five activities. First, most chemical reactions in the cell occur in the cytoplasm. It also receives substances from outside sources and converts them into viable energy sources for the cell. The cytoplasm also synthesizes new materials for the cell. The cytoplasm can take these materials and package them for transport to other parts of the cell. Finally the cytoplasm eliminates wastes from the cell. The cytoplasm occupies a large area of the cell and is easily identified when seen. The cytoplasm also holds all the organelles except the nucleus.

The student went through a peer-review workshop and then asked for a teacher conference. She knew she had a serious problem with the paper, but even the peer review had not given her enough information to help her revise effectively. The teacher and student first looked for revisions that the style analysis could not address, such as audience and purpose. The student was writing an analogy paper—comparing a cell to a city—for high school biology students and felt that the general plan of the paper was sound. When the teacher and student looked at the arrangement of parts of the paper, though, both agreed that paragraphs needed to be reorganized or, in one instance, deleted.

The teacher and student then turned to the style-analysis printout. Even though the student was writing for a high school audience, she had seriously oversimplified sentences. The sentence structure was short, choppy, and, in places, incoherent. The style analysis confirmed what both the teacher and student felt from reading the paper—too many short, simple sentences. The printout showed that 70 percent of the sentences were simple, 30 percent repeated forms of "to be," 20 percent were shorter than thirteen words, and 80 percent began with the subject. Although the writer wanted to accommodate readers who might not be familiar with technical information, she had broken apart too many sentences and removed too many of the logical connectors between ideas. Thus sentence cohesion suffered in the draft. With suggestions from peers, the teacher, and the style-analysis program, this student was able to revise successfully to meet her own intentions and her readers' needs. The revised paragraph follows:

> The city must have a basic layout, and the cytoplasm fulfills this function in the cell. The cytoplasm contains the organelles. Most of the chemical reactions in the cell take place in the cytoplasm. The cytoplasm also receives substances from outside the cell and converts them into viable energy sources for the cell. Also functioning as the receiving site, the cytoplasm packages materials and transports them to other parts of the cell. Thus, the cytoplasm has many functions including transport, synthesis, packaging, and receiving.

While a style analyzer may not always suggest useful revisions, students are often reassured that their intuitions—that "something is wrong with the way this paper sounds"—are reasonable and that they can revise to strengthen their writing.

Commenting on Final Papers

On final drafts, teachers can collect style-analysis printouts with the final copy of the paper. Having commented on the paper as a whole, many teachers find that the style analysis confirms or reinforces a point they have made about the paper. Often a teacher commenting on lack of specific detail will note later that a vagueness program identified 10 percent vague words. Simply circling that percentage on the printout and pointing out that vague words substitute ineffectively for detail will remind students to revise for specific language in a subsequent paper.

In commenting on papers, teachers we have polled find that at the editing stage, basic writers benefit from programs that flag vague and wordy diction. More experienced writers benefit from programs focusing on sentence variety. Thus style analyzers extend the learning process from one paper to the next by showing students what features of style they have improved and how they can continue to strengthen their revision skills.

Teaching Teachers: Suggestions for Inservice Programs

For teachers unfamiliar with style analyzers, the following sequence of activities might be followed to introduce teachers to the concepts covered above. The inservice program might be as short as one day or as long as a week.

I. Teachers Use the Programs
   A. Teachers compose or transcribe their own texts, written for a specified audience and purpose, into a word-processing program.
   B. Teachers conduct a peer review of their writing to get suggestions for rhetorical revision for audience, content, and style.
   C. Teachers run a style-analysis program and, if possible, get a printout. Workshop leaders describe each program with transparencies and remind participants of the advantages and pitfalls of each analysis.
   D. Teachers pair up to compare the peer reviews with the style analysis, focusing on appropriate and inappropriate suggestions from the style program.

II. Teachers Focus on Student Writing
   A. Based on perceived strengths and weaknesses of the style analyzer, teachers collaborate on selecting programs, sequencing them for effectiveness, and planning student exercises and workshops. Different groups might concentrate on different sets of skills; for example, revising for specific detail, revising for sentence variety, or revising for audience (tone, clarity).
   B. Time for final questions and discussion. Teachers work toward consensus on which analyses should be introduced early and which should come later in the the writing instruction sequence.

Conclusion

Teachers prepared to incorporate style analyzers, such as *Writer's Workbench*, *Grammatik*, *HBJ Writer*, *MacProof*, and *Right Writer*, into their writing courses can find them valuable aids in teaching revising and editing. Integrated carefully with peer revising, conferencing, and workshop activities, style analyzers can assist students with revising and editing processes. In context, style analyzers provide an additional response and prompt for possible changes; with proper guidance and clear rhetorical contexts, many writers can learn to choose wisely from these programs as they revise and improve their writing.

Works Cited

Dobrin, David. 1986. "Style Analyzers Once More." *Computers and Composition* 3 (August): 22–31.

Reid, Stephen, and Gilbert Findlay. 1986. "Writer's Workbench Analysis of Holistically Scored Essays." *Computers and Composition* 3 (March): 6–32.

Sommers, Nancy. 1980. "Revision Strategies of Student Writers and Experienced Adult Writers." *College Composition and Communication* 31: 378–88.

17 Using Computers in the Literature Class

Frank Madden, Westchester Community College

Background

Computers have been used in connection with literary study for over twenty-five years. As early as May 1965, the *Newsletter* of the American Council of Learned Societies reported nearly seventy cases of research in progress using computer technology to analyze language and literature. Literary scholars doing attribution and influence studies, comparisons of variant texts, and thematic analyses were employing computerized word counts and content analysis, machine-constructed concordances, and parsing of sentences to support their research.

Literary critics often gather evidence by looking for patterns, classifying them, and discovering connections. Using computers to seek and sort out elements of text has enabled scholars to gather data with remarkable speed and reliability, to reorder this information however they wished, and to store it for future access.

Recently, however, in an experiment which employed the computer in an undergraduate literature course, Elgin Mellown (1986) obtained mixed results when he asked students to analyze novels with a concordance program, an alphabetical listing of all the words in a text, showing the contextual occurrence of each. Students were asked to trace natural phenomena and occurrences of colors in *Jacob's Room*, references to drinking in *Dubliners*, and the association of good and evil with white and black in *The Heart of Darkness*. Mellown concluded that the largest obstacle in this classroom application was "offering specialized research techniques about difficult literary works to students who, for the most part, had only a general preparation for literary studies. They could take the computer part of the course without batting an eye—but not Virginia Woolf and James Joyce."

And so, while sophisticated programs of this nature continue to benefit the specialized research of professors and graduate students, they seem of dubious value to the halting inquiry of students unsure of the place, if any, that literature has in their lives.

Of what value are computers in the literature classroom? The emergence and popularity of the personal computer as a teaching tool has created new and exciting possibilities, and the computer's most valuable literary function may now lie in its potential to help inexperienced students understand, appreciate, and write about literature.

Students and Literature

For many students, the study of literature is an intimidating impersonal experience. Unlike most of us who teach literature and who learned to appreciate it first in a personal way, many students feel no personal attachment to it. They read for the information in a work of fiction in the same way they read for information in a science text. They confine themselves to seeking a single "correct" interpretation matching that of the instructor, instead of exploring the many supportable possibilities arising from their own experience with the work.

Computers alone will not change this, but when used in conjunction with carefully chosen software and by a teacher who is aware of the need to involve students personally with the literature they study, computers can provide valuable support.

Teachers and Computers

For many teachers, using computers in a literature class is not a simple adjustment. Often, because they have little experience with computers, they must overcome prejudices and misconceptions about what these machines can and cannot do, and they must slowly discover how to use them. Having been cast as experts in literature, they may find the role of novice a trying one.

Very few assumptions should be made, therefore, when training teachers to use computers. During a demonstration of a literature program in a workshop for my department, for instance, a colleague cried out in amazement, "How did it know my name and the name of the novel?" Well, of course, it did not *know* anything. It simply stored her earlier responses to an inquiry about her name and the name of the novel by coding them, and then it presented them back to her as part of a subsequent question. Explaining what computers "do not know" may be the most important step in the orientation process. Debunking myths many teachers have about computers might convince them, contrary to their fears, that they, not the computer, are in control.

The most effective workshops and orientation sessions "patiently" allow participants hands-on experience, with space and time for "screwing up" and "achieving" modest triumphs. For example, teachers might learn a great deal in a session in which they are given the space, time, and guidance to create sample literature lesson files by using their own lecture notes and questions applied to short stories, novels, or poems covered in their classes.

Word Processing

For teachers desiring a personal touch but wary of the commitment which programming requires, literature lesson files may provide a relatively easy alternative. Lesson files are simply text files containing questions or prompts which have been typed with a word-processing program and saved on a data disk for subsequent student use (see Helen J. Schwartz, Chapter 14).

If teachers leave instructions on carefully designed screens, students may write their responses and, by pressing appropriate command or function keys, work their way back and forth through prompts and questions. "Throughout the lesson, they can be told to refer back to their previous ideas, notes and drafts, thereby reinforcing the notion of writing as a recursive process" (Rodrigues 1986).

For example, lesson files might begin with questions and prompts which emphasize a student's initial, personal response to a work customized for each work of literature. (See Sample Screens 1 and 2.)

Sample Screen 1

****

1. How we respond to characters in fiction is often influenced by our identification with them.

Sometimes, we identify with characters because we see aspects of our own personalities in them.

At other times, we identify with characters because we admire aspects of their personalities and wish we had them ourselves.

PRESS THE OPEN APPLE AND DOWN ARROW KEY TO GO ON

****

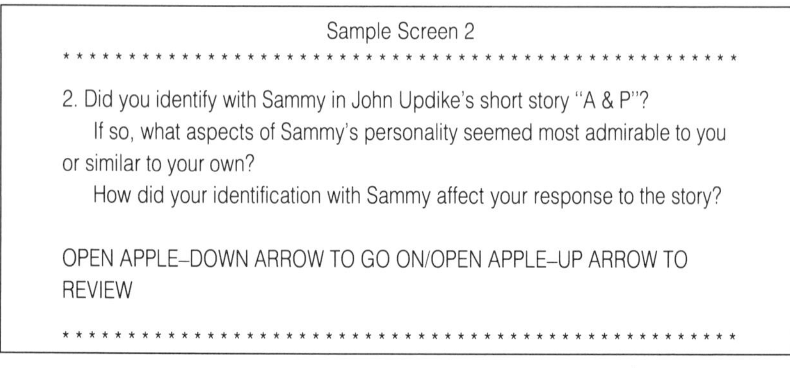

Sample Screen 2

* *

2. Did you identify with Sammy in John Updike's short story "A & P"?

If so, what aspects of Sammy's personality seemed most admirable to you or similar to your own?

How did your identification with Sammy affect your response to the story?

OPEN APPLE–DOWN ARROW TO GO ON/OPEN APPLE–UP ARROW TO REVIEW

* *

After students examine personal responses of this kind, subsequent explanations and questions might encourage them to return to the text, where they are likely "to observe rather than to participate" and to "move toward the discovery of a coherent pattern of meaning" (Flynn 1983). (See Sample Screen 3.)

Sample Screen 3

* *

When characterization is most convincing, we are not told about the characters directly. We observe them and learn about them indirectly through their thoughts and actions. This type of characterization is called "development through implication" or "indirect presentation."

Which of Sammy's "thoughts and actions" in "A & P" are most important to his development as a character?

OPEN APPLE–DOWN ARROW TO GO ON/OPEN APPLE–UP ARROW TO REVIEW

* *

Subsequent questions might ask students to examine and compare their earlier personal "participating" responses with their later detached "observing" ones. The process of using a lesson file this way "reflects a reenvisioning of the text, and often students discover a new focus. The result . . . reveals growth, expansion, metamorphosis" (Flynn 1983).

By pressing a command or function key, students might have access to helpful definitions and examples of literary concepts placed at the beginning or end of the file. While lesson files do not offer the interactive features of programs, they do offer ease of authorship for teachers and the numerous advantages of word processing for students. And sound advice and suggestions are available (see Rodrigues and Rodrigues 1986).

Choosing Software

Software development has progressed a great deal since its early days when electronic drill-and-practice workbooks passed for computer-assisted instruction (CAI). Programs now are faster, friendlier, more interactive, and often designed by or in consultation with experienced teachers.

Nonetheless, while all of the programs mentioned in this section support the ways teachers actually teach literature, not all these programs are on the cutting edge of pedagogical or mechanical innovation. We are still in the early stages of discovering how to use the computer's unique capabilities, and the development of educational software has followed a pattern consistent with the history of technology. "The earliest steel buildings followed the architecture of wood and stone. The first automobiles were modeled on the horse-drawn carriage" (Costanzo 1988). So too, many of these programs are modeled on traditional classroom practices.

Given our knowledge of how students learn and what computers can do, the following criteria represent a high but reachable standard. Teachers should require literature programs to meet these criteria:

1. *They are easy to operate.* For some students, using computers can be a frightening experience. Confusion about how to run a program will only increase the anxiety they already feel about responding to literature. The best programs provide easy access to "help" menus and "forgive" minor keyboard errors.
2. *They encourage personal response and reflection.* An overwhelming amount of evidence indicates that each person's initial response to a work of literature is unique, that this personal response is the most basic part of the literary experience, and that it underlies all criticism (see Purves and Beach 1972). Thoughtfully examining this response may improve students' capacity to respond adequately and to find personal meaning in the literary experience (Rosenblatt 1976).
3. *They require writing.* Writing is thinking and learning.
4. *They allow students to revise their responses.* Invention is recursive

and occurs in many different stages of the writing process, prewriting through proofreading (Sommers 1980). By the time students reread earlier responses, their views may be informed or altered by later discoveries in the literature or subsequent thinking. Allowing them to revise these responses enables students to clarify and express their views in light of their fully developed intentions.

5. *They emphasize process before product.* The best tutorial programs are temporary crutches which help students learn to walk on their own. If literary concepts are clearly explained for them, explanations are reinforced as they apply them, and support is provided as they sort out and organize their responses to one work of literature, students may learn, through the process, to respond adequately to other works—with or without the program. And by learning such a process, they may come to understand that the quality of an assertion lies not in itself but in the nature of its supporting commentary.

   For example, prior to having students identify the theme of a story, a program can provide students with a clear definition. As it works with a sample story, it can give them a model for the process of finding the theme. And finally, it can have students identify the details of their own stories, deduce conclusions, and verify their conclusions against these details. Only then can it ask students to make the leap to generalization and theme. That is, it can take them step by step through the process. Ideally, this "knowledge by experience" can be applied to other stories and without reliance on the computer program.

6. *They are consistent with the philosophy and objectives stressed in the classroom.* Students must be able to recognize the program as a natural extension of the course, a complementary tool in a larger process which includes class discussion and individual conferences. Demonstrating and discussing the program in class prior to sending students to use it in a lab may solidify this connection and may answer many practical questions.

7. *They allow students to print a hard copy of their work or save their work as a text file for transfer to a word-processing program.* Being able to walk away with something in print gives students a product upon which they may reflect at their own convenience. Being able to save their work as a text file is not only a convenience and

safeguard, but it enables students to refashion their responses to literature into a polished essay, with all the attendant benefits of that process.

Programs and Approaches

Comprehensive Packages

Literature software is now available which guides students all the way from initial response to finished essay. In one program, *Macmillan Literature and Composition Software* (Macmillan 1987), students begin by reading the text of a poem or short story on the screen or by choosing one they have read on their own. The program then brings them through three stages: prewriting, writing, and revising. In the *prewriting* stage, they are encouraged to brainstorm, invent, answer questions, and support and revise hypotheses. For instance, if students choose to analyze a poem, they will be asked to freewrite continuously for three minutes and to explore specific questions about the speaker, sound effects, imagery, and figures of speech. (See Sample Screen 4.)

Sample Screen 4

* *

Prewriting   Writing   Revising

Answer the following questions.

3. IMAGERY:
What do the images make me see, hear, smell, taste, or touch? What do these images add to the meaning?

A–N to review
Type your answer.   A–? for help

* *

When students move into the *writing* section, they write their essays on a full-function word processor built into the program. Here they may call up definitions of literary concepts or their earlier ideas in a scrolling text window at the bottom of the screen, thus encouraging and supporting invention and revision. (See Sample Screen 5.)

Sample Screen 5

****

Edit   Format   [Notes]   Help   Disk   Print   Quit

Browning uses several poetic devices to pull the reader into the mood of "Meeting at Night." I feel as if all my senses have been involved. The images are especially clear.

> IMAGERY:
> I "see" the light of the moon shining off the ringlets and "hear" the oars make the ringlets in the still water and "smell" and "hear" the scratch of the match.

Press Escape for menu.

****

During the *revising* portion of the program, students are aided as they polish their essays. They may consult checklists for fundamental information pertinent to writing about literature, overall revision, words and sentences, and editing and proofing.

Apart from its comprehensive nature, the most innovative feature of this software is that it uses the unique capabilities of the computer to recognize and support the recursive nature of invention and revision throughout the writing process.

Heuristics

Computer-based heuristic programs provide literature students with opportunities for invention, analysis, organization, and thesis support. By asking open-ended questions which allow students space to discover their own views and to develop and support hypotheses, these programs give students a personal stake in their interpretations.

The pioneer program in this area, Helen J. Schwartz's *SEEN*, or *Seeing Eye Elephant Network* (Schwartz 1984), asks students to build on their personal responses to literature by having them create a hypothesis about a fictional character and respond to prompts for evidence supporting the hypothesis. (See Sample Screen 6 for one in a series of twelve questions.)

Sample Screen 6

* *

4. What does Ferdinand DO that shows Ferdinand is a loving gentleman?

\+ + + + + + + + + + + + Your answer + + + + + + + + + + + +

\+ + + + + + + + + + + + Function keys + + + + + + + + + + + +

F1	F2	F5	F6	F7	F8	F9	F10
Go on	Go back	Advice	Sample	Help	Review	Menu	Quit

* *

A valuable feature of this program is a built-in response network. After students post their ideas under a pen name in the network, they are encouraged to read and comment about each other's work, providing them with an audience and peer collaboration. By returning to the menu, they have access to a bulletin board and may choose to read and comment on the files left by other students, or they may choose to read comments left by classmates on their own file.

While initial, personal responses are important, they are naturally limited by a student's background and perspective. The peer exchange provided by this network enables students to reshape or enhance their interpretations when someone else's interpretation makes more sense or helps them see the work in a more meaningful way. (See Sample Screen 7.)

During subsequent sessions, students may return to earlier ideas and revise them. The "elephant" part of the program keeps a record of students' comments and peer responses and enables them to "trace the development of their ideas."

Originally written for the Apple II, the *SEEN* program is now available in a revised IBM version. While maintaining the sound pedagogy of its predecessor, the new version has been updated to take advantage of an 80-column screen; function keys to access help, menu, and special options screens; and a larger memory and faster operating system.

Heuristic programs which were not designed exclusively for literary study, but which contain sections for that purpose or which are flexible enough to allow instructors to create or alter prompts and questions for application to literary analysis, may also be quite useful. *Idealog*, developed by Fred Kemp at the University of Texas, is one such program. When students choose to do literary analysis, they are pro-

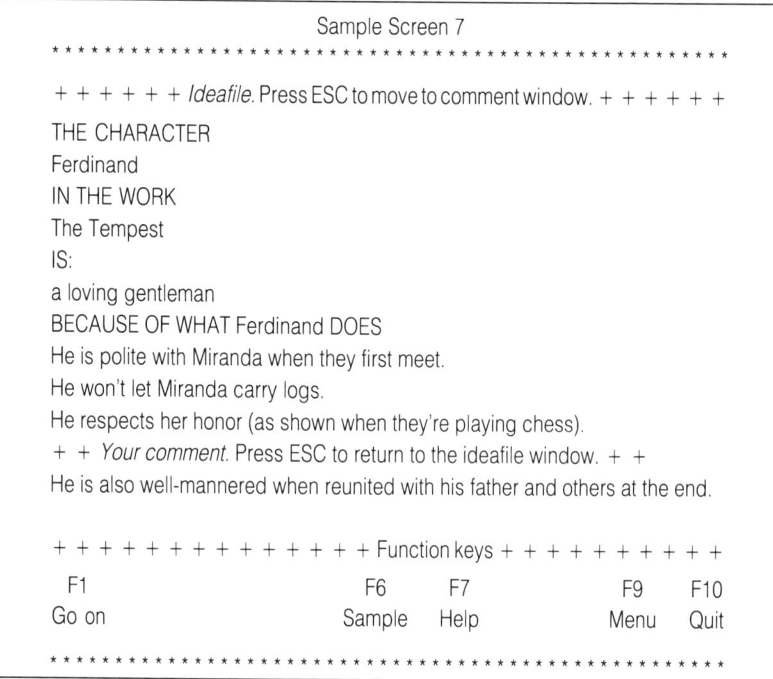

Sample Screen 7

* *

\+ + + + + + *Ideafile.* Press ESC to move to comment window. + + + + + +

THE CHARACTER
Ferdinand
IN THE WORK
The Tempest
IS:
a loving gentleman
BECAUSE OF WHAT Ferdinand DOES
He is polite with Miranda when they first meet.
He won't let Miranda carry logs.
He respects her honor (as shown when they're playing chess).
\+ + *Your comment.* Press ESC to return to the ideafile window. + +
He is also well-mannered when reunited with his father and others at the end.

\+ + + + + + + + + + + + + + Function keys + + + + + + + + + +

F1	F6	F7	F9	F10
Go on	Sample	Help	Menu	Quit

* *

vided with an "expert system" which asks them if they would like to emphasize symbol, character, plot, theme, or style. Depending on students' responses to questions about what they know or do not know about their topics, the system selects a heuristic format for them which may be applied to a particular assignment. Students may view or change earlier responses in the program at any time and are periodically asked if they wish to change their thesis statement or subject. Finally, the text of the program may be saved and brought up on a word processor for revision and polishing.

Another program, *Invent,* created by Michael Spitzer at the New York Institute of Technology, encourages teachers to create their own "scripts" by writing in their own questions. Thus, it is possible for each instructor to custom-design questions to fit literary analysis, a particular work of literature, and even a specific analytical approach (see Michael Spitzer, Chapter 15).

Notable Others

According to the particular needs of the class and the instructor, there are many other programs which might be of value in a literature course. For instructors who understand or who are willing to learn how to use *PFS:File,* Stephen Marcus's *PFS:File / Analyzing Fiction* (Marcus 1986) could be a very useful tool for teaching literary analysis, while Marcus's *Compupoem* may be of benefit to students learning to write short poems. *Poetics,* a creation of John Plummer at Vanderbilt University, provides tutorials, exercises, and an authoring system for teaching versification to college students. "For students who genuinely want and need to be walked slowly through a poem by an intelligent and articulate teacher," comments Rose Norman (1986), "*Poetics* is invaluable." Even commercially popular "interactive fiction" programs like *Fahrenheit 451* or *The Hitchhiker's Guide to the Galaxy,* which require the reader to be an active participant in the writing of the story, may be quite valuable in the hands of a creative teacher.

Do It Yourself

In addition to creating a more interactive experience for the student, the obvious advantage of writing your own software is that it can be custom-made to fit your course, method of instruction, and even your personality. It becomes, ideally, an extension of the support which you provide in your classroom and office. And it is available when you are not.

A colleague and I have each written a program which helps students analyze literature. My own program, *Literature Journal* (Madden 1987), initially emphasizes the role which personal factors may play in students' responses. Students are asked to compare their personality traits, backgrounds, and experiences with those of characters in a story and then to write about the ways in which these factors have affected their responses. (See Sample Screen 8.)

Sample Screen 8

****

Seeing aspects of our personalities in characters may influence our feelings about them. Let's look at some similarities between you and the boy in "Araby."

You have described both yourself and the boy as

Reserved

Tender

Unsure

How have these similarities affected your feelings about the boy?

****

Examining these choices and others derived from the affective domain, and questioning the effect such choices have on their judgment, students build a personal foundation for their responses and then add analysis based on traditional text-related and author-related approaches.

My colleague's program, *Story Tutor* (Costanzo 1987), emphasizes such visual concepts as setting, point of view, and symbolism, in addition to plot, characterization, and theme. (See Sample Screen 9.)

Sample Screen 9

```
*****************************************************

HERE IS YOUR BRIEF SKETCH OF THE SETTING
TIME: 1940's
PLACE: New York City
USE THE SPACE BELOW TO ENLARGE YOUR DESCRIPTION:
The story begins in a boarding house. Peter is staying there illegally
because
TYPE UP TO 40 LINES
PRESS DELETE TO ERASE / -> TO GO ON

*****************************************************
```

In each case, what we have emphasized in our programs is based on what we emphasize in teaching our classes. These emphases, no doubt, are influenced by related academic interests: in my case, psychology; in my colleague's, film. Even without seeing our names on the programs, our students can easily identify who wrote which program. The approaches are our signatures, and the programs are a natural extension of our classes.

Because programming "calls for logical thinking, clear expression, and a working knowledge of the standard rules of syntax," English teachers make outstanding programmers (Costanzo 1987). And excellent guidance is available (see, for example, Selfe 1986). But though the pedagogical and personal rewards are considerable, teachers who want to write their own programs must be prepared to spend a substantial amount of time planning, writing, testing, and revising.

Epilogue

The progress made over the past few years in computer-assisted instruction in writing is inspiring and serves as a model for what can be done. And while the potential for using computers to support the teaching of literature remains comparatively untapped, its promise is just as inviting.

The computer is neither magic box nor Pandora's box, and its value is measured by the quality of the teaching it supports. When employed by teachers who have learned about the technology, adjusted their teaching methods to use it, and committed themselves to fostering literary involvement as much as literary criticism, computers can be an exciting and powerful tool in the literature classroom.

Works Cited

American Council of Learned Societies. 1965. "Computerized Research in the Humanities: A Survey." *ACLS Newsletter* 16 (May): 13–24.

Costanzo, William V. 1987. "The English Teacher as Programmer." *Computers and Composition* 4 (August): 65–76.

———. 1988. *The Electronic Text.* Englewood Cliffs, N.J.: Education Technologies.

Flynn, Elizabeth A. 1983. "Composing Responses to Literary Texts: A Process Approach." *College Composition and Communication* 34: 342–48.

Macmillan Literature and Composition Software. 1987. New York: Scribner Educational Publishers.

Madden, Frank. 1987. "Desperately Seeking Literary Response." *Computers and Composition* 4 (August): 17–34.

Marcus, Stephen. 1986. *Analyzing Fiction Software: Literature and Composition Data Base for PFS:File.* New York: Scholastic.

Mellown, Elgin. 1986. "The Use of the Computer in Literary Studies: An Experimental Course." *The Computer-Assisted Composition Journal* 1(1): 55–61.

Norman, Rose. 1986. "Poetics." *Computers and Composition* 3 (November): 99–111.

Purves, Alan C., and Richard Beach. 1972. *Literature and the Reader: Research in Response to Literature, Reading Interests, and the Teaching of Literature.* Champaign, Ill.: National Council of Teachers of English.

Rodrigues, Dawn, and Raymond J. Rodrigues. 1986. *Teaching Writing with a Word Processor, Grades 7–13.* Urbana, Ill.: ERIC Clearinghouse on Reading and Communication Skills and National Council of Teachers of English.

Rodrigues, Raymond J. 1986. "Creating Writing Lessons with a Word Processor." *The Computing Teacher* 13, no. 5 (February): 41–43.

Rosenblatt, Louise. 1976. *Literature as Exploration,* 3d ed. New York: Noble and Noble.

Schwartz, Helen J. 1984. "SEEN: A Tutorial and User Network for Hypothesis Testing." In *The Computer in Composition Instruction: A Writer's Tool,* edited by William Wresch, 47–62. Urbana, Ill.: National Council of Teachers of English.

Selfe, Cynthia L. 1986. *Computer-Assisted Instruction in Composition: Create Your Own.* Urbana, Ill.: National Council of Teachers of English.

Sommers, Nancy. 1980. "Revision Strategies of Student Writers and Experienced Adult Writers." *College Composition and Communication* 31: 378–88.

18 Databases for English Teachers

Stephen Marcus, University of California at Santa Barbara

My first work with computer-assisted writing, back in the early days, involved developing a program that helped students study and write poetry. I quickly learned to keep quiet about my work when talking with some people. They had a hard time accepting the notion that technology could be integrated into that particular curriculum. For many, it constituted "unnatural practices . . . unspeakable acts."

Times have changed. Now, people routinely see computers as a "natural" resource for English teachers. Word processing remains the crucial technological tool for enriching the language arts curriculum, for providing students with new powers and incentives. And it is no wonder. Arthur C. Clarke has noted that "any sufficiently advanced technology is indistinguishable from magic." Word processing, which allows students' words to be written in light instead of carved in stone, has worked its subtle but profound magic on many of us, changing our views of what writing entails and of what we can do as writers—of who we are as writers.

There are other kinds of software now having a major impact on the English and language arts curriculum. Telecommunications, style checkers, networking software—these and others are all a part of any comprehensive integration of technology into the curriculum. Still another tool is database software, something with which I personally had virtually no experience at the time I was asked to develop some language arts applications for a popular database program.

What I eventually discovered was that a database provides a means of organizing, storing, and retrieving information. Your wallet is a database. So is a dictionary. So is a novel. Each of these provides a way to organize, store, and retrieve information, whether the information is about you, about your language, or about an author's insights on life. A computerized database has its own special qualities, of course. If a word-processing program can be thought of as a fancy typewriter, a database program can be thought of as a fancy 3 × 5 card-filing system. (Both these comparisons obscure as much as they reveal, but they do help make the strange familiar.)

There are databases that are stored in central computers and that are available to people with the right hardware, software, account number, and password. Some of these "subscription" databases (such as *CompuServe)* require that you register in advance and agree to pay an hourly rate whenever you use them. They give you access to such items as the *Grolier's Encyclopedia, Dialog* (a database similar to the *Reader's Guide,* allowing you to search for magazine or book titles related to a topic), or *Cendata* (a database which includes census data from all parts of the country).

There is a growing availability of databases for teachers of English and language arts who do not want to take the time to create their own—including some new "hypertext" databases being designed for the Macintosh. Hypertext databases can include text, graphics, and even sound. A literature database named *Rosetta* is currently being designed by John McDaid. It includes a variety of writing exercises based on describing, interpreting, and responding to remarkably clear pictures that have been stored on the disk. Teachers can add their own graphics and text to the exercises included on the disk.

At Brown University, developers are working on a hyptertext project which stores material related to the life and works of Robert Browning. A more modest example of hyptertext is such software as *Prose* by Nancy Kaplan, which connects teachers' comments to student papers with specific points in the text to which the comments relate. Other related software allows people to write and sometimes to illustrate or animate their own interactive letters and choose-your-own-adventure stories (e.g., *AdventureMaster, Story Tree, Bank Street Story Book).* In all these cases, the writer/reader becomes an "architect of knowledge." The text on the screen is just the currently visible part of an amorphous structure that a person creates new with each "reading."

There are also disk-based databases that are more under your control, databases that you and your students can custom-design and use whenever you want. In this latter case, you determine what kind of information, in what area of knowledge, you want to organize and store. You use a database program (e.g., *PFS:File, Bank Street Filer,* and the database portion of *AppleWorks)* to design a computerized form that can be filled with the information you want.

The more ingenious your form, the more filled in it gets, and the more forms you fill in, the more you can "interrogate" the database.

That is, you can ask it questions and get answers that will be more or less interesting—depending on the nature of your questions and the basic structure of the form.

In collaboration with Beverly Hunter, I created three database curriculum units (Marcus 1986). The one package contains *AESOP, FICTION*, and *PAPERS*. The *AESOP* file is based on Aesop's Fables (and includes seventy-five of them). *FICTION* is designed for reading and responding to any novel or short story. *PAPERS* is for students to use for recording information about writing done in class. It, too, stresses reading-writing connections, only instead of reading and responding to literature, students have the opportunity to read and connect with one another's writing.

The following discussion of *FICTION* should give some idea of how database software can be used to help students learn how to respond personally to literature as they develop critical thinking and writing skills in English classes. Keep in mind as you read it that the technique described could be adapted to any database program that a school or department happens to have. Teachers would, of course, have to type in their own fables or stories (unless they have access to optical scanners, devices that translate text characters into computer information), but with students or other teachers collaborating, the task is surmountable, and the software that teachers create will be enormously flexible. In a teacher-training course or in an inservice workshop, teachers could learn how databases work as they collaborate to create their own classroom tools.

The *FICTION* form can be applied to any number of works, but to give students material to work with, *FICTION* comes supplied with seventy passages from two novels (*The Red Badge of Courage* and *Lord of the Flies)* and one short story ("The Lottery"). Each passage is contained on its own form, along with other information, such as students' responses to the passages.

It is important to emphasize that while numerous forms contain filled-in fields (to serve as examples and working material), the real point of the *FICTION* file is to give students the chance to read, think about, discuss, and respond to literature as they add their ideas to the *FICTION* database. As teachers use this file or a similar one that they design themselves, they will gradually learn how to help students learn to use the database program to explore the nature of fiction in general and the "fiction" portion of the database in particular. Teachers and students can fill in the forms (and add new ones) with passages and information about the same or different literary works.

As students add their responses to the *FICTION* file, the database becomes richer. They can then use it to help answer questions like the following:

> I'm writing a paper on the theme of "courage." Which stories can I draw on for ideas?
>
> I think that Henry in *The Red Badge of Courage* is a coward. I wonder what other students think?
>
> How does a character develop an understanding of himself or herself?
>
> Is there a difference between what boys in this class think about courage and what girls think?

Part of the educational goal with this material is to help students learn how to frame productive questions and how to think about what kinds of information will help them answer their questions. As readers of literature, they are encouraged to pay careful attention to the text they are studying, but they are also invited to respond personally to every text. As writers "publishing" their thoughts and insights in the database, they are provided with a tool to help themselves get "raw material" for class discussions and writing assignments.

It is also important to note that *FICTION* rarely supplies the actual answers to the questions. Instead, the students must apply such thinking skills as identifying and organizing information to solve a problem. They must also synthesize and evaluate that information in order to apply it to the particular writing assignments they are working on.

As noted, *FICTION* can be used with any novel or short story. Using the database program itself (*PFS:File,* in this case), teachers and students can redesign the form's structure to reflect other interests in the literature. They can also create a different version to use with drama or poetry. Their classes can even prepare special collections of passages and comments on topics chosen by the students, such as "Growing Up," "Leaving Home," or "Succeeding in Life."

Creating, enlarging, and maintaining a database is a challenging and rewarding task. Many people, in fact, succumb to what is known as "database fascination." The experience is like browsing through an electronic book shop. You can peek into other worlds and other people's responses to those worlds.

Every database program has its own special strengths. *PFS:File,* for example, allows relatively large passages of text to be stored. Whatever program you use, you will find that database applications provide intriguing new opportunities for integrating technology into the English and language arts curriculum. Students can develop important research skills, become more computer literate, and enrich their study of literature.

Work Cited

Marcus, Stephen. 1986. *Literature and Composition Data Bases for Scholastic's PFS:File.* New York: Scholastic.

19 Teaching in Networked Classrooms

Trent Batson, Gallaudet University

Educators considering adding a microcomputer network[1] should understand that networks were developed for business, not teaching. They are really just a bare-bones technology designed to share software and peripherals[2] and to provide E-mail,[3] scheduling, and a bulletin board. Some of these are useful in the classroom or microlab, but by themselves they might not justify the considerable expense of a network. In schools we have different populations, purposes, and economics. Also, the office kind of specialization—computers dedicated to printing, communication, databases, and word processing—is inappropriate in education since almost all users have similar needs. Finally, electronic mail, news items, and an electronic calendar may have little use in a computer-writing lab. At about a thousand dollars per computer, it may be hard to justify the expense of a network in a writing lab solely on the basis of practical or fiscal advantages.

But what about customizing networks to make them more useful for writing labs? Networks are virtually untapped territory for educators. Almost no applications have been developed specifically for networks. Part of the reason is that programming on networks is a lot more difficult than for single computers. Therefore, to exploit networks educationally requires that we step back, forget our preconceptions about educational computing, and focus on the ways that networks can improve practice in the writing lab. There are two main advantages to having networks in the lab: they make it easier to manage a writing lab, and they allow computers to communicate with each other, thus opening the door for collaborative learning.

To demonstrate these advantages, imagine yourself as the director of a writing lab. You are considering networking your computers for the following reasons:

1. I want to add a laser printer[4] with graphics abilities. It is faster and quieter and produces camera-ready copy. With it, teachers can make overhead transparencies directly from printouts. But

the computer I attach it to will have to be dedicated to that use only. A network would let me keep that computer in operation because print commands can be issued from any computer.[5] Once I have the laser printer hooked into the network, I can get rid of some of the printers in the room, reducing clutter and noise.[6]

2. I also want to buy more software, but I hate buying copies for each computer. Currently I have to have a user aide on duty during open hours to check out the software; despite policing by user aides, some of the software is stolen, erased, or damaged. A network would let me put the software on just one machine, and the students could access it from their own computers.
3. I would like to simplify the start-up procedure of the computers. We waste a lot of time teaching each new student how to "boot up" and get into a word-processing program. I could make a menu[7] disk for each machine, or I could create just one for a network.
4. I can, therefore, reduce the number of user aides I need on hand, eliminate the need to check out software (and spend less on software by getting network versions), reduce the number of printers, and create one easy-to-follow menu system for the whole lab.

The only disadvantages you can think of are the cost and more cable clutter, for there would be one more cable on the floor. Otherwise, everything would run the same as before, and each microcomputer could still be used independently of the network. Your conclusion: a network looks promising and possibly worthwhile.

However, the setup envisioned by this lab director sounds sophisticated, and it is. A nonnetworked microcomputer lab can be managed by the average computer-literate teacher; a network needs a technician. Someone has to design and support the whole web of software and peripheral sharing. Even if a teacher is willing and able to take on the job, he or she probably will not have the time or be available constantly. Without technical support, network abilities will be underused and the investment wasted.

Communication: Moving toward Collaborative Writing

From a time and money perspective, the idea of a network is intriguing, but not compelling. But let us see what networks can really do.

Computers, alone, make writing easier because the writer can manipulate and display text easily. Computers in a network open the possibility of *shared text.* Teachers and students can actually work dynamically with emerging text in class. This may not sound earthshaking at first, but that is only because we have become accustomed to the limitations (and the slow feedback) of the traditional writing classroom.

When teachers in a traditional classroom assign in-class writing, they may wander about the room, peering over the shoulders of students, but they are not able to interact easily with students or to comment on their writing.

In a computer lab equipped with a video-switching network,[8] you as teacher can wander and peer while sitting at your own computer—without having to struggle through illegible handwriting. Through the video network, you can, for example, provide immediate feedback to one student, then display his or her work to all, and, finally, display your own way of writing the same passage. While you display work, you can comment aloud. This sharing of work is a first step toward peer review and a more collaborative approach to teaching writing.

You can move a step further toward collaboration by using a "real" network, which allows data transfer between machines.[9] The video network displays work, but each person's work is kept separate at his or her station, as if each person has a separate chalkboard; the "real" network allows for a mingling of work, like sharing one large chalkboard. This ability introduces a whole new kind of writing classroom.

Existing Collaborative Programs

A few educational and research facilities have begun experimenting with cooperative work using a shared workspace. The "cooperative work" done by computer scientists is a process similar to the "collaborative learning" in which writing teachers and students engage. Several examples are described below.

One network vendor includes a "CB"—"citizen's band"—utility with its network.[10] This utility—intended for office communication—has become the workhorse for a new approach to teaching writing on networks in universities. At the time this chapter is being written, there are four colleges and universities that are using the communication utility: Ohlone Community College in Fremont, California, the University of Minnesota, Northern Virginia Community College in Annandale; and Gallaudet University in Washington, D.C.; several other universities are getting started. Behind this movement is the

ENFI Project (English Natural Form Instruction), which originated at Gallaudet University.

The CB utility allows students and the teacher to "talk" to each other on their screens. They type a message in a little private window at the bottom of their screens (the window is an area of the screen where they write while other things are happening in the rest of their screen; that is, the computer processes the two windows separately). When they finish writing, they enter a command, and the message moves up to the main window. Everyone sees the messages in the main window. The program attaches the writer's name to each message, and the "Conversation" scrolls up the screen like a play dialogue.

Combining this interaction ability with the display ability of the video network produces the tools for true collaborative writing. Now writing can serve *as a means of communication.* The computer supplies the missing link between speaking and writing. We can use writing for many more purposes than just producing something for evaluation because we have opened the whole spectrum of social writing.

Imagine in your own class that students sit at computer stations instead of desks. Instead of only talking to them, you can also write to them. Your written discussion itself becomes a model of writing; you can instantly demonstrate writing samples that the students see on the screen before them; they see *you* writing, a new experience for them; you can all jointly freewrite, brainstorm, and organize. In short, this particular network application, the communication utility, offers revolutionary possibilities to the writing teacher.

Another approach to shared-workspace cooperative work was developed at Xerox Palo Alto Research Center (PARC), the developmental site of many innovations, including the Macintosh interface. This program, *Cog Noter,* allows students and the teacher to brainstorm and organize ideas collaboratively. Instead of writing a message, each participant uses a mouse[11] to position a phrase or a word anywhere on the screen. To clarify a particular phrase, a participant writes additional text in a separate window which others can "open."[12] To indicate that an explanation has been added, the original phrase now appears in boldface on the screen. When participants agree the screen is full enough, or they run out of ideas, they start drawing lines on the screen to connect related ideas, forming a kind of "mind map," which participants use when writing an outline for a paper.

These are only two examples of collaborative work on networks. Software supporting collaborative work is becoming common in the business world. Companies are beginning to perceive that using computers to support work-group collaboration provides a competitive edge, according to Robert Johansen of the Institute for the Future. At meetings, one person may sit at a computer with a projector and help organize the meeting by using such software as *The Consensor* or *The Option Finder*, or simply by using a database. Voice-data transmission is also growing in use, to support meetings at a distance. There are many presentation preparation programs available, such as *Power Point*, *More*, and *MacDraw*, which improve collaboration. Some software helps groups do their calendaring, speeding up consensus. Some programs foster collaborative writing, such as *For Comment*, *Compare Write*, *Manuscript*, *Red Pencil*, and *Build*. These keep track of drafts, identify who added what, and generally support group editing of manuscripts. *WordPerfect* and *Microsoft Word* will offer some group-oriented features soon. More adventurous are the programs that allow screen-sharing, such as *In Synch*, *Carbon Copy*, and *Interceptor*. True coprocessing of shared data is difficult to program, so this area will be slow to develop.

Up until now, two people sitting next to each other could work on the same legal pad, three could share a white board, but larger groups did not have a convenient collaborative medium. A writing teacher could move toward collaborative *learning*, but collaborative *writing* remained out of reach. Now, networks bring that ability within reach.

Possibilities for Networked Classrooms

It does not take a visionary to see the possibilities inherent in a shared workspace for improving writing instruction. For example, teachers who use the writing-process approach to teach composition often encourage their students to freewrite as a way of coming up with a topic for a paper. In a traditional class, the students are on their own, using pen and paper. Even in a computer lab, students are mostly on their own. Some computer programs coach freewriting by prodding and by providing advice and text-management tools, but the student still does all the thinking.

With a CB-like utility, students and teacher can freewrite together, throwing their ideas into a common "pot." The blank-page (or blank-screen) trauma is eliminated. Or the teacher can create smaller work groups by having students team up on the network. On a private CB channel, they jointly brainstorm the topic, keeping the emerging text in one window and typing to each other in a second window, transporting phrases between windows at will.

Using the network's displaying and manipulating abilities, the teacher can also demonstrate his or her own text-generation process, explaining the thinking process as he or she freewrites, brainstorms, composes, revises, and edits. Normally, students see static examples of writing; the network allows them to see a dynamic model of the writing process.

These examples only hint at the power of the computer as a manager of classroom communication. The success of the network applications described above, and these are just examples, depends on a new and different approach to teaching. Attempting such applications will fail if teachers simply transfer their normal teaching approach—their syllabuses, goals, and manner—to the network. Changing the medium, as Marshall McLuhan warns us, changes the message.

Training for Collaborative Work

In preparation to use this new network approach, teachers first need to become familiar with collaborative learning. Shifting to the network is a dramatic shift in the locus of activity and control, which the teachers need to welcome and not resist. If they understand the value of the shift, they will make the shift more readily.

The issues teachers generally bring up when starting to use networks collaboratively are "coverage" and control. They find as they give over some control to the students, they often cannot stay strictly with their syllabuses; they have lost the absolute control they had over pacing. Those teachers who prefer having control and going strictly by a syllabus, therefore, will not take very well to collaborative learning, even without computer networks in the picture. One teacher lamented that before switching to the network, she had stood tall in her class. All eyes were on *her* as she lectured. "Now, I'm just one line among many" on the screen. Even teachers who claim to prefer "student-centered" education are bothered when it actually happens. Teachers have to be prepared for changes like these when they move to the network. They have to alter their expectations, syllabuses, strategies, manner, and sometimes their understanding of what education means.

The best training approach, therefore, is to combine forces with those who are behind other composition theories, such as collaborative learning, writing across the curriculum, or the writing process. Form an alliance by showing how computer networks can implement one or more of these theories. Select teachers to train from those who are already interested in trying a new approach in class. Combine training in use of the network with training in the new approach.

During your training sessions, do not separate technical training from theory. If you do, those who believe they can transfer their usual teaching practices intact to the network will have that belief misleadingly reinforced.

A number of universities are using the network approach to teaching writing (the ENFI method), and staff members at these schools may be able to help in setting up a training program: the University of Texas, the University of Minnesota, New York Institute of Technology, Carnegie-Mellon University, Northern Virginia Community College in Annandale, Gallaudet University, Lehman College of CUNY, Ohlone Community College in Fremont, California, and the University of Southern Mississippi.

Gallaudet University, at this writing, is preparing a teacher manual. Formal training in the ENFI method is offered at Gallaudet in June of each year. At that time, we meet for three days from 9:00 a.m. to 4:00 p.m. and alternate between discussion of writing theory—writing process, collaborative writing, writing across the curriculum, natural language acquisition—and practice on the network. We demonstrate how a teacher can use the network to interact dynamically during collaborative work on invention, for example. We also prepare trainees to adjust to the grammar of "talking" on the network, where time is altered and patterns of group interaction (taking turns, especially) are disturbing and unfamiliar at first.

We compare the goals and dynamics of the traditional classroom, based on a model of education as knowledge transfer, with the networked classroom, where knowledge is socially constructed, and we demonstrate the practical ways that this is so—students are able to write to a live and present audience, and group collaboration reduces the artificiality of the traditional writing classroom.

After this three-day period of intense theory and practice, we have follow-up one-day training sessions before each semester begins, when teachers are feeling anxious. At the end of the year, we have a debriefing session. One-day training workshops also have been given, but these were not as effective. We also have experimented with tuition charges. When we first began the network project on campus, we paid the teachers to attend training; now our trainees pay the tuition themselves and receive continuing-education credit.

Summary

To summarize, the following guidelines seem most effective in establishing a networked classroom:

1. Choose the already converted.
2. Combine theory and practice.
3. Demonstrate the teacher's loss of control to prepare trainees for that experience.
4. Build in follow-up workshops.

It is important to remember that when computers are networked, they cease being like fancy typewriters and take on new powers: the power to change how people relate to each other and the power to speed up classroom processes. Both powers can be brought to bear on the writing classroom, but only with training that is far different than the usual computer training. The normal computer training is like learning to drive: you still move along the ground but faster; training in networks is more like learning to fly: you have to become comfortable in a new medium.

Notes

1. There are many kinds of networks. I use "network" here to mean a local-area network run entirely on personal computers. In educational institutions, these networks are usually limited to one room, though they can extend several hundred feet. Local-area networks require cabling between work stations, software at each station, and often a file server (a computer with a hard disk).

2. Peripherals are equipment that is "peripheral" to or outside of the central processing unit, including the disk drives, display unit, and keyboard as well as printers, modems, computer projectors, and other add-on devices.

3. Electronic mail lets you write a message to one, two, or more people, which they can read at their leisure and then print out, save on a disk, or delete.

4. Laser printers look and act like photocopiers. They produce camera-ready copy quickly and quietly, making them ideal for the writing lab, except that they currently cost up to ten times as much as inexpensive dot-matrix printers.

5. Print jobs do not get mixed up because the network automatically creates a print queue, taking each job in turn.

6. One laser printer can do the work of five to ten dot-matrix printers. Lasers use regular copier paper, eliminating those little squibbles of tractor-fed paper edges, the need to change ribbons, awkward paper feeding, and all that noise.

7. A menu is a list of options. The student merely has to press one key (usually) to make his or her choice.

8. A video-switching network hooks together only the video displays, allowing the work done at one computer to be displayed at another. This kind of network costs less than half of what a regular network costs. Since it allows

the teacher to stay at one station and to share work, it has important teaching advantages.

9. A "real" network wires together the processing units of the computers, which allows people to create joint text, so it is a step up from the video network.

10. Fox Research of Dayton, Ohio, sells the CB utility on 10Net in the United States and around the world. CompuTeach, of Washington, D.C., sells CB-like software ("CTC"—*CompuTeach Classroom*) for other networks. *Classroom Communicator* is another communication utility.

11. A mouse supplements the keyboard, either replacing some key functions or adding a free-form ability; it can be used on all brands of computers.

12. Before you "open" a window on a computer screen, you see only the "foreground," like seeing only the inside wall of your house. Opening a window means that a rectangle opens somewhere on the screen, and you see "background" information, but you do not lose the foreground, like looking outside your house through a window even though you can still see the inside wall. The window blocks out part of the screen, but it does not permanently affect that part. Once the window is closed, there is no trace of it.

20 Computer-Supported Writing Classes: Lessons for Teachers

Cynthia L. Selfe, Michigan Technological University

Billie J. Wahlstrom, Michigan Technological University

Computers change the way we plan and teach writing in writing-intensive classes within the English curriculum. Teacher-training programs need to allow time for teachers to share pedagogical experiences so that they can discuss those changes. Without such exchanges, each teacher operates in an instructional vacuum.

This chapter describes what happens in different kinds of computer-intensive courses. We discuss suggestions for planning and teaching such courses, and we outline the advantages and disadvantages we see to using computer support in these writing-intensive courses. We focus on the so-called computer classroom, the kind of classroom/laboratory that houses a sufficient number of computers for an entire class to use during a class session.

Background: Computers and Writing Classes

Classroom/laboratories allow teachers to make use of what they already know about such strategies as process-based writing instruction, the use of multiple drafts, assignments designed to produce expressive transactional writing, peer feedback at all stages of students' writing processes, frequent teacher-student and student-student conferences, the carefully planned and structured use of journal writing, and occasional nongraded writing assignments.

If the computers in these settings can be netted, or linked, together electronically, labs can also provide additional instructional advantages for writing-intensive courses. Students can, for example, use the "private" section of the network to store initial drafts of a piece, journal writes, expressive discourse, or notes in files where access is protected by a personal password. Students can also use the network to share work at later stages of the composing process by posting their papers on a "public" section of the system so that their peer-group members, classmates, or teachers can respond to or critique their work. Teachers can use the network to store their lecture notes or class handouts, making them available in "read-only" files for students who have missed class.

Teachers are already using computer classrooms in a variety of ways. Some teachers prefer to provide their students with the choice of using the classroom/lab on a walk-in basis; other teachers actually hold classes in the facility or require every student in their classes to do all written assignments on the netted computers.

Planning Computer-Supported Writing Courses

Most instructors agree that planning an effective writing-intensive course is nearly as difficult as teaching it. Computer-supported writing courses present additional difficulties. They require all the planning that traditional writing courses do, and given that most professionals in our field often have limited experience in teaching with computer support, the decision to use computers means that special attention needs to paid to their role in the class. We recommend three unique considerations for planning computer-supported writing courses: deciding if a course would be improved by computer support, deciding how and to what extent computer support would be used, and deciding how computer support would change both the nature of written assignments given and the teacher's response to them.

Will This Course Be Improved by Computer Support?

One of the early lessons we have learned in wrestling with curriculum design in the wake of the computer revolution is that computers are not right for every course, every teacher, or every student. In fact, unless the use of computers has distinct advantages for presenting the course content, assisting teachers, and aiding students, the additional work involved in redesigning a class may not be worth the effort.

Content has to figure as a central concern for teachers who plan to integrate computers into a particular course. Classes, for example, that require highly personal journal writes, that involve constant risk taking in writing assignments, or that stress the use of field notes do not always prove to be the best choices for computer support. Often the writing done in such classes involves additional privacy requirements or on-the-spot writing that could not be supported by the semi-public classroom/lab to which many students find themselves assigned.

In addition, classes requiring students to learn other kinds of sophisticated electronic equipment (such as video-production classes involving the use of complicated cameras, computerized character generators, mixers, and sound systems) might also be less than optimal choices, despite the fact that they might be writing-intensive courses. Computers take time to learn, even when word processing is the only application involved, and it is important to be realistic about the out-of-class time students are asked to commit.

The classes which seem to benefit most from computer support are those which involve a great deal of writing and which stress writing assignments that can be done during the hours the classroom/lab is in operation. Obvious choices include basic, technical, and business writing classes, as well as courses in style, grammar, journalism, or advanced composition. Courses in such areas as philosophy, communication, or art history in which substantial interaction occurs between the teacher and the student or among students about what they have written may also benefit from computer support.

Teachers as well as students should benefit from the addition of computer support to their classes. Unless computers facilitate some aspect of planning, teaching, or evaluating course materials, no instructor will choose to incorporate them into his or her class. Computers can provide several personal advantages. If, for example, a course involves the extensive use of structured journal writes, the computer can be a boon to the instructor. It is much easier on a teacher's eyes (and the back if she or he has to carry home thirty 200-page journals) to have students write their journals on computers. Printed type, whether on a computer screen or on a printout, is easier to read than handwriting and makes grading go much quicker. Twenty-five computerized journal assignments could also be stored on a single disk and carried home or to the office for a grading session.

Computers can also be helpful in communicating and conferencing with students, especially when the computers are in a network. Mailboxes for both teachers and students can be up on the network so that messages about drafts, writing assignments, and conferences can be sent and received electronically. Drafts in progress can be reviewed electronically when students leave them on the network for their teachers, and one-on-one conferences can be conducted more effectively when teachers and students can experiment with text revision on the computer screen.

Finally, computer support has to provide benefits for the students in our courses. Because many computer classes carry with them both lab fees and the burden of learning a word-processing system, students are likely to avoid computer-intensive courses until they are convinced such classes offer distinct advantages.

In actuality, students seem quick to see the advantages of computer-intensive courses. In many cases, students themselves identify the benefits they see in taking such classes. At Michigan Tech, for example, our students mention frequently that they value the chance to learn or to use a word-processing package even though doing so costs them increased time and effort in connection with a class. They report that writing, revision, and proofreading done on the computer are easier and faster to accomplish; that they prefer "doing papers on the computer" to composing on a typewriter; that screen copy and printer copy are easier for them to read than handwritten copy; and that computer use would be important for them in the future "on the job."

Our students have also mentioned that they enjoy the increased level of collaborative writing activity some computer-intensive writing courses provide. They like the electronic exchange of drafts that allows them to fit peer critiques into their busy schedules and to communicate with teachers or with each other. They also enjoy working in the lab, which provides the space for a ready-made writers' community composed, at least for a term, of all the students in the class.

How and to What Extent Will Computer Support Be Used?

Planning a writing-intensive class involves defining an appropriate degree of computer support. Ironically, such definitions often prove to be quite complicated because of the wide range of choices available to teachers who elect to use computers in their classes. Most departments, in designing their computer-supported writing facilities, opt for maximum flexibility. They create a room that can accommodate a large group of students, for teachers who choose to hold class sessions in the lab, or individual students, for teachers who prefer to let individuals use the lab during out-of-class hours.

This flexible classroom/lab setup can be used in a number of ways. For some classes, all students can be required to use the facility for all writing assignments. Such an arrangement assures that every class member as well as the teacher has access to the same kind of computer, a common word-processing system, and a central location for electronically storing and retrieving text. For other classes, computer support can be optional; therefore, students who have their own computers or access to a roommate's computer can use the machines they prefer.

To distinguish between the two approaches, we can label such classes "computer-intensive" and "computer-supported," respectively. Both kinds of classes have advantages and disadvantages. Computer-intensive classes have the advantage of employing a common system on which all class members and the teacher can work and exchange text. Teachers can then elect to meet with their students during class hours in the classroom/lab or choose to hold classes in a conventional classroom setting and simply require students to do all written assignments on the computers during out-of-class hours. Because both teachers and students use a common system, the exchange of text, assignments, and messages is enhanced.

However, disadvantages to this arrangement are also evident. At Michigan Tech, for example, each student in a computer-intensive class is required to pay an accompanying lab fee of twenty dollars per term to offset the cost of expendable supplies. Teachers of such classes generally felt obligated to learn to operate the computers themselves in order to help their students with the assignments when questions arise. Students in these classes, even if they did have access to another computer, had to learn our system and to complete assignments in the semi-public setting of our computer laboratory, unless their computers were compatible with those in the lab.

Computer-supported classes have the advantage of allowing for more choice. In these classes, students have the option of using the facility to support their out-of-class work on assignments. Students for whom the lab fee is too much of a financial burden can elect not to use the lab that term. In such classes at Michigan Tech, only a third to three quarters of the students in any given class choose to use the facility. As a result, teachers do not necessarily feel obligated to learn the computer system. Without a common system, however, we found that teachers and students could not easily exchange drafts, finished products, or assignments.

Even among computer-intensive classes, there is room for remarkable variation in planning writing assignments. Courses that follow a lecture-and-discussion style do not seem to lend themselves to a computer classroom/lab setting. Computers in such courses can be used to support only the written work done during out-of-class hours. Some classes can meet in the lab during sessions when peer-group critiques are being conducted. Students can conduct peer-group critiques more easily with the electronic aid of the computer network. In still other classes, every session can be conducted in the computer classroom/lab, and students can be required to complete all written assignments, both in and out of class, on the computers in the lab.

Decisions on this matter are best determined by the course content. For example, when much of students' in-class time is spent writing and rewriting short, stylistic exercises, these short in-class writings can often be done more quickly with the aid of a word-processing program, and the resulting products can be more easily shared and critiqued using the computer network.

How Will Computers Change Writing Assignments?

In planning for computer-supported writing classes, it is also necessary to rethink the assignments that were designed for use in a traditional classroom setting. Adding a component of computer support even to those courses which a teacher has taught many times requires changes both in the assignments given and in the ways in which teachers respond to these assignments.

Much of what we, as teachers, take for granted about giving writing assignments in a traditional classroom changes when we move into a computer-supported classroom. Assignments, for example, no longer have to be printed out in hard-copy form—no dittos, no stencils, no photocopies need to be used. All assignments can be stored and displayed on the network in a computer classroom/lab. Students can then access the assignments and choose whether to read them on the screen or in hard copy. For other classes, writing assignments can be available in both hard-copy and electronic form. Exceptionally long assignments or assignments accompanied by model student essays can be stored on the computer to reduce the cost of reproduction.

Preparing for written assignments that are to be delivered to the teacher in an electronic form also requires some new planning strategies. Writing assignments of this kind need to include instructions about how to label electronic drafts with names that allow the teacher to recognize the file easily on the electronic network. For instance, drafts of exercises handed in to the teacher on the computer network can be identified with the number of an exercise and the student's initials: *EX12.LMS*. Journal entries can be stored in each student's file with a designation indicating the date submitted: *Journal.216*.

Teachers also need to consider the rhetorical nature of the writing assignments in connection with appropriate computer support. In some courses, given the personal and speculative nature of students' journal entries, especially if they deal with such issues as ethics and responsibility, individuals can be required to store written assignments under secret passwords in invisible subdirectories on the computer network so that no unauthorized readers could access them.

Privacy also needs to be planned for in classes which involve students in group writing projects. If, for example, student groups compete against each other in producing an effective brochure involving integrated text and graphics, teachers might want to suggest that each group keep its writing on a "private" floppy disk that is accessible only to other students in the same group. In classes where students produce transactional prose or are encouraged to share their writing in the draft stage, elaborate precautions might not be necessary, although students in all supported classes probably should be encouraged to keep their important or personal files on a "private" floppy disk.

Teachers' responses to student writing also have to change when classes become computer-intensive. This is especially true in courses requiring students to hand in electronic copy. How does one mark an electronic essay, for example, when the teacher's input is printed in the same type as the student's writing? In classes for which teachers have to mark electronic copies, we need to develop computer-based strategies for responding to written assignments. Many of these strategies can take advantage of the computer's large storage capacity. If a teacher wants to keep students' drafts unmarked and intact to encourage their sense of ownership of their writing, then the instructor can electronically make two copies of the file containing each student's draft. The basic file name remains, but the teacher adds his or her initials or another symbol to the version that will contain his or her remarks.

Other response strategies can use the computer's ability to display text in different colors. With some computers and software, it is quite easy to access a student's file on the computer network and to display a response to this text in a strikingly different color. Teachers can also respond in all capital letters (by pressing the "caps lock" key), display responses within the lines of a text (by using the "insert" key), and identify particular text components by making them blink or appear in a different color on the screen. Students quickly learn these tricks and invent many of their own, and papers often resemble Fourth of July fireworks after extended teacher-student exchanges. Thus, even though we might lose some of the ease associated with writing directly on a student's paper in the ink of our choice, we gain, after a bit of thought, a whole new repertoire of responses.

Teaching Computer-Supported Writing Courses

Although planning a computer-supported writing curriculum is a complicated matter involving considerations of teachers, students, and course materials, teaching within such a curriculum can be equally as challenging. Just as the addition of computer support changes the way in which teachers have to prepare for their courses, it also alters the way in which these classes are conducted—affecting the location of classes, the nature of class sessions, and the focus of classes.

The Location of Computer-Supported Classes

An important issue involved with teaching computer-supported courses is the location. When teachers decide to use the more intensive forms of computer support in their classes, they have to think differently about how those class sessions would work and where the classes would best be conducted.

Often, the solution is that computer-intensive classes need to meet in more than one location. A class could meet in the computer classroom/lab for one class session each week during which students critique each other's written assignments. For this class, the teacher could reserve the classroom/lab and indicate the appropriate class location on the course syllabus. For other classes, however, students can work in a traditional classroom for part of the class session, listening to a short lecture or holding a discussion about an out-of-class reading, and then adjourn to the computer classroom/lab to do an in-class writing activity, the results of which could be shared on the electronic network. In such cases, teachers have to schedule courses in traditional classrooms near the computer classroom/lab.

Location is an issue even for classes conducted entirely in the computer classroom/lab. If this room is used both for classes and as a place students can use on a walk-in basis, teachers will have to post a sign on the door indicating when students will be able to come in and use the machines. If scheduling is not made clear, students who never meet with their classes in the lab may be unaware that other classes do hold sessions in the lab.

The Nature of Computer-Supported Writing Courses

Instructors who teach a computer-supported, writing-intensive course, especially one held in a computer classroom/lab, quickly learn that such classes are different in both nature and focus. The extent of computer support in a course seems to be directly proportional to change in the nature and focus of that class. Increasing the computer support in any particular course involves a concomitant commitment to increased discussion about the new writing technology. Often teachers devote five to ten minutes of each class period to a discussion of computer-related concerns. Students have to be told, for instance, how to label and date the electronic drafts they hand in so that the teacher can recognize these files, how to back up drafts so that they have "insurance" copies in case of an electronic failure; and how to guard their computer journals against electronic plagiarism and voyeurism.

"Paperless" courses, which involve a high level of computer support, require teachers to devote even more class time to a discussion of technology. Students have to be taught, for instance, how to exchange papers electronically, how to set up mailboxes on the network, how to use increasingly complicated software packages, and how to respond effectively to classmates' electronic drafts.

The time spent on such matters is viewed both negatively and positively by teachers. Teachers beginning to teach computer-supported classes often feel the time they spend discussing writing technology takes away from the already limited time they have to discuss course content or writing itself.

As teachers become more experienced in teaching such classes, however, two things seem to occur. First, they learn how to reduce the time devoted to the discussion of writing technology by refining the strategies of computers within the framework of the class, communicating such strategies more efficiently to the students, and documenting the techniques for the use of fellow teachers. Second, teachers of writing are coming to realize that discussing writing technology is an important part of the writing processes of students who use computers. By showing these students various strategies for manipulating and changing text files, protecting drafts, and using the computer to exchange information, we are equipping them with the valuable, process-based writing skills that they need for success in a world where writing and information sharing are technologically controlled.

The Focus of Computer-Supported Writing Courses

Teachers, especially those whose classes meet occasionally or entirely in the computer classroom/lab, are learning interesting lessons about focus. As teachers in traditional classrooms, many of us are used to a classroom environment that minimizes distractions and maximizes focus on the teacher.

In traditional courses, the teacher stands at or near the front of the classroom, lectures or gives instructions for small group discussions and activities, and enjoys a relatively high degree of control over students' attention. Little is present in our traditional classroom to distract students; as teachers, we choose when to write on a chalkboard, when the students should split up into groups, and when those groups should rejoin the larger class.

In a computer classroom, such a teacher-centered focus quickly dissipates. The physical layout of the computer classroom/lab and the lure of the CRT are certainly two of the major factors for this change in focus. Many computer-supported writing classrooms across the country are set up with the computers facing each other in clusters so that students can collaborate freely as they work on their electronic writing. In a room without a real "front," with no podium or teacher's table, teachers often feel lost. Contributing to this feeling is the difficulty, especially for those of us who are short, of maintaining eye contact with students who sit behind a CRT.

An additional factor in dissipating focus is the inviting nature of the blank computer screen. Even students who are most attentive in a traditional classroom setting cannot withstand the powerfully attractive draw of the computer. Teachers quickly discover that their introductory remarks, tailored for the relatively sedate atmosphere and pace of a traditional classroom, are soon punctuated by keyboard sounds, first from one corner of the room and then from another as students are seduced into jotting phosphorescent messages on the computer monitors.

Making the Switch to Computer-Supported Courses

Our initial attempts to guide an entire class through a computer-supported exercise were disconcerting. If twenty-five students started at the same moment, all twenty-five would be at different stages of the activity at the next moment. Students with extensive computer experience would sprint ahead, quickly discovering how to broadcast electronic messages to their peers after completing a task. Students without computer experience needed extensive help from the teacher in getting the technology to perform. Those students somewhere in the middle experimented playfully with the new writing technology and quickly left their teacher behind. Added to this whirlwind of writing activity was the clatter of twenty-five keyboards and four printers, which distracted even the most flexible teachers among us.

The end result of these factors is that teachers learn slowly how to modify their teaching styles when conducting classes in the computer classroom. They may find themselves lecturing less and circulating more among clusters of students seated at the computers. Those who use the classroom/lab frequently will certainly discover how to give concise directions about a computer-supported writing task—covering aspects of both the writing activity (purpose, audience, length, time limits, collaborative work) and the necessary components of the writing technology (file names, necessary word-processing strategies, electronic text exchange)—and then sit back and enjoy the writing energy that consumes the students.

Guidelines for Computers in the Classroom

Some specific suggestions for procedures in a computer-intensive classroom follow:

1. Have your handouts typed on a disk and put it on reserve in the computer classroom/lab for your students. They can read the handouts on the computer screen (a paperless classroom) or print out hard copies as needed.
2. Put certain writing activities on a disk and use it for those class meetings held in the lab. In one class period, for example, you might plan to have students meet in small groups and rewrite a memorandum on the computers.
3. Put past quizzes, tests, and student papers on a disk and keep it on reserve in the lab so students have access to valuable study and writing guides for your class.
4. Have students write their journals on the computer. Put sample entries (labeled "successful" or "not-so-successful") on a disk and put it on reserve in the lab.
5. Set up a dialogue or letter disk on which students record their questions about your class or write you letters, and keep it on reserve in the lab. Once a week, you can read these questions and letters and respond to them by computer. Some teachers might want to put their responses on individual student's disks; others might want to respond on a public disk so that all the students in the class can benefit from each other's questions.
6. Ask your students to keep their disks in the lab so that you can leave on-line messages. Be sure to negotiate "privacy" guidelines with your class before you do this. Students may not want you to

have access to disks which contain their rough drafts. They may want to have separate disks for private and public material.

7. Schedule one class period in the first or second week during which appropriate staff members can introduce your entire class to the word-processing software. Schedule other class periods for introduction to a spelling checker, a graphics package, or the electronic mail system.
8. Schedule a half-hour session in which you meet with a computer expert in your department, school, or university to discuss alternative ways of using computers in your class.

Where Do We Go from Here?

The lessons to be learned from teaching computer-supported writing classes are not all pleasant ones. For teachers, the effort of adding a computer-support component to a course generally requires a great deal of time and flexibility—sometimes more than overworked faculty are capable of providing. The choice of making this effort, however, is no longer ours. Computers have already changed the way in which humans communicate and exchange information, and our students will be intellectually crippled unless we provide them with successful strategies for using computerized writing technology in their communication efforts.

As teachers of writing, we do, however, still have the choice about how to use computer support in the teaching of writing-intensive classes. To take full advantage of the new writing technology, we have to take the time to describe our classroom efforts to each other, share our pedagogical successes and failures, and publicize the results of systematic observations that grow out of computer-supported classes.

21 Evaluation of Computer-Writing Curriculum Projects

Raymond J. Rodrigues, Colorado State University

Once teachers have developed and implemented computer-writing programs, they need to prepare for continuing evaluation—both programmatic evaluation and teacher evaluation. In both public schools and universities, teachers new to computers need to be sensitized to the problems that can arise when computer projects and computer classroom teaching are evaluated. If the complete project is being evaluated internally, the problems are minimized. But frequently the evaluators are external consultants, administrators unfamiliar with the program's goals, or curriculum-area specialists using evaluation instruments designed for noncomputer environments. Teacher-training projects should prepare teachers to deal with the less-than-ideal climate in which evaluation is likely to occur in their schools. They should also help teachers begin to develop their own notions about how evaluation of computer projects can best be accomplished. In this chapter I will review some salient points about curriculum evaluation in general before suggesting an inquiry model for evaluating computer-writing curriculum projects.

Background: Curriculum Evaluation

A standard approach to evaluating any curriculum project would be to establish objectives and to conduct formative and summative evaluations. However, whenever we attempt to evaluate any curriculum program, we need to consider how politicized the process typically is. Public schools are held accountable to such public agencies as departments of education and must answer to a myriad of demands for improvement from pressure groups that include parents, national professional organizations, business, industry, and legislators. In their most simplified versions, the demands for accountability rely upon product measures for their judgments rather than process measures.

Thus, for example, standardized test measurements, rather than actual student writing samples, or demonstrations of editing skills, rather than the development of ideas, may dominate curriculum evaluation and thereby dictate curriculum.

Even at the university level, standardized measures dictate budgetary decisions. Thus, the number of student credit hours generated, grant proposals funded, and articles published are easily quantifiable and therefore often count more in the evaluation of programs and faculty than do quality measures, such as student satisfaction or ability to think. Unlike public school teachers, university professors must deal with a complicated balance of tenure standards, proprietary turf battles, and hierarchical struggles characterized by university-wide committees and professorial ranks. Most university instructors, however, need not deal with the burden of constraints that limit the efforts of public school teachers, constraints such as textbook adoption policies, classroom discipline regulations, and limited time to reflect and work on curriculum development.

Public school curriculum development, which must include evaluation, typically follows a limited number of models. The most common model is that identified with Ralph Tyler (1949). Essentially, Tyler's curriculum development model is characterized by a needs assessment, the development of objectives, an accumulation of activities to accomplish the objectives, and evaluation of the curriculum, namely, a determination of whether the objectives have been achieved. However, recent curriculum evaluation procedures have moved beyond such mechanistic approaches.

Most recently, curriculum evaluation has focused upon a "clinical supervision" approach, an approach that emphasizes the teacher as the key to any improvement in results. The literature and school practices have emphasized clinical supervision as the means both to determining the quality of instruction and to bringing about improvement in instruction and, by extension, the curriculum itself. The most common example of the clinical supervision model employed by administrators appears to be the "Madeline Hunter/UCLA Model," a model that includes observation of the teacher by a supervisor, analysis of a "script" or record of observations, determination of cause-effect relationships, and then a conference between the supervisor and teacher that is designed to reinforce what the supervisor views as positive behaviors as well as the elimination of behaviors that do not lead to positive learning. (See *Educational Leadership* 1987 for a series of articles explaining the Hunter model and the varieties of coaching techniques that are used to develop teachers' abilities and to recognize that teachers are professionals and colleagues.)

In the current debate about curriculum development, including evaluation, both the Tyler curriculum-development model and the Hunter teacher-evaluation model have engendered criticism. While criticizing the Tyler model, MacDonald and Purpel (1987) argue, nonetheless, that understanding the Tyler rationale is essential to understanding today's curriculum-planning methodology since it remains the foundational and functional paradigm for the profession. However, they fault the Tyler rationale for ignoring the human dimensions of teaching and learning and for being based upon classical economic decision-making theory. Thus, the model carries in it the ethos of our technical and engineering culture. The model further complements the general climate of cost accounting, efficiency, and accountability, with its focus upon student and teacher competency, and fits perfectly with metaphors of school as business or factory, metaphors that stress quality control of the presumed product of schooling: student achievement. The model also lends itself well to certain political dimensions of schooling, inasmuch as it clearly communicates a simple and logical technique to nonprofessionals, thereby functioning to serve the status quo by focusing on *what,* not *why.* Efficiency becomes key.

Instead of the industrial approach of Tyler or the clinical supervision approach of Hunter, MacDonald and Purpel favor an approach that involves inquiry. Their model is characterized by data gathering, participant observation, and interpretation. The interpretation involves considerable dialogue among the participants, requiring "intellectual rigor, aesthetic sensibility, and free-flowing imagination. [The dialogue] will very likely be conducted in a context of inadequate information, insufficient understanding, differing interpretations, that is, with uncertainty."

Because the Hunter model rests upon the notion of the supervisor as expert and the teacher as patient, it has been criticized by such clinical supervision theorists as Noreen Garman (Garman et al. 1982), who argues for the supervisor to collaborate, to be a colleague, to provide skilled service, and to act ethically, working *with* the teacher to construct knowledge about what happens in a classroom. We can consider this approach to be an "inquiry-based evaluation" model. With that in mind, Decker Walker's cynical view (1986) regarding the context of computers in the schools is appropriate:

> It is, I think, the implementation problems that will determine the type and extent of uses to which computers are put in schools, not

> the philosophical or theoretical claims and not the objective benefits to be gained from any given use. Put simply, so long as matters proceed through the existing channels of change in school programs, only those uses of computers will be implemented that do not disturb the older, more accepted, tried-and-true ways of doing things.

Thus, teacher trainers will probably find themselves working in an educational environment that emphasizes evaluation by objectives and improvement of teaching through the expertise of the supervisor. Yet we may be in the midst of a paradigm shift that suggests that evaluation by objectives is artificial, that the process of change may be more important than the change itself, and that the infinite variety of contexts within which computers are used to teach composition may dictate how evaluation should be carried out. Ultimately, teachers must determine criteria for evaluation at the onset of any computer-writing project, and evaluators must work hand-in-hand with teachers to understand the varieties of factors that may influence results in any given classroom.

Inquiry-Based Evaluation of Computer Programs and Teaching

How should we go about evaluating computer-writing programs? To develop evaluation procedures that have the greatest potential to effect real, meaningful change, those who are responsible for evaluation need to involve as many representatives as possible of the practitioners who will use the technology. Curricular change has often been followed by frustration when not everyone involved understood the purposes for the change. "Well-intentioned, hard-working people appear locked into a school structure that contradicts the expressed goals of schooling," Jeannie Oakes (1986) reminds us; she continues:

> Unless research knowledge is supported by *inquiry within schools, local school districts, and state education agencies themselves,* little change is likely to occur. . . . Changing . . . will require the careful, open, tolerant, and generous probing of the experiences, assumptions, values, and knowledge of those whose lives are most affected by it: students, teachers, administrators, and communities.

Inquiry-based evaluation involves the participants in designing their own questions about their teaching and seeking their own answers. Inquiry-based evaluation needs to begin with a careful exploration of the constraints surrounding whatever computer-writing project is to be evaluated. What do the participants expect? Do teachers expect writing to improve? Do they expect their teaching to be easier or harder? Do they understand the teaching conditions that will change when computers are introduced? Do they know enough about both writing as process and the technologies to be employed—hardware and software? Have they had an opportunity to explore specialized software, such as invention or style-analysis software, and to judge the value of that software against word-processing software for *pedagogical purposes?* Do they know how much access to computers they and their students will have? When teachers have been acquainted with and helped to design such questions *at the outset* of the project, then they can begin to gather the information that will help them answer the questions and make critical choices when necessary.

What about administrators? What are their reasons for supporting a computer-writing project? Some may be truly committed to improving student writing. Others may recognize the public relations value of having computers in the schools and may expect everything else to remain the same. How do they intend to evaluate the teachers who are learning how to employ the technologies within their teaching? Are the administrators willing to tolerate initial disruptions, unexpected costs, and an evolving curriculum? Most important for the political future of the teachers, does the evaluation system that the administrators use to judge teaching ability reflect the conditions under which teachers will most effectively teach writing with computers? If a school district is locked into an evaluation checklist that is based upon some conception of the essentials of teaching, does the checklist reflect conditions that can be expected in a computer-writing environment? Teacher trainers can serve an important function here: that of educating administrators about what they can expect while preparing the teachers to implement the new curriculum.

Both teachers and administrators should know what kinds of students they will be trying to help, what their computer abilities are, what their writing abilities are, and how they learn. Indeed, how can the students help address the evaluation questions themselves? As the project evolves, if teachers can be allowed and encouraged to ask their own questions as informal researchers, then the evaluation itself will evolve from the results of that informal research. Teacher trainers can help teachers and administrators frame the key questions, determine how to gather appropriate observations, and establish a schedule for addressing the data, reflecting upon what is discovered, and summarizing the conclusions.

An inquiry-based evaluation system assumes a partnership of all participants. Teachers, in both public schools and universities, are, first and foremost, to be treated as professional colleagues. Dawn Rodrigues and I saw teachers in the El Paso, Texas, School District excited by the possibilities that were opened up to them. They began to view what they and we were doing as vital, as meaningful, and as worth doing, not simply a fad that a couple of university types were promoting and that administrators did not really want to support. The administrators wisely recognized the enthusiasm of the teachers and gave them the freedom to act. When encouraged and allowed to ask their own questions, and when shown how those questions will be reflected when the computer-writing project is evaluated, teachers can proceed on their own, weaning themselves from the teacher trainer and setting a standard for administrators to follow.

Computer-writing projects have evolved at the same time that the school reform movement has generated interest around the country. The Holmes Group and the Carnegie Report have placed an appropriate emphasis upon the professionalization of teachers. Although it was discussing collaborative mathematics projects, the Ford Foundation's *. . . And Gladly Teach* (1987) captured the essence of what I am arguing for:

> The larger issue is the degree to which teaching has been conceived as a narrowly instrumental activity, improvable by "in-service" days and other specific "technical fixes" aimed at updating the skills and knowledge of teachers. Good thinking, learning, and exploration can only be done under conditions of high expectations, firm support, and adequate time to struggle with ideas and talk about them with others.

In this context, evaluation as inquiry is ideally suited for computer-writing projects, for evaluation becomes as much a process as is writing.

To review the process of inquiry-based evaluation, first, both the evaluators and the teachers should approach the evaluation process as ongoing classroom research, research to construct meaning out of the events that occur. Second, before any conclusions may be drawn, the context in which computer writing has occurred must be fully considered. And third, ultimately what matters is how and how well students are learning to write with computers, not the pros or cons of the technology.

The rapid change in both technology and teaching techniques complicates the scene. Both early programs and machines soon became technological dinosaurs—slow-moving, inefficient writing tools. For example, the early *Bank Street Writer* interfered with writing. Excited by what computers and early programs could do, teachers spent more time on computer-program evaluation rather than on evaluating whether those programs helped or hindered students learning to write. Schools rushed to develop computer "literacy" courses rather than to find ways that teachers could integrate the computers into their classrooms. And even when computers were first integrated into those classrooms, early computer enthusiasts hoped for a technological "fix." Naively, we assumed that the advent of computers would make teaching easier, rather than change the ways that we teach (as reported by Paul LeBlanc and Charles Moran in Chapter 9 and by other contributors in Part I).

Thus, the best evaluative procedures that we use will involve careful inquiry by both teacher and evaluator. Both must work with the understanding that what they experience may change with the next semester as a result of what they have learned about both the technology and the interaction of learners with that technology in a very specific context. We can develop a set of guiding questions to help our inquiry:

I. How do the intentions of the computer-writing program and the context in which students write with computers complement each other?
   A. What intentions do teachers and administrators have for the computer-writing program?
      1. Teachers
         a. Is the teacher's purpose to teach writing as process or some other purpose?
         b. Does the teacher want to improve student writing or to hope for a technological fix to classroom problems?
         c. Did the teachers initiate the program or did the administrators?
      2. Administrators
         a. Is the administrator looking for schoolwide improvement or selected improvement?
         b. Is the administrator committed to student writing or merely fascinated with technology?
   B. What is the context for computer writing?
      1. Are computers available for all or some students at any time?
      2. Are computers in a common laboratory shared by others?
      3. What other associated equipment is available?
         a. Printers, modems, video-data projectors?
         b. Networking capabilities?

4. What is the quality of the software vis-à-vis writing-process functions?
    a. Centrality of word processing?
    b. Reliance upon special software to supplement word processing, such as prewriting programs?
    c. Integration of style-analysis programs?

C. How will student writing be measured?
   1. Attitudinal changes?
   2. Mastery of writing processes?
   3. Changes in student products?
   4. Emphasis upon surface features or development of ideas?
   5. Quality of revision?

Such a checklist can serve as much as an educational tool for faculty being educated in computer-writing techniques as it can serve as an evaluation device. Teachers and university instructors are still very much in a transitional stage. As Dawn Rodrigues notes at the beginning of Chapter 13, many English teachers and administrators have not yet accepted writing-process theory as something that has to do with the ways that writing can be taught. For them, the advent of the computer may be simply an opportunity to produce end results more quickly and in more readable form. Many administrators may still view word processing as a device that will give their students more marketable skills. They may support computer-writing programs because that seems an appropriate thing to do, rather than out of any belief in or commitment to the opportunity to improve students' writing skills while also changing the ways that teachers will teach.

In any training program, the issues raised by evaluation questions ought to be confronted at the outset. By doing so, the teacher educator, composition director, consultant, or vitally interested colleague can determine what expectations the teachers and faculty have for computers in the writing classroom. When those expectations are different from those of the instructors in charge of the training, then the training program will have to be adjusted to bring the teachers and instructors to a point where they can understand the opportunities that computers can facilitate.

Evaluation can bring about positive changes if it is ongoing, or formative, rather than something applied at the end of a semester or year—summative evaluation. In the El Paso, Texas, public schools, Dawn Rodrigues entered the classrooms of teachers involved in the project as a colleague, not as an external expert expected to make a judgment about what she observed. When a teacher asked for advice about how to involve a student who was not participating, Dawn demonstrated by involving the student personally. When Dawn saw something positive occurring that the teacher might not have had time to notice, she called it to the attention of the teacher, and together they tried to determine why it had occurred and how it might be replicated. By treating the teachers as colleagues, Dawn showed them that she respected their abilities and their knowledge about their own students and the conditions under which they had to work. It was to the school district's credit that they were willing to support such long-range evaluative efforts, such "coaching" (*Educational Leadership* 1987), for too often school districts have invited consultants to present workshops without any opportunity to adjust the recommended methods to actual classroom conditions.

Without evaluation permeating the development of a computer-writing program, too many variables can interfere with its success. Administrators or teachers of low-ability writers might assume that the computer could never help those students see the joy of writing, be motivated to write more, and improve through writing. At the other end, writing teachers who work only with high-ability writers might assume that these students already write well enough, and might not help their students tap the full potential of the technology. All along the spectrum of writing classrooms, some administrators and teachers may look to the computer for automatic improvement of student writing and may abandon the computer when they realize that little happens automatically and that working with computers may actually be harder than working without them; but for the diligent administrators and teachers, the results will be better. And always, as educators of writing teachers, we must argue for their right to teach differently, often having to give them the ammunition to fight for what they believe in and to convince administrators, parents, and even other teachers that our current ways of teaching may actually hinder student learning once computers become part of the writing program.

MacDonald and Purpel (1987) summarize the good that can result from collaboration throughout the curriculum process:

> The hope is that this curriculum planning process will provide liberating experiences that will promote the personal and social development of the curriculum planners. . . . the process is not to be seen as prescriptive except in the sense that it is designed to be in harmony with the educational framework. A key element in this model is that it provides a diversity, pluralism, and most importantly is intended to allow for openness. . . . Curriculum planners . . . are also inquirers and critics of education responsible for conceptualizing and posing problems and issues. . . . this process

. . . is characterized by constant reexamination, research, and reevaluation.

Such was the effort described by Sondra Perl and Nancy Wilson (1987) as they became participant observers when they attempted to determine how effective their writing project had been. How else can we work with individual teachers who, even in the same school, have different personalities and different students? Any evaluation effort must take such normal variations into account and involve the teachers as active inquirers, as classroom researchers who are willing to ask questions and keep working.

In short, how we evaluate computer writing in the curriculum must be based upon the contexts in which teachers teach. Those who train teachers—whether through inservice sessions, in university classes, or as colleagues working side by side—must understand how teachers' efforts are judged. Just as the microcomputer in the classroom provides the opportunity for students and teachers to be collaborators in learning to write and enables them to realize that we can often accomplish more in a writing task by sharing our efforts with others, so computer-writing programs can bring together teacher educators, administrators, and teachers. Together, we can collaborate to liberate ourselves from artificial boundaries just as we liberate our students to explore language more freely and to experience both a fascination with the written word and a love for the fluidity of language through the technological capacity of the computer.

Works Cited

Educational Leadership. 1987. Vol. 44(5).

Ford Foundation. 1987. . . . *And Gladly Teach.* New York: Ford Foundation.

Garman, N. B., C. D. Glickman, M. Hunter, and N. L. Haggerson. 1987. "Conflicting Conceptions of Clinical Supervision and the Enhancement of Professional Growth and Renewal: Point and Counterpoint." *Journal of Curriculum and Supervision* 2(2): 157–77.

MacDonald, J. B., and D. E. Purpel. 1987. "Curriculum and Planning: Visions and Metaphors." *Journal of Curriculum and Supervision* 2(2): 178–92.

Oakes, Jeannie. 1986. "Keeping Track, Part 2: Curriculum Inequality and School Reform." *Educational Leadership* 43(2): 148–54.

Perl, Sondra, and Nancy Wilson. 1987. *Through Teachers' Eyes.* Portsmouth, N.H.: Heinemann Educational Books.

Tyler, Ralph. 1949. *Principles of Curriculum and Instruction.* Chicago: University of Chicago Press.

Walker, Decker. 1986. "Computers and Curriculum." In *Microcomputers and Education: The Eighty-Fifth Yearbook of the National Society for the Study of Education,* edited by J. A. Culbertson and L. L. Cunningham, 22–39. Chicago: University of Chicago Press.

Appendixes

Appendix A: Survey of Computer Uses in English Education Programs

William Wresch, University of Wisconsin–Stevens Point

In November of 1985 NCTE's Committee on Instructional Technology chose to explore current practices in English teacher training. The committee was interested in knowing if prospective teachers were receiving any training in computer uses and, if so, what kind of training. As one part of that effort, the committee mailed a survey to 1800 members of NCTE in the spring of 1987. There were 176 teacher educators who returned the survey, and their answers have been summarized below. Because the mailing list used included comprehensive members of NCTE, some high school English teachers also received the survey, and many were kind enough to answer it as well. Their answers were separated from the 176 listed below and were tabulated separately.

The survey was broken into three major parts. The first asked about the English education methods course itself. The committee wanted to know if computers were becoming part of that course. The second part of the survey sought to discover what kind of exposure to computers English majors were receiving in their other English courses. The last part of the survey asked about the school districts where student teachers were placed—were student teachers finding computers there, and if so, how were they being used?

English Education Methods Courses

The following questions and responses to the survey pertain to the methods courses.

1. Does your English Education Methods course contain instruction in computer use? *Yes = 89; No = 87*
   If so, please check areas of instruction:

	Number	*Percent*
word processing	*76*	*85.4*
software evaluation	*42*	*47.2*
CAI use	*35*	*39.3*
databases	*9*	*10.1*
spreadsheets	*7*	*7.9*
invention programs	*30*	*33.7*
spelling checkers	*44*	*49.4*
style checkers	*25*	*28.1*
other (please specify)	*12*	*13.5*

2. How many class hours during the semester are devoted to instruction in computer applications? *Average = 5.7 hours*
3. Does your department offer a specific class such as "Computer Applications in English"? *Yes = 12; No = 164*
4. Place a check mark in front of any materials available for your majors:

	Number
sample computer software	*113*
sample word processors	*121*
books on computer use in English classes	*90*
computers reserved for use by English majors	*49*
on-line database searches	*59*
graphics software	*60*
desktop publishing software	*40*
other (please specify)	*11*

5. If your students DO NOT use computers as part of English Education Methods courses, what are the major reasons?

	Number
lack of equipment	*36*
lack of training by EE faculty	*48*
lack of interest by area school districts	*8*
a determination by EE faculty that it is unnecessary	*7*
other (please list)	*37*

60%: "Covered in another course"
40%: "No time"

While the number of methods instructors who include instruction in computer use is only slightly greater than the number who do not, question 5 shows that many additional students are getting such instruction in other classes. In sum, then, it would appear a substantial majority of English education majors are getting training in computer use as part of their teaching preparation. A number of respondents mentioned California's new requirements in computer literacy for teacher certification or similar requirements by other states as a spur to this kind of training.

According to question number 2, word processing is the major emphasis of instruction such students receive. Spelling checkers were mentioned next, possibly because they pose a special dilemma for teachers, or possibly because they are increasingly built into word processors. The frequency with which software evaluation was included as a major activity may result from the normal inclusion of such instruction in computer-literacy classes.

While the average time allotted to computer instruction was 5.7 hours, the average masks major variances from one college to another. The majority of instructors replied that they used two or three hours for computer instruction. Opposing them were a small number of instructors who used eight, or ten, or even fifteen hours for discussion of computers. As a result, the average is a little misleading. It may be more accurate to say that most instructors spend approximately one week on computer instruction.

Question number 4 seems to indicate a growing catalog of resources available to prospective English teachers. Almost two thirds of respondents reported that sample word processors and other software were available to their majors, and one half had begun to collect books on computer uses in English classes. Fully one third of responding professors noted the availability of graphics programs and on-line database searches. The fact that such resources are available, of course, does not mean that all students use them, but it does give some sense of the commitment of the institution.

As for the English education faculty who do not include computer instruction, more than half gave lack of their own training as a reason. Another problem was lack of equipment. Less than 10 percent felt the training was unnecessary. Of those who gave "other" as their reason for not including computer uses in the methods course, a common comment was that there was little time for such training in an already crowded course. Theirs was the familiar question, "If I put computers in, what do I take out?" The other most frequently mentioned "other" reason for not including computer uses was the existence of a separate course where such material was already covered.

All in all, responses to the survey indicated that computers had already taken on a much larger role in preservice teacher training than most observers would have suspected.

English Department Attitudes

The questions pertaining to the attitudes of regular English department faculty help explain why computer instruction was increasing in English education. These questions were added to the questionnaire to see if the experiences future English teachers had in general English classes were consistent with the instruction they were receiving in their methods class. The two questions from this section demonstrate great consistency between student experiences and department attitudes.

1. What is your perception of the attitudes of English faculty on your campus? How would they feel about the statements below?
   1 = strongly agree 2 = mildly agree 3 = neutral
   4 = mildly disagree 5 = strongly disagree

	Average
a. English teachers should be able to use a word processor.	*1.82*
b. English teachers should be able to program a computer.	*3.95*
c. Computers are a passing fad.	*4.37*
d. Computers are a useful writing tool.	*1.74*
e. Computers will improve writing instruction.	*2.59*
f. Business teachers, not English teachers, should teach word processing.	*3.81*
g. There should be a designated computer writing lab on campus.	*1.90*
h. Computers can be useful in literary analysis.	*3.18*

2. As part of other English courses are your majors encouraged to use

	Number
word processors	*113*
on-line database searches	*41*
personal databases	*12*
graphics software	*18*
other (please specify)	*9*

Several respondents remarked on the survey that they were uncomfortable trying to gauge the attitudes of fellow faculty, but the answers were consistent enough to portray departments as being generally pro-computer. There was general agreement that English teachers should be able to use a word processor, that computers are useful for writing, and that there should be a computer-writing lab on campus. These attitudes were supported by question 2, which showed that nearly two thirds of responding universities encouraged students to use word processors as part of general English courses.

While respondents generally felt computers were useful for writing, they were much more neutral on whether computers would help writing instruction. One or two comments in the margin of the survey noted the lack of empirical research proving the value of computers in writing instruction.

Area School Districts

The third section of the survey was an attempt to determine what kind of student teaching experience new English teachers are having. Are they encountering computers when they student-teach, and if so, for what purposes are the computers being used? Teachers were asked to respond to the following questions based on the school districts where their students were placed as student teachers.

1. What percentage of school districts have computers available for use in English classes? *Average = 57.8%*
2. For those districts, what is the average number available per school?

	Number
1–3	*11*
4–6	*17*
a computer lab	*62*

3. For those districts, what percentage of computer time goes for each of these applications (estimate as best you can)?

	Average
word processing	*58.3%*
grammar and spelling drills	*20.7%*
prewriting software	*7.2%*
spelling and style checks	*6.0%*
databases	*1.8%*
library searches	*1.6%*
other software (please name)	*4.5%*

4. What are the two or three computer programs you see fairly often in English classrooms?

Bank Street Writer	*38*
AppleWorks	*31*
AppleWriter	*16*
WordStar	*11*
WordPerfect	*9*
Fred Writer	*6*
MacWrite	*6*
PFS Write	*5*
MECC Writer	*5*
Writer's Helper	*4*
Magic Slate	*4*
Sensible Speller	*4*
Grammatik	*3*
Newsroom	*3*
Writer's Workbench	*3*

The number of reported school districts with computers available in English classes seems incredibly high. The answer may be skewed because only districts with student teachers were included, or it may be the question was badly worded. Since the vast majority of districts mentioned were said to have a computer lab available for English classes, it may be the respondents were including any school in which a computer lab was available to English classes on occasion. Since sharing computer labs is becoming more common, this would help boost the numbers reported in the survey.

The use of computer time by English classes seems consistent with other surveys: drills are decreasing in popularity at the secondary level, while word processing and other "tool" use of computers is gaining acceptance. In fact, if the percentage for prewriting and revising programs is added to the word-processing percentage, we see that over 70 percent of estimated computer time goes for writing activities. If this figure is accurate, the computer is definitely being used as a writing tool rather than for grammar drills.

This use of the computer is consistent with the software mentioned. Of the fifteen programs listed most frequently by respondents, *all* are programs used for writing. No drill program was mentioned more than once or twice.

Other Comments

The survey concluded with an opportunity for respondents to make any comments they wished about the use of computers in an English teacher's preservice experience. There were a few unusual responses. One person felt the survey was printed using an unpleasant type font (12-point Geneva). Several people pointed out a spelling error I made in the form. More typical comments were these:

> It's essential in my opinion.
> Essential given WP presence in college and industry. . . .
> Should be required. . . .
> Many of my students already have computer skills.
> Too much CAI software seems modeled after the worst instructional approaches.

Many preservice and inservice teachers are anxious about computers.
I wish I had more time for more training and for more inservice (for myself).
Many demands compete for the students' attention. Some topics will need to be dropped if we are to include enough computing instruction to be useful.
Vital!
Usual complaint—what do we cut out of the curriculum?
Word processing is certainly useful to any writer, but right now I don't feel it is important enough to devote a substantial part of an Eng Ed course to it.
Each teacher should be a competent user.
Area high schools surpass the university in this area.
English Educators should not act as if micros are going to save English Education. They aren't.
English Education professors *must* become more knowledgeable about computers and their use in English.
It's absolutely *vital.*
The trend is clear. . . .
Knowledge and evaluation of English software should be part of any valid methods course.

Besides commenting on the role of computers in English education, some professors offered suggestions for helping preservice teachers gain more computer ability. One instructor described using English education majors as tutors in the college writing lab as good preparation. Another described having students do all their own work on computers so they would learn about writing software through personal experience.

In general, the tone of all the responses was supportive of computers, if somewhat cautious. Few respondents used the survey as an opportunity for a tirade against technology. Many voiced regret that budget limitations kept them from doing as much as they wanted with computers. Many described plans already in place to increase the role of computers in their classes. All respondents showed that they were aware of computer uses in English and had given some thought to the appropriate role of the machine in specific teacher-training courses. It is clear the profession is well aware of the machine and is moving to respond to it.

Appendix B: Computer Access for English Classes

Elizabeth Foster, Chelmsford High School, Chelmsford, Massachusetts

Irene D. Thomas, Fort Bragg, California

Lawrence Frase, AT&T Bell Laboratories

The Issues

Literacy has traditionally been the business of the English and language arts curriculum. But literacy in the information society in which we live requires more than books, paper, and pencils. Our schools lag far behind in preparing people to live and work in that society. Students must be introduced to and must experience the technology they will live with, learn with, and eventually work with. While the first rush was to computer literacy, mathematics, and drill applications, prominent educators now realize that teaching "real-life" application, such as word processing and database management, should occupy a higher priority. Indeed, our traditional notion of "literacy" is being redefined. The message changes as the medium does.

A global movement toward computer literacy exists in Italy, France, Japan, and the Soviet Union. While the value of mandated computer literacy is questionable to some American educators, the fact remains that students in these countries will have more exposure to computers than our students. And their governments are assisting in ways that ours is not. Access to computer technology represents a major expense to school districts, which have various sources for basic funding. School budgets differ from state to state and even from district to district within some states.

We all recognize that computers are a legitimate tool for the English and language arts classes. However, we English teachers are faced with a two-level problem. In acquiring access to computers for the school system and within the school, the English teacher has to overcome barriers, not only those created by fiscal restraints but also those caused by misconceptions held by administrators and other departments.

English and language arts classes need equal access to computers because a computer is a language machine as well as a number machine. Word processing suppports the writing-process model of instruction. With word processors, students gain the ability to revise easily and to produce neat, legible copy.

Additionally, problem solving and critical thinking are as applicable to verbal literacy as to computer literacy.

Strategies for Action

Computers are expensive equipment, and many schools are operating with limited budgets because of declining enrollments and taxpayer demands for lowered expenditures. Since the goal of providing computer access for English teachers is such a complex issue, guidelines that might be followed by teachers would be helpful. The following are some approaches that any classroom teacher might find valuable.

Guidelines

First, explore all the possibilities available to you. Use research guides to help brainstorm resources for classroom computer implementation. For instance, the American Psychological Association publishes the *Guide to Research Support,* which contains a wealth of information on funding from all manner of federal and nonfederal sources. In addition, it contains advice on how to approach organizations for support. Use the resources of national organizations, such as NEA, to identify other funding sources. Many education organizations have collected useful information on funding sources for the schools.

Work through professional computer organizations. The American Federation of Information Processing Societies (AFIPS) has a project called Technology in Education, which has run workshops at which computer specialists helped teachers understand how to use computers in their classrooms and what to look for when purchasing hardware and software.

Once you have begun to gather information, be sure to consider the possibility of acquiring computer access through some source outside the local school system. Working through a large organization is helpful since grants and awards are rarely made to individuals; they usually go to schools or larger system units.

One idea is to contact businesses or industries with established computer grants. In 1981, corporations such as AT&T, Apple Computer, IBM, and Exxon gave away $3 billion. Companies give grants for various purposes, and an area representative from the company can put you in touch with appropriate personnel. These programs change frequently; hence, current information is essential. Even if an outright grant is not available, large discounts are often available for innovative computer use in education.

Philanthropic organizations associated with industry could also be helpful. Many large companies have employee organizations that teach computing, give demonstrations, or provide other benefits for the general public. For example, the Pioneers of AT&T are known for their community contributions. The work of such people provides a community service that can be helpful to the schools, especially in those areas with minority populations.

In addition to business and industry, charitable foundations are clearly another potential source of funding. Many of these foundations are regional. In 1981, over 22,000 foundations gave $4.1 billion in grants. Charitable contributions for computing have come from the Murdock Charitable Trust (Washington), the Pew Memorial Trust (Pennsylvania), the Hillman Foundation (Pennsylvania), the Cleveland Foundation (Ohio), the Gannett Foundation (New York), and many others.

Another approach would be to explore contacts with researchers at universities and colleges. Often researchers can obtain funding that includes equipment to be used for experimental purposes in the school. Experimental research requiring the use of computers may also be carried out by state or regional education consortiums.

Find out what technological issues are included in the curricular guidelines published by your state department of education. Investigate the legislation and funding in other states (for example, California's AB 803, Technology in the Classroom Program, and Summer Institute). Urge your own legislators to draft and implement similar programs. Letter-writing campaigns to state legislators can be effective in those areas where most education budgets are derived from state funds, while a similar campaign on the local level would be more appropriate where funds are mainly from local sources. Initiate a letter-writing campaign to your legislators, citing the importance of computer instruction.

Since another facet of the issue of gaining computer access for English and language arts teachers is the problem of increasing availability within the system, take steps to familiarize all departments and the administration with the necessity of using computers in the English classroom.

Promote inservice workshops by local specialists who work with and understand the value of using computers in the classroom. Collect articles on how word processing has been used in writing instruction, and circulate them among your colleagues. Help teachers overcome "computer anxiety" by allowing them to borrow a computer and software to take home over a weekend. Teacher exposure is the best way for teachers to decide how computers can best be used in their curricula. Alternatively, purchase several word-processing programs and encourage teachers to borrow one for personal writing. Teachers who are comfortable with word processors tend to see the enormous impact this tool can have on writing instruction.

Another way to increase teacher knowledge of computer use is to identify school districts in which a limited number of computers have been successfully integrated into the English or language arts curriculum and ask representatives from those districts to make presentations.

Excellent information can also be gained through having teachers attend conferences. Insist that at least one representative from your school attend the major computing conferences, such as CUE, and report back on information learned. Assign a representative to attend computer-application sessions at the major language arts conferences (NCTE, IRA, CCCC). Urge that your local National Writing Project director devote a summer institute to the topic of writing with computers.

Editors

William R. Oates, Education Director of the American Welding Society, continues a unique career combining technology with education writing and media work. After ten years as a science writer for the General Motors Research Laboratories, he taught mass communication at Indiana University, the University of Alabama, and the University of Miami. As an educator, he pioneered applications of computer technology to education in writing and journalism. His presentation at the 1979 NCTE convention was the first ever made at an NCTE convention on the subject of using computers in teaching writing. His eclectic career mirrors his four-degree education (engineering sciences, journalism, marketing, and mass communication). In addition to his articles and monographs, from 1983 to 1988 he wrote a regular column devoted to computer-based education for *Journalism Educator*. A continuing member of the NCTE Committee on Instructional Technology since its inception in 1981, he was chair from 1984 to 1987, during the development of this book.

Dawn Rodrigues is Associate Professor of English and Director of the Computer-Assisted Writing Center at Colorado State University. She has been a language arts consultant for computer projects in El Paso, Texas, and in Denver, Colorado. In addition to her journal articles, reviews, and book chapters, she collaborated with Raymond J. Rodrigues on *Teaching Writing with a Word Processor* and with Richard Gebhardt on *Writing: Processes and Intentions*. She makes presentations regularly at meetings of NCTE and the Conference on College Composition and Communication and has twice been a consultant for the CCCC Winter Workshop.

Cynthia L. Selfe is Associate Professor of Composition and Communication at Michigan Technological University, where she directs the undergraduate program in Scientific and Technical Communication. She has chaired both the NCTE Assembly on Computers in English and the NCTE Committee on Instructional Technology and has served as a member of the CCCC Executive Committee and the CCCC Committee on Computers. In addition to her journal articles and book chapters on computers, she is the author of *Computer-Assisted Instruction in Composition: Create Your Own* and, with Gail Hawisher, a co-editor of *Critical Perspectives on Computers in Composition Instruction.* With Kate Kiefer, she founded the journal *Computers and Composition,* and now, with Gail Hawisher, she continues to serve as editor of that publication.

Contributors

Bruce C. Appleby is Professor of English and Professor of Curriculum and Instruction at Southern Illinois University–Carbondale. He has taught at all levels of instruction, from preschool through graduate school, and is currently involved in an extensive inservice training program on literacy through literature, as well as an NSF-funded program on the use of writing in teaching biology. He spent a recent sabbatical in Australia, Thailand, and the People's Republic of China, training university and secondary teachers on the use of the computer in teaching English composition. He is a former chair of the Conference on English Education and former member of the NCTE Executive Committee.

Trent Batson was an average, desperate teacher of writing as late as 1982, when he discovered how his own personal computer changed his approach to writing. Coming off a sabbatical year with greater than usual energy, he started the ENFI Project (English Natural Form Instruction), using local-area networks as a vehicle for rich collaborative work in college writing courses. The Project soon had won a major grant from the Annenberg/CPB Project, an equipment grant from IBM, and funding from the ADAPSO Foundation to help it spread nationally. He continues to direct the ENFI Project from Gallaudet University. He was a visiting professor at Carnegie-Mellon University in 1987–1988, and in 1989 he cochaired the Fifth Computers and Writing Conference.

Stephen A. Bernhardt is Associate Professor of English at New Mexico State University, where he works with the graduate programs in rhetoric and professional communication. He has taught secondary English, worked with school reform efforts in Illinois, and worked with a number of schools and teachers on elementary and secondary curriculum development. He has published articles on scientific and technical writing, computers and composition, and teacher training in *College Composition and Communication*, the *Journal of Technical Writing and Communication*, *Written Communication*, and *Research in the Teaching of English*. His current research interests involve hypermedia documentation and workplace literacy. He makes frequent presentations at NCTE conventions and meetings of its affiliates and is active in the Society for Technical Communication and the Association of Teachers of Technical Writing.

Eleanor Berry works as an independent scholar in rural Wisconsin. Besides computers and writing, her primary research interest is language and form in twentieth-century poetry. She is writing a book tentatively titled *Language in*

Modern American Poetry and serves as book review editor for the *William Carlos Williams Review*. As a lecturer at the University of Wisconsin–Milwaukee, she coordinated the English department microcomputer classroom from 1983 to 1986 and trained teachers to use the classroom for a wide range of writing courses. Since receiving her Ph.D. from the University of Toronto in 1981, she has published papers on prosody and poetic language in anthologies and several journals, including *Language and Style* and *Contemporary Literature*, and has made presentations on the topic of computers and composition and on language and form in poetry at many conferences and conventions, including ICCH, CCCC, MLA, and MMLA.

W. Edward Bureau is Supervisor of Language Arts in the Springfield School District (Delaware County), Pennsylvania. He has taught high school English, graduate courses at Widener University, and numerous workshops in the areas of writing, teaching for thinking, and computers. As a fellow of the Pennsylvania Writing Project, he teaches school administrators how to implement successful writing and language arts programs. The focus of his doctoral work in progress at the University of Pennsylvania is on elements of change which influence successful implementation of language arts programs.

Barbara L. Cambridge is Associate Professor of English and Associate Department Chairperson at Indiana University–Purdue University at Indianapolis. She serves as Executive Director of the Indiana Teachers of Writing, consultant/evaluator for the National Council of Writing Program Administrators, and member of the NCTE Commission on Inservice Education. She is editor of the *Journal of Teaching Writing* and has published on gender issues in writing, collaborative learning, and assessment in the undergraduate curriculum.

James L. Collins is Associate Professor of English Education at the State University of New York at Buffalo. He has taught high school English and has served as monographs editor for the New York State English Council. He has been a member of the NCTE Standing Committee on Research and the NCTE Task Force on Class Size and Workload in Secondary English Instruction. Currently, he is a contributing editor for *Composition Chronicle* and directs his university's Software Evaluation Project. In addition to his articles, research reports, and book chapters, he co-edited *Writing On-Line: Using Computers in the Teaching of Writing* with Elizabeth A. Sommers.

Ulla Connor is Associate Professor of English and Coordinator of English as a Second Language at Indiana University–Purdue University at Indianapolis. She has taught English, K–12, in two large school systems. She was co-principal investigator in a recent research grant from the Exxon Education Foundation to study cross-national trends in persuasive high school writing. Her research findings have been published in such journals as *Language Learning*, *Text*, and the *TESOL Quarterly*. She is co-editor of *Writing across Languages: Analysis of L2 Text* and *Coherence: Research and Pedagogical Perspectives*.

Joan Dunfey is Instructor at Lesley College in Cambridge, Massachusetts. She has taught English at the junior high, high school, and college levels and

English education courses at the graduate school level. She is an active consultant for many school systems in the area of effective computer uses in the language arts, particularly in reading and writing. Her publications include reviews of software for *Electronic Learning* and articles on curriculum for *Teaching and Computers* and *The Computing Teacher*. She makes presentations at NCTE conventions, conferences of its affiliates, and computer conventions.

Jane Zeni Flinn is Assistant Professor of English and Education Studies at the University of Missouri–St. Louis and Director of the Gateway Writing Project. She has edited two books of articles by Gateway teachers, *Reflections on Writing* and, with Archibald, Spina, and Krater, *New Routes to Writing*. Her own articles have appeared in *Computers and Composition, English Education, Educational Leadership*, and the National Writing Project *Quarterly*. As a consultant, she has been working with suburban teacher-researchers to improve their black students' performance in writing. She is currently doing research on successful writing environments using computers. She now publishes under the name of Jane Zeni.

Elizabeth Foster is a teacher at Chelmsford High School in Chelmsford, Massachusetts. She has taught in both senior and junior high schools and worked as a consultant for the QUILL Pilot Project. In collaboration with Rebecca Burnett Carosso, she has written *Shakespeare Persona* and *American Persona*. In addition, she has been project editor for *Intermediate Persona I* and *Intermediate Persona II*. She has made presentations at NCTE and affiliate conferences and currently serves on NCTE and NEATE committees.

Lawrence T. Frase is a Distinguished Member of Technical Staff at AT&T Bell Laboratories. He has published over seventy papers on human learning, reasoning, instruction, writing, text design, and software design and applications. While on leave from AT&T Bell Labs, he was Chief of the Learning Division at the National Institute of Education. He serves on the editorial boards of several journals, including *Contemporary Educational Psychology, Journal of Educational Psychology, Knowledge-Based Systems*, and *Written Communication*, and he reviews papers for *Research in the Teaching of English*. He is a fellow of APA and a member of ACM, AERA, IEEE, and NCTE, serving on the NCTE Committee on Instructional Technology. His current work involves expert system development.

Oscar M. Haugh is Professor Emeritus of Curriculum and Instruction at the University of Kansas in Lawrence. He has taught in junior and senior high schools in Minnesota and in universities in Wisconsin, India, Costa Rica, and Kansas. As president of the Kansas State Planning Commission and the Kansas Association of Teachers of English, he served as a consultant and workshop leader in many schools and colleges in the Midwest. He was the originator and first editor of *English Education*, as well as a consulting editor for *Research in the Teaching of English*. The author of five books, four workbooks, numerous monographs and teachers' manuals, and over one hundred journal and magazine articles, he is currently active in evaluation and research in the language arts as the author of twelve standardized tests and the coauthor of fourteen others.

Amy L. Heebner is Instructor in Educational Technology and Media at Teachers College, Columbia University. As a research fellow at the Center for Intelligent Tools in Education, an IBM-funded research and development project at Teachers College, she conducted classroom research and served as a liaison between CITE and the Teachers College Writing Project. Her dissertation concerns the effects of word processing on the writing of young children.

Deborah H. Holdstein is Director of Writing Programs at Governors State University in University Park, Illinois. She has written extensively on the use of computers in composition instruction and on other issues in composition. In addition to journal articles, book chapters, and textbook materials, she is author of *On Composition and Computers* and *Process Writer Guide to Writing* (forthcoming) and is co-editing a collection of essays called *Issues in Computers and Writing.* She is a member of the CCCC Executive Committee, serves on several editorial boards and as consultant reader for *College Composition and Communication* and *College English,* and presents papers regularly at professional meetings that include MLA and CCCC.

Sandra Hooven is a teacher of secondary English at Glendora High School in Glendora, California. She has taught junior high and high school language arts for many years and still relishes her experiences with American youth. The latest exciting addition to her teaching repertoire was a summer spent as a fellow at the Technology Institute of the University of California at Irvine. The institute delved into the strange and sophisticated world of computer as word processor and telecommunications device. She has not previously published any of her many writings, but with her trusty Apple sidekick is hopeful that she might publish other teacher-oriented materials.

David Humphreys is Professor of English at Cuyahoga Community College and a computer-writing consultant to local schools. He has twenty years of experience teaching both secondary and postsecondary English. Since 1984 he has taught area teachers to use the computer in teaching writing. He has attended NCTE conventions regularly and is past chair of the NCTE Assembly on Computers in English. He received the 1986 Innovator of the Year Award from the League for Innovation in the Community College and currently serves on several editorial boards.

Kate Kiefer is Professor of English at Colorado State University. She has written and presented papers on the applications of computers to composition instruction. In addition to teaching undergraduate and graduate courses in composition and composition theory, she supervises the basic writing program. She is author of two basic writing texts and coauthor of *Writing, Brief, 3e.*

Paul LeBlanc is Assistant Professor and Chair of the Department of English at Springfield College. He is continuing his research in computer-based writing software and has published in *Computers and Composition* and *Thalia.*

Frank Madden is Associate Professor of English at Westchester Community College and chair of the NCTE Assembly on Computers in English. He makes presentations regularly at NCTE national and regional conferences and teaches graduate courses in English education, computers, and telecommunications at the City College of New York. He has received grants from the SUNY Research Council and IBM and has written a computer program called *Literature Journal*, which helps students analyze literature. His articles have appeared in *English Journal*, *College Literature*, *Computers and Composition*, the *New York Times*, and *Insight*.

Chris Madigan taught the summer institute and inservice programs for the Gateway Writing Project and codirected the University of New Mexico Writing Institute, for which the New Mexico Council of Teachers of English honored him with their Excellence in English Education Award. He has published on computers and writing in *English Education*, the *Computer-Assisted Composition Journal*, and *Computers and Composition*, and he consults with schools and businesses about computers and writing from his home in Albuquerque, New Mexico.

Stephen Marcus is Associate Director of SCWriP, a National Writing Project site in the Graduate School of Education, University of California at Santa Barbara. He has spoken and published extensively in the United States and abroad in the area of computer-assisted English and language arts; his published work includes ten software packages ranging from first-grade applications to advanced college composition materials for business and professional writing. In Great Britain, he helped develop guidelines for computer use in British language arts classrooms. In the United States, he has served on the advisory board of the Apple Education Foundation and is currently on the NCTE Commission on Media and the National Software Advisory Board for Scholastic, Inc. His current work includes directing a HyperCard/multimedia project for writing teachers.

Charles Moran is Professor of English at the University of Massachusetts at Amherst, where he directs the University Writing Program. He is past director of the Massachusetts Writing Project. He has published articles in leading journals and is on the editorial boards of the *Massachusetts Review* and the *Journal of Basic Writing*.

Stephen Reid is Associate Professor of English at Colorado State University. He has served as Director of Composition and currently runs the placement program at CSU. He has published articles in NCTE journals and presented numerous papers at NCTE conventions. He is the recent author of a college composition textbook, *The Prentice-Hall Guide for College Writers*.

Raymond J. Rodrigues is Associate Vice President for Academic Affairs at Colorado State University. He has taught high school English in Las Vegas, Nevada, and Las Vegas, New Mexico, and has been the president of the Southern Nevada Teachers of English and the Utah Council of Teachers of English. He currently is on the NCTE Editorial Board. His NCTE publications include *Teaching Writing with a Word Processor, Grades 7–13,* coauthored with Dawn Rodrigues, and *Mainstreaming the Non-English Speaking Student,* coauthored with Robert White. In addition, he has published several high school and junior high school textbooks and written numerous articles on English methods and multicultural concerns in English.

Helen J. Schwartz, Professor of English at Indiana University at Indianapolis, is author of *Interactive Writing,* articles on computers in writing, and the computer programs *ORGANIZE* and *SEEN.* Along with chairing the CCCC and MLA committees on computer use, she has headed a national panel of EDUCOM to assess the use of computers in composition and to recommend a blueprint for future use. She has lectured and consulted with teachers across the United States, in China, in Sweden, and, as a Fulbright Senior Scholar, in the Netherlands. As a Dana Fellow at Carnegie-Mellon University, she has begun research on how people read to write about literature.

Elizabeth A. Sommers is Assistant Professor of Rhetoric at Boston University, where she has constructed a computer-assisted writing program for the College of Basic Studies. She completed her Ph.D. at SUNY at Buffalo in 1986, investigating college writers receiving process-oriented instruction while using word processing as a writing tool. With James L. Collins, she co-edited *Writing On-Line: Using Computers in the Teaching of Writing,* a book for teachers interested in integrating computers into their English curricula. Her current research interests and publications continue to focus on computers, revision, and process-oriented instruction.

Charles R. Smith is Professor of English at Colorado State University, where he teaches medieval literature, composition, and humanities. In 1981 he began the Department of English project for computer-assisted composition and served in the early years as its codirector. He has spoken and published on *Writer's Workbench* and text analysis and is joint editor of *WUG,* a newsletter for users of *Writer's Workbench.* A developer and producer of the collegiate edition of *Writer's Workbench,* he has continued work in text analysis, including work on *CRITIQUE,* IBM's package for natural language processing and text analysis.

Michael Spitzer is Dean of the School of Humanities at New York Institute of Technology, where he formerly chaired the Department of English. He regularly makes presentations on computers and writing at NCTE, CCCC, and other conferences and is a member of the NCTE Committee on Instructional Technology and chair of the NCTE Assembly on Computers in English. His recent publications have dealt with computer conferencing and using computer networks in the writing classroom.

Irene D. Thomas, a charter member of the NCTE Committee on Instructional Technology, is a writer and software designer.

Neil A. Trilling is Director of the Computing Services Division at the University of Wisconsin–Milwaukee. As a computing professional and university administrator, he has been interested in the application of computers in education for over twenty-five years. Of particular interest are applications in the humanities and the education of faculty. In designing faculty computer-literacy programs, he has specialized in teaching computer-phobic or computer-anxious faculty. He has presented papers in this area and consulted on several such programs.

William Van Pelt is Assistant Professor of English at the University of Wisconsin–Milwaukee, where he teaches composition, technical writing, writing for computer technology, and Romanticism. He helped establish the university's microcomputer writing lab and has coordinated the lab since 1984. His research includes several articles on technical writing, the impact of computers on the writing process, and collaborative learning in the computer classroom. He is also working on a book entitled *Using Computers for Applied Writing: Process, Products, and Applications.*

Billie J. Wahlstrom works in the field of communication. She has written extensively for numerous publications, including the *Journal of Popular Culture*, the *Writing Instructor*, *Collegiate Microcomputers*, *Computers and Composition*, and *Computers in the Humanities*, and is the author of a forthcoming book, *Perspectives on Human Communication.* She has served as a communication consultant to state agencies, educational institutions, government, and business, including Paramount Pictures. She makes presentations regularly at CCCC and is active in the Council for Programs in Technical and Scientific Communication.

William Wresch is Associate Professor and Chair of the Department of Mathematics and Computing, University of Wisconsin–Stevens Point. He taught college composition for ten years and has published three books: *The Computer in Composition Instruction*, *A Practical Guide to Computer Uses in the English/Language Arts Classroom*, and *Writing for the 21st Century*. He is also the developer of *Writer's Helper Stage II*, a computer-writing tool named Best Writing Software by EDUCOM.